ADULT LEARNING

Linking Theory and Practice

Sharan B. Merriam and Laura L. Bierema

JB JOSSEY-BASS™
A Wiley Brand

Copyright © 2014 by John Wiley & Sons, Inc. All rights reserved.

Published by Jossey-Bass
A Wiley Brand
One Montgomery Street, Suite 1200, San Francisco, CA 94104-4594—www.josseybass.com

Jossey-Bass books and products are available through most bookstores. To contact Jossey-Bass directly call our Customer Care Department within the U.S. at 800-956-7739, outside the U.S. at 317-572-3986, or fax 317-572-4002.

Wiley publishes in a variety of print and electronic formats and by print-on-demand. Some material included with standard print versions of this book may not be included in e-books or in print-on-demand. If this book refers to media such as a CD or DVD that is not included in the version you purchased, you may download this material at http://booksupport.wiley.com. For more information about Wiley products, visit www.wiley.com.

Library of Congress Cataloging-in-Publication Data

Merriam, Sharan B.
  Adult learning : linking theory and practice / Sharan B. Merriam, Laura L. Bierema. – First edition.
    Includes bibliographical references and index.
    ISBN 978-1-118-13057-5 (hardback)–ISBN 978-1-118-41910-6 (pdf) – ISBN 978-1-118-41631-0
(epub)   1. Adult education.   2. Adult education–Research.   3. Education and globalization. 4. Activity programs in education.   I. Bierema, Laura L. (Laura Lee), 1964–   II. Title.
  LC5215
  374–dc23

                                        2013026292

Printed in the United States of America
FIRST EDITION
HB Printing   10 9 8 7 6 5 4 3 2 1

THE JOSSEY-BASS HIGHER AND
ADULT EDUCATION SERIES

CONTENTS

LIST OF TABLES, FIGURES, AND EXHIBITS

PREFACE

Adults are learning all the time. Whether we are searching the Internet to learn more about a recently diagnosed health problem, having a coworker show us how to navigate a new reporting procedure, or taking classes to get a certificate or a degree, learning is firmly embedded in our work, family, and community activities. The sites and programs where adult learning takes place are also endless—from human resource development programs at work, to seminars and workshops sponsored by libraries, museums, religious institutions, hospitals, and so on, to more formal programs offered by schools, colleges, and universities—and all of these can be accessed in online environments. At the heart of such a diverse field, and what unites us as practitioners, is the adult as a learner. And the more we can understand our own learning, the better we can be as practitioners who design and facilitate learning activities for adults.

Most likely you are reading this book because you are interested in knowing more about adult learning. However, unlike Malcolm Knowles who, as director of adult education at the Boston YMCA in the 1940s, could not "find a book that would tell me how to conduct a program of this sort" (1984, p. 2), and added "that although there was general agreement among adult educators that adults are different from youth as learners, there was no comprehensive theory about these differences" (pp. 3–4)—there is now voluminous literature on adult learning. This literature ranges from "how-to" guides, pamphlets, handbooks, and books, to scholarly theoretical discussions to well-designed research studies.

Purpose and Audience

So, with all of these resources on adult learning available, why this book? A quick survey of some of the books published in the last 10 years reveals that most focus on a particular aspect of adult learning such as motivation (Wlodkowski, 2008); andragogy and its application to workplace learning and human resource development (Knowles, Holton, & Swanson, 2011); critical thinking (Brookfield, 2012b); experiential learning, (Fenwick, 2003); dialogic education (Vella, 2008); and transformative learning (Taylor & Cranton, 2012). Others are highly theoretical (Illeris, 2004b; Jarvis, 2006a) or theory and research intense (Merriam, Caffarella, & Baumgartner, 2007). What we felt was missing from the literature on adult learning is a book that gives an overview of the major theories and research in adult learning in language that those new to adult education can understand, and at the same time points out applications of these ideas to practice. We have presented adult learning theory to the reader mindful that our readers are themselves adult learners as well as practitioners who design and facilitate educational programs for adults. In keeping with our goal of writing a book that is reader- and practitioner-friendly, we have included activities and resources at the end of each chapter for personal and instructional use.

There are three intended audiences for *Adult Learning: Linking Theory and Practice.* The primary audience for our book are students in adult education and human resource development programs in the United States and Canada. All of these programs have a core required course in adult learning. Whether these are undergraduate, masters, or doctoral-level programs, typically this course is the student's first introduction to adult learning. A second audience for our book are graduate students in professional preparation programs whose work may involve the education and training of adults, such as school administrators, public health personnel, social workers, corporate consultants and trainers, the military, counselors, government administrators, higher education faculty and administrators, and community educators. A third and growing audience are students in undergraduate and graduate programs in other countries. These programs go by different names such as Lifelong Learning, Social

Education, Adult and Professional Education, Community Education, and so on, but all offer a course on adult learning.

Overview of Contents

Based on our many years of teaching adult learning courses and also conducting seminars and workshops on adult learning, we have organized this book according to what we have found "works" in terms of acquainting readers with adult learning theory and practice. The first two chapters review (1) the present context of adult learning, and (2) the emergence of specific theories of learning. Chapter 1, Adult Learning in Today's World, sets the framework for the book by examining the forces that make continued learning in adulthood so important. Globalization, the knowledge society, technology, and demographic changes are shaping the landscape of adult learning today. Lifelong learning is indeed becoming a reality with adults engaging in learning in formal, nonformal, and informal settings. We define who the adult learner is, and review characteristics of participants in formal learning settings. Chapter 2, Traditional Learning Theories, begins with a brief exploration of the concept of learning, then moves historically through the development of learning theories beginning with the earliest scientifically developed learning theory, behaviorism. Going in somewhat chronological order, the following orientations/perspective/theories are presented: behaviorism, humanism, cognitivism, social cognitivism, and constructivism. These five are considered traditional learning theories and are foundational to what we have come to understand about adult learning.

Again, going loosely in order of their appearance in our field's literature, the next three chapters present major, foundational theories of adult learning: andragogy, self-directed learning, and transformative learning. Chapter 3, Andragogy—The Art and Science of Helping Adults Learn, is a review of Malcolm Knowles's theory, later characterized as a set of assumptions, which distinguishes adult learners from pre-adult learners. Andragogy is the oldest and best-known set of principles used to guide instruction of adult learners. In this chapter we review the theory and latest research, and offer a number of examples of application. Chapter 4 is on self-directed learning. One of the assumptions of andragogy is that because adults are self-directing in their work, family, and community lives, they can also be self-directing in their learning. Along with andragogy, self-directed learning developed as one of the major foundational pillars of adult learning theory. Reviewed are various models of self-directed learning and ways in which self-directed learning has been applied in practice. Chapter 5 is on Transformative Learning, which joins andragogy and self-directed learning as a major theory explaining learning in adulthood. In the last twenty-five years we have seen a burgeoning of theorizing and research around the notion that learning can profoundly change the way adults view themselves and act in the world. Beginning with Mezirow's breakthrough formulation of transformative learning and the research and development around his theory, we then review other conceptualizations of transformative learning, discuss promoting and evaluating transformative learning, and close with a review of several issues yet to be resolved in promoting this type of learning.

The next four chapters explore several dimensions of adult learning, all of which are important to a full understanding of the adult learner and the process of adult learning. Chapter 6, Experience and Learning, looks at the central role of adult life experiences in generating as well as acting as resources for learning. Beginning with formative works of Dewey, Lindeman, and Kolb, and moving to contemporary conceptualizations including several models from adult educators, we explain how life experiences and learning are integrally related. Also reviewed is the role of experience in reflective practice, in "authentic" real-life experiences as explained in the learning theory of situated cognition, and in communities of practice. Chapter 7, Body and Spirit in Learning, addresses the holistic nature of learning. More than a cognitive activity, learning also involves acquiring knowledge through the body, which is called somatic or embodied learning, and for some adults, learning may also include a spiritual dimension. Chapter 8, Motivation and Learning, is a review of what we know about the motivation to learn, its cultural and biological components, and how meeting needs and motives through learning becomes reinforcement for continued learning. We also offer suggestions as to how readers can identify their own motivations for learning as well as how to take motivation into consideration when planning learning activities with adults. Chapter 9, The Brain and Cognitive Functioning, reviews how the brain actually functions in learning. We begin the chapter with a short overview of how the brain works, then go on to discuss some of the exciting new work in neuroscience and learning. Several dimensions of cognitive functioning including memory, intelligence, cognitive development, and wisdom are also reviewed—all with an eye to how learning maximizes each of these functions.

In the last three chapters we explore in more depth the importance of context to learning. Although this theme is present throughout the book, we thought the context of learning was so crucial to really understanding adult learning that we have featured it in these last three chapters. Chapter 10, Adult Learning in the Digital Age, addresses the pervasiveness of technology in our lives, a factor that both engages and distracts our learning. How do we maximize this medium in learning, and at the same time enable adults to be savvy consumers of massive amounts of information at the tap of a keyboard? Understanding how adult learners engage with technology and how that technology is shaping their learning is critical to our role as adult educators in helping adults navigate this new learning context. Just as technology defines the context of our learning, so too do the social and global contexts of the 21st century. In Chapter 11, Critical Thinking and Critical Perspectives, we situate critical thinking in its broader context, considering its philosophical underpinnings and contemporary counterparts. The chapter begins with a discussion of what it means to be critical and introduces critical theory, critical thinking, and critical action as a framework for learning and teaching. Our final chapter, Chapter 12, Culture and Context, Theory and Practice of Adult Learning, considers how culture and context affect learning, explores the role of theory and practice in adult education, and offers a framework that integrates culture, theory, and practice.

Although in our minds we had a rationale for the order of chapters, the chapters can be read in whatever order is most helpful to the particular instructional situation; further, individual chapters can be used in single session workshops and seminars. At the end of each chapter we have a section titled Linking Theory and Practice: Activities and Resources where we have included activities we have used to engage learners in each of the topics. These activities and resources are meant for readers to explore their own learning as well as to use in instructional settings. Finally, each chapter closes with a list of Chapter Highlights where we have captured what we consider to be the salient points or "takeaways" discussed in the chapter.

Acknowledgments

We would like to acknowledge the students in our classes as well as participants in our workshops and seminars across the world who have been the inspiration for this book. They have challenged us to think through how best to engage people in understanding what we know about how adults learn. The order in which we have presented the material in this book, as well as suggested activities and resources have had trial runs, so to speak, with our students and workshop participants. Their candid feedback is much appreciated. We also want to thank the three reviewers of our manuscript whose comments, insights, and suggestions were most helpful in strengthening this book. We also want to acknowledge our editor, David Brightman, and his colleagues at Jossey-Bass who were extremely supportive and helpful throughout the process of bringing this book to fruition. Finally, a special thanks goes to our University of Georgia PhD students and graduate research assistants, Nan Fowler and Leanne Dzubinski. Nan assisted us in the early stages of the book with library research. Leanne accessed resources for our book, tracked down references, assisted in editing, and saw to the technical matters of getting the book ready for the publisher. To all of you, including our family and friends, we thank you for your support and encouragement.

Sharan B. Merriam and Laura L. Bierema
Athens, Georgia
October, 2013

THE AUTHORS

Sharan B. Merriam is Professor Emerita of Adult Education and Qualitative Research at The University of Georgia in Athens, Georgia, United States. Merriam's research and writing activities have focused on adult and lifelong learning and qualitative research methods. For five years she was coeditor of *Adult Education Quarterly*, the major research and theory journal in adult education. She has published 26 books, several of which have been translated into Chinese, Korean, Japanese, and French, and over 100 journal articles and book chapters. She is a four-time winner of the prestigious Cyril O. Houle World Award for Literature in Adult Education for books published in 1982, 1997, 1999, and 2007. Based on her widespread contributions to the field of adult education, Merriam has been inducted into the International Adult and Continuing Education Hall of Fame and was the first to receive the American Association of Adult and Continuing Education's Career Achievement award. Her most recent books are *The Jossey-Bass Reader on Contemporary Issues in Adult Education* (2011), *Qualitative Research: A Guide to Design and Implementation* (2009), *Third Update on Adult Learning Theory* (2008), *Learning in Adulthood* (2007), and *Non-Western Perspectives on Learning and Knowing* (2007). She has conducted workshops and seminars on adult learning and qualitative research throughout North America and overseas, including countries in southern Africa, Southeast Asia, the Middle East, and Europe. She has been a Fulbright

Scholar and a Senior Research Fellow in Malaysia, and a Distinguished Visiting Scholar at universities in South Korea and South Africa.

Laura L. Bierema is professor of adult education, learning, and organization development at the University of Georgia, Athens. Bierema's research and writing activities have focused on creating a critical human resource development (HRD) stream of research and practice, exploring women's learning and development in the workplace, and incorporating a feminist analysis to HRD discourse, research, and praxis. She has published four books and over 50 journal articles and book chapters. Bierema's research and writing have been recognized by The Academy for Human Resource Development (AHRD) with four Cutting Edge Awards. She is also the recipient of the *Highly Commended Award* at the Literati Network Awards for Excellence 2009; winner of the University of Georgia, 2012 College of Education Russell H. Yeany, Jr. Research Award; recipient of the 2012 Sherpa Trailblazer of the Year Award in recognition of innovation application of the Sherpa Executive Coaching Process; and 2013 winner of the AHRD's Outstanding Scholar Award. Bierema is a former coeditor of *Adult Education Quarterly*. Her other books include: *Women's Career Development Across the Lifespan: Insights and Strategies for Women, Organizations and Adult Educators* (1998), *Philosophy and Practice of Organizational Learning, Performance, and Change* (2001); *Critical Issues in Human Resource Development* (2003); and *Implementing a Critical Approach to Organization Development* (2010).

CHAPTER ONE

ADULT LEARNING IN TODAY'S WORLD

"Anyone who fails to learn . . . is regarded as *oku eniyan* (the living dead)," says an African proverb that captures not only how embedded but how necessary learning is in today's world (Avoseh, 2001, p. 483). Indeed, the daily lives of most people on the planet require constant learning, not just in a classroom, but as we go about our everyday activities. The way we communicate with others, deal with personal and family problems, conduct our work, and build our communities, all require us to learn new information, new procedures, and new technologies.

In this opening chapter we take a look at the social context of learning today, a context characterized by globalization, the knowledge age, technology, and demographic changes. We then turn to a focus on *adult* learners, how their life situation differs from that of children, and how participation in even formal learning activities has continued to grow over the years. In the last section of this chapter we describe the various settings where learning occurs, ending with a brief discussion of the global concept of lifelong learning.

The Social Context of Adult Learning

Learning, Jarvis (1987) writes, rarely occurs "in splendid isolation from the world in which the learner lives; . . . it is intimately related to that world and affected by it" (p. 11). From learning to use the newest version of your smartphone, to dealing with a diagnosis of Type II diabetes, to navigating your city's public transportation system, learning is embedded in the world in which we live. In this chapter we first step back and paint a large backdrop of forces shaping the world today against which we can more specifically address who the adult learner is, and what forms of learning an adult might be engaged in. Factors we see as important for understanding the context of adult learning are globalization, the information society, technology, and changing demographics.

Globalization

Of the many factors affecting our lives today, globalization is often mentioned more than anything else. In fact if you Google the term "globalization," you get more than 40 million "hits," a number that increases daily. The widespread use of the term not only speaks to its many meanings and applications, but to its vagueness. For our purposes, we define globalization as the movement of goods, services, people, and ideas across national borders. Of course for centuries people and goods have moved across national boundaries. What is different today is the speed and intensity of this movement. As Friedman (2011), one of the major commentators of this phenomenon writes, we have moved from "connected to hyperconnected."

What first comes to mind when most people hear the term "globalization" is outsourcing of manufacturing to low-income, low-wage countries. Indeed, something of a scandal arose in the summer of 2012 when it was learned that the U.S. Olympic team's uniforms had been outsourced to China! The economic component also makes people think of huge multinational or transnational companies that operate worldwide and are not held accountable by any single nation-state. The "market economy" underpins this accelerated version of globalization. Today, "corporations not only control the means of production—both economic and technological— but they also control the means of spreading knowledge about their products as they seek to convince the public to purchase what they produce" (Jarvis, 2008, p. 20). Thus, not only goods and services, but information and ideas are brokered across the globe, which in turn creates more demand for goods and services. One writer has wryly observed that the market economy and consumerism dimensions of globalization have resulted in the world becoming "one big shopping mall" (Cowen, 2003, p. 17). The downside of global commerce is the exploitation of workers worldwide, even children(witness, for example, the May 2013 collapse of a garment factory in Bangladesh killing more than 1100 workers), along with increasing pollution and environmental exploitation. The rise of "corporate social responsibility" campaigns and a movement toward sustainability in the market are closely linked to globalization. Scherer, Palazzo, and Matten (2010) argue that because nations have declining capacity to regulate socially desirable corporate behavior with commerce crossing national, social, political, cultural, and economic borders, it is becoming more incumbent on organizations to bear this political responsibility.

Education itself has become a commodity of the marketplace. Friedman (2005) gives numerous examples of this in his groundbreaking book on globalization titled, *The World Is Flat.* For example, parents in the United States are hiring math and science tutors for their children—that is, they are hiring tutors who are living in India. Students arriving home from school in the afternoon get on the Internet and are greeted by their Indian tutors who are up early to meet their students in real time (and at a considerably cheaper cost than hiring tutors in the States). Students are now consumers who "shop" worldwide for the educational program that best fits their needs and pocketbooks and which promises the results they seek. There is even a growing area of research and writing on what is being called "academic capitalism." Here institutions of higher education become a commercial enterprise in "the pursuit of market and market-like activities to generate external revenues" (Slaughter & Rhoades, 2004, p. 11). So while students may "shop" for their education, colleges and universities are also shopping for students!

The Knowledge Society

Intricately related to the market economy in a globalized world is the "knowledge economy." Companies will locate where there is a workforce with the knowledge and educational system able to sustain and develop the business. For example, the skill and educational base of potential workers was a major factor in Caterpillar, the world's largest manufacturer of heavy construction and mining equipment, which recently chose to locate a new plant in our university's hometown of Athens, Georgia (Aued, 2012). Not only do companies move to where the qualified workers are, but workers also relocate to where they can utilize their knowledge and training. Spring (2008) talks about moving from a "brain drain" phenomenon to a "brain circulation" trend "where skilled and professional workers move between wealthy nations or return to their homelands after migrating to another country" (p. 341).

The "knowledge economy," or, as it is more often labeled, the "knowledge society," has replaced the industrial society and has great implications for learning and educational systems across the globe and throughout the lifespan. As Dumont and Istance (2010) point out, "21st century competencies" include "deep understanding, flexibility and the capacity to make creative connections" and "a range of so-called 'soft skills' including good team-working. The quantity and quality of learning thus become central, with the accompanying concern that traditional educational approaches are insufficient" (p. 20). They go on to say that "knowledge is now a central driving force for economic activity, and the prosperity of individuals, companies and nations depends increasingly on human and intellectual capital. Innovation is becoming the dominant driving force in our economy and society (Florida, 2001; OECD, 2004; Brown, Lauder, and Ashton, 2008). Education and learning systems, for which knowledge is their core business, are clearly right at the heart of such a mega-trend" (p. 21).

The knowledge society is much more complex than what is implied by the earlier term, "information" society. While we are inundated with bits and pieces of information (note the millions of Google hits for the term "globalization" above), for information to become useful and meaningful, it needs to be weighed, organized, and structured into meaningful units of knowledge; information and data are the building blocks of knowledge. It is with knowledge that we build new insights, new understandings, and even new products, all of which can contribute to a more enriching context for learning. There are some caveats about this seemingly utopian concept of the knowledge society. Some places in the world are so torn by strife, poverty, and illiteracy that a knowledge society has not evolved, leaving these countries far behind and utterly unable to compete in the developed world. And some groups of citizens, discriminated against because of gender, race or ethnicity, disability, or age, are marginalized in their own societies and prevented from meaningfully participating in the knowledge society. "Women," for example, "make up 70 percent of the 1.3 billion absolutely poor, more than half the population of women over age fifteen worldwide are illiterate, and 75 percent of refugees and internally displaced are women" (Merriam, Courtenay, & Cervero, 2006, p. 92).

Everyone is challenged by the speed of change in this knowledge society. Most feel it is no longer possible to "keep up," for according to some estimates, information doubles every two years and World Wide Web

information doubles every 90 days (www.emc.com/about/news/press/
2011/20110628–01.htm). Change is at such an accelerated pace that even
some of the routine tasks of daily living require new learning. To buy
groceries at your local supermarket, for example, you may have to figure
out how to automatically scan your items and check out without dealing
with a person. Or, you may make your purchases in front of your computer
screen, never setting foot in the actual store. Tinkering with your car in
your own garage may not be possible without some knowledge of computer diagnostic systems. You can make a banking transaction or check-in at
the airport for a flight without ever making human contact. Even our trips
to the library can be conducted from the comfort of our homes where we
can electronically check out articles and books.

It is also clear that one cannot learn in the first two or three decades
all that a person needs to know for the rest of his or her life. Most professional preparation becomes outdated before one gets situated in a career.
Hewlett Packard has estimated that what one learns in a Bachelor of Engineering program is outdated or "deconstructs" in 18 months, and for
technology-related fields the half-life is even less. Students need to be
prepared as self-directed, lifelong learners "for jobs that do not yet exist,
to use technologies that have not yet been invented, and to solve problems
that we don't even know are problems yet" (Darling-Hammond et al.,
2008, p. 2)

Technology

Globalization and the knowledge society are promoted and sustained by
communications technology and the Internet. From multinational companies who conduct much of their work through technology-assisted
means, to friends in different parts of the world talking in real time over
Skype, to social media enabling social change as in the Arab Spring revolution, technology has irrevocably affected how we work, carry out our daily
lives, and interact with other people. There is little doubt that the "technology infused lives of today's learners" (Parker, 2013, p. 54) is shaping
not only the context of learning, but the learning itself. Even traditional
educational systems from elementary through higher education are using
technology in designing and delivering curriculum. Teachers in California, for example, are experimenting with the "flipped classroom" where
students watch videos for homework, "then go to class to demonstrate
their learning" (Webley, 2012, p. 39). Public libraries now loan out e-books.
Even prestigious higher education institutions are opening up access to

learning through the Internet. In 2012 Stanford University offered a free online course on artificial intelligence that drew 160,000 students from 190 countries. This experiment has evolved into what are being called MOOCs (massive open online courses). Stanford recently partnered with Princeton, University of Michigan, and University of Pennsylvania to offer 43 courses enrolling 680,000 students (http://www.nytimes.com/2012/ 07/17/education/consortium-of-colleges-takes-online-education-to-new -level.html?_r=1&src=me&ref=general). Harvard and Massachusetts Institute of Technology (MIT) are engaged in a similar partnership estimating that half a million students would enroll in their free, online courses (http://www.bbc.co.uk/news/business-18191589). Indeed, Friedman speculates that these MOOCs are likely to transform higher education into a credentialing system where participants, rather than getting "degrees" will get "certificates that testify that they have done the work and passed all the exams" (Friedman, 2013, p. SR11).

Technology is also changing how adults learn. Adult basic education programs through continuing professional education are incorporating technology in both the design of curriculum and its delivery. And the field of adult education is becoming particularly attentive to the Net generation, those born between 1981 and 1994. These young adults "bring with them a set of traits that includes familiarity with technology, optimism, ability to multitask, diversity, and acceptance of authority (Bennett & Bell, 2010, p. 417). They are also characterized by "shallowness in reading, lack of critical thinking, and naïveté about intellectual property and information authenticity of Internet resources" (p. 417). And while technology is certainly affecting formal learning, its impact on informal learning, that which we do as part of our everyday lives, is limitless. As King (2010) writes, "Ubiquitous (but not always obvious) informal learning opportunities make it possible for adults to tap the exploding information and learning resources of our times. Informal learning today goes beyond book-based self-study to include a plethora of Web-based, digital, and community resources, along with opportunities for worldwide collaboration with people of similar interests and needs. The world is rich with new learning opportunities—for example, iPods, TV programs, digital radio and virtual simulations—that can fit anyone's schedule and learning style" (p. 421). The availability of massive amounts of information 24 hours a day, seven days a week also challenges us, Bryan (2013) points out, in terms of dealing with information overload and learning how to critically evaluate all this information. The informality of twitter, texting, email, emoticons and so on is also bringing about changes in our language. How do tech-savvy young people know "what language formats are best suited for the workplace, or to use for technical language in the sciences and math fields, or for scholarly writings, or marketing, and the list goes on and on" (Bryan, 2013, p. 10).

As pointed out earlier, technology cannot be separated from globalization and the knowledge society. However, it is important to note that "although some may say the digital divide has been bridged, visiting impoverished inner-city, small rural, and violence-torn areas around the globe reveals scores of people who do not have access to electricity, technology, and the outside world" (King, 2010, p. 426). Further, it has been estimated that only 12% of the people in the world have computers, and of that, only 8% are connected to the Internet (http://www.miniature -earth.com). There is still much to do to address the basic needs of marginalized people and nations before all can benefit from participation in this digitalized, globalized, knowledge society.

Changing Demographics

Globalization and all that it entails has enabled people everywhere to see the diversity of the world's seven billion people. It is much more difficult for certain societies to be inward-looking and ethnocentric, that is, seeing themselves as the center of, and superior to the rest of the world when we see the diversity of the world on our televisions and computer screens and indeed, even as we are out in our local community. It is enlightening to look at the statistics through an analogy of presenting the world as a community of 100 people, keeping all of the proportions the same as in our world of seven billion. For example, if the world consisted of 100 people, 61 would be Asian, 14 North and South Americans, 13 Africans, and so on. Table 1.1 presents some of these statistics.

Of particular interest to our field of adult education, is the fact that 16.3% of those over 15 years of age would be illiterate, and only seven would have a secondary education, and one a college education. And in reference to our discussion of technology above, 12 out of the 100 would have a home computer (http://www.miniature-earth.com; http:// stats.uis.unesco.org; https://www.cia.gov/library/publications/the-world -factbook/). A UNESCO (2008) report concluded: "Equalizing opportunities in education is one of the most important conditions for overcoming social injustice and reducing social disparities in any country . . . and is also a condition for strengthening economic growth" (p. 24). Further, global illiteracy continues to plague the world, especially among women who make up two-thirds of the 774 million adults lacking basic literacy skills (UNESCO, 2009). So, back to the analogy of 100, almost 11 of the 16 illiterate would be women.

There are other demographic shifts that are of particular interest to adult educators. Many countries, for example, are experiencing a dramatic growth in their aging population. Due to a decline in fertility and an increase in longevity, it is estimated that "in less than 10 years, older people will outnumber children for the first time in history" (Withnall, 2012, p. 650). In 2010 older adults comprised 11% of the world's population and are expected to grow to 22% in the year 2050 (World Economic Forum, 2012). As can be seen in Table 1.2, this growth is uneven but all

TABLE 1.1 IF THE WORLD CONSISTED OF 100 PEOPLE

61 Asians	21 live on less than $2 (U.S.) a day
14 Americans (North and South)	14 are hungry or malnourished
13 Africans	16.3 are illiterate (15 years of age and above)
12 Europeans	
1 Australian (Oceania)	Only 7 are educated at the secondary level
70 Non-White	Only 1 would have a college education
30 White	If you keep your clothes in a closet and food
67 Non-Christian	in a refrigerator, you are richer than 75%
33 Christian	of the entire world population
8 are 65 years and above	
12 are disabled	
30 are Internet users	
12 have a home computer	

Source: http://www.minature-earth.com; http://stats.uis.unesco.org; www.cia.gov/library/publications/the-world-factbook/

TABLE 1.2 PERCENTAGE OF POPULATION AGED 60 AND OLDER

	2010	2030	2050
World	11	17	22
More Developed Regions	22	29	32
Less Developed Regions	9	14	20
Africa	5	7	10
Asia	10	17	24
Europe	22	29	34
Latin America & Caribbean	10	17	25
North America	19	26	27
Oceania	15	20	24

Source: World Economic Forum, 2012.

regions are experiencing growth. And while the *percentage* of the population over 60 is greater in developed countries, the actual number of older adults is greater in developing countries such as China, India and Brazil (WHO, 1999). There were 171 million older adults in China in 2010, for example. Even more dramatic are the top 10 countries experiencing the greatest growth in their elder populations. As can be seen in Table 1.3, Japan currently leads the world with 22% of its population 60+, rising to a projected 45% by the year 2050.

This worldwide demographic trend presents both opportunities and challenges to nations and communities, and education is coming to play an important role is meeting these challenges. International bodies such as the United Nations, the World Health Organization, and the European Commission, nation states, and even local communities are developing educational policies and programs in response to global aging. The European Commission has identified five challenges with regard to older adult learning and stated that "there is a need for better insight into the benefits of adult learning and the barriers to its uptake, and for better data on providers, trainers, and training delivery" (European Commission, 2006, p. 10). And in line with this 21st century context of globalization, information, and technology, computer-based, online delivery systems have been successful in improving access (see Swindell, 2000). Further, computer literacy and social media are also topics of interest to older adult learners (Kim & Merriam, 2010).

Another worldwide demographic trend is the movement of people across borders, usually related to employment opportunities, but also in

TABLE 1.3 THE TOP 10 COUNTRIES WITH THE HIGHEST PERCENTAGES OF 60+ POPULATIONS IN 2011 AND 2050

2011		2050	
Japan	31	Japan	42
Italy	27	Portugal	40
Germany	26	Bosnia & Herzegovina	40
Finland	25	Cuba	39
Sweden	25	Republic of Korea	39
Bulgaria	25	Italy	38
Greece	25	Spain	38
Portugal	24	Singapore	38
Belgium	24	Germany	38
Croatia	24	Switzerland	37

Source: World Economic Forum, 2012.

search of a better life, and in some cases escaping war and violence. With regard to work, we have already mentioned the "brain circuit" phenomenon created by the knowledge society wherein people with specialized training are in demand, irrespective of national borders. Due to low birthrates in many developed countries, workforce shortages are being addressed by importing immigrants to fill low-skilled jobs. Singapore, for example, has had to bring in immigrants from China and Southeast Asia to fill service and construction-industry jobs. China itself is struggling with a huge flux of internal migrants moving from rural to urban areas.

The U.S. experience with the growing diversity of today's immigrant population mirrors what is taking place worldwide. As Alfred (2004) explains, the immigration pattern reflects an hourglass: "There are those immigrants who are quickly achieving upward mobility, primarily through education and high-tech jobs, while on the opposite end of the hourglass, large numbers of low-skilled workers find themselves locked in low-wage service jobs." As a result, "planners of adult and higher education programs face a challenging task as they attempt to meet the variety of needs and expectations that immigrants bring to the new country" (p. 14).

As with the global aging phenomenon, the growing cultural and ethnic diversity of most countries presents both challenges and opportunities. For example, according to the latest U.S. Census (Humes, Jones, & Ramirez, 2011), between 2000 and 2010 the Hispanic population accounted for 43% of the total population growth, Asians about 43.3%, and African Americans 12.3% (U.S. Bureau of the Census, 2012). Another measure of growing diversity in the United States is something called the USA TODAY Diversity Index (Nasser, 2013). This index measures on a scale of 0 (low diversity) to 100 (high diversity) the probability that two people chosen randomly are of different races or ethnicities. In the 1990 census the probability was 40; in 2000 it was 49; in 2010 the Diversity Index rose to 55. Such demographic changes as these create tension between how much a group's culture and language is to be preserved versus adopting the norms of the dominant culture. And of course such diversity presents challenges for adult education in terms of aligning learning needs and learning styles of different ethnic and cultural groups with the design of curriculum and instruction.

In summary, in drawing the context of adult learning, we have only touched on several major trends, any one of which has dozens of book-length treatments and will elicit millions of hits on Google. Globalization, the information society, technology and changing demographics are so interrelated it is difficult to consider one without reference to the others.

The learning that adults are engaged in both reflects and responds to these forces.

The Adult Learner and Learning in Adulthood

Adult learning is at the heart of our practice as adult educators. Whether we are offering training on new equipment at the workplace, designing continuing professional education for accountants or nurses, enrolling adults in a college course, or teaching adults English, our practice is enhanced by knowing as much as we can about who our learners are as well as how they learn. While of course our entire book is about learning in adulthood, it is important to first review what we know about adult learners themselves, including participation data, and the types of learning activities in which adults are likely to be engaged.

The Adult Learner

A discussion of the adult learner often begins with defining what it means to be an "adult." Of course this may seem obvious to most of us, but for funding and policy guidelines it may not be so clear. If, for example, we use age, say 18, which is a legal definition of adult in the United States, then what about high school dropouts who enter adult education programs to complete their secondary education? Typically, age 16 is the minimum for engaging in adult secondary education programs. If we define an adult as one who has assumed the social roles and responsibilities expected of an adult, what about adults who are institutionalized, incarcerated, or in the fulltime care of family? Perhaps the only way out of this maze is to broadly define adult as Merriam and Brockett (2007) have as part of their definition of adult education—"activities intentionally designed for the purpose of bringing about learning among *those whose age, social roles, or self-perception, define them as adults*" (p. 8, italics added).

More important than defining what constitutes an adult is understanding how an adult's life situation typically differs from that of a child and what implications this has for learning. An adult is in a different position in the life span than a child. A child is dependent on others for care, learning is a child's major activity in life, and much of this learning is in preparation for assuming the tasks and responsibilities of adulthood. Going to school is a child's full-time job! Adults, in contrast, have many other roles and responsibilities. They may be going to school, even full-time, but they *add* the role of student onto their other often full-time roles as caretaker, worker, and citizen. Another dimension that differentiates adult learners from children is an adult's life experiences. Observers going back to the beginning of the field of adult education have noted this as a key characteristic of adult learners. Lindeman (1926/1961) is often quoted as saying "the resource of highest value in adult education is the learner's experience" (p. 6). Experience becomes "the adult learner's living text-book" (p. 7). Kidd (1973) was even more explicit in writing that "adults have more experiences, adults have different kinds of experiences, and adult experiences are organized differently." It is these experiences that set adults "off from the world of children" (p. 46). And of course one of the major tenets of Knowles's andragogy (1980) (see Chapter 3) is that adults' life experiences not only define who they are as adults, but these life experiences are also a rich resource for learning.

A third way in which adults differ from children that has implications for learning is that adults are developmentally at different stages in the life cycle. Children of course are also developing, but much of this development is biological, both physical (as in learning to walk) or cognitive (learning to communicate). Adult development has more to do with social roles (learning to be a parent or a worker) and psychosocial tasks such as establishing intimacy in young adulthood, or generativity in middle age (Erikson, 1963). Theories of cognitive (Kegan, 1994; Perry, 1981), moral (Kohlberg, 1973), and faith (Fowler, 1981) development all posit qualitatively different stages of development for children and adults. Interestingly, the social context of our world today may be fostering a new stage of adult development, that of "emerging adulthood." According to its main proponent, Arnett (2000; also see Arnett & Tanner, 2006), emerging adulthood is neither adolescence nor young adulthood, but that period between 18 and 25 years of age when young people in America are allowed a "prolonged period of independent role exploration" (2000, p. 469).

Because an adult is in a different position in the lifecycle than a child, and because adults' life experiences are greater and more varied than those of children, adults' learning needs and interests vary from children. This difference is reflected in the research on what motivates adults to participate in learning activities (see Chapter 8). Briefly, adults participate in learning for a number of reasons, all of which link back to their position in the life cycle as adults. Adults are motivated by wanting to improve their situation in adult life, whether that situation is work-related, personal (such as improving their health, dealing with family issues), or social/community-related. Some adults like to learn for the joy of learning of course, but even what they choose to learn "for fun" most likely has something to do with their life stage and previous experiences.

Participation in Adult Learning Activities

Participation in adult education has grown some, yet remains "unacceptably low" in most countries according to a 2009 UNESCO *Global Report on Adult Learning and Education.* The percentage of adults 25 and older who have not finished primary schooling or its equivalent speaks to the large unmet demand for adult basic education. According to the report, "at least 18% of the world's adults have not completed primary schooling or ever been to school. This rate reaches 30% in Latin America and the Caribbean, 48% in the Arab States, 50% in sub-Saharan Africa and 53% in South and West Asia. Given that for many of the poorest countries in the world, no data are available at all, it is certain that were these countries to be included in the estimates given . . . average rates of adults not completing primary schooling would be even higher" (p. 62).

In Europe and North America where participation data are tracked, the percent of adults who participate in various adult education activities has increased over the years. For example, Finland saw a doubling of participation between 1980 and 2000. U.S. data have shown a slight increase from 40% in 1995, to 46% in 2001. U.S. participation decreased slightly in 2005 to 44% (U.S. Department of Education, NCES, 2007). Participation in Europe varied widely by country in its inaugural European-wide adult education survey from 2005 to 2006, covering 29 countries. Results showed a variance in participation from the European average of 35.7%, with Sweden having the highest participation rate at 73.4% and Hungary having the lowest at 9.0%. The UNESCO report identified four different levels of participation as depicted in Table 1.4.

Research in the U.S. has also given us a sociodemographic profile of the adult learner, so that we do have a picture of the typical adult learner, especially those who participate in formal educational programs. Participation in formal adult education can take many forms: English as a second language (ESL), adult basic education (ABE), general education development (GED), credentialing and apprenticeship programs, work-related courses, continuing professional education (CPE), continuing education, higher education, and personal development courses. This list does not include the range of informal and nonformal learning adults engage in such as self-directed learning projects. The first national study of participation in adult education was conducted by Johnstone and Rivera (1965).

TABLE 1.4 COUNTRY GROUPINGS BY PARTICIPATION IN ORGANIZED FORMS OF ADULT EDUCATION IN THE PREVIOUS YEAR, POPULATION AGED 16–65

Group	Participation Rate	Description
Group 1:	>50%	Nordic countries, including Denmark, Finland, Iceland, Norway and Sweden.
Group 2:	35–50%	Countries of Anglo-Saxon origin: Australia, Canada, New Zealand, the United Kingdom and the United States of America. A few of the smaller Central and Northern European countries, including Austria, Luxembourg, the Netherlands and Switzerland, as well as the Caribbean archipelago of Bermuda, are also among this group.
Group 3:	20–35%	Northern European countries including Belgium (Flanders) and Germany as well as Ireland. Also among this Group are some Eastern European countries, namely Czech Republic and Slovenia, and some Southern European countries including France, Italy and Spain.
Group 4:	<20%	Southern European countries, namely Greece and Portugal, as well as some additional Eastern European countries, Hungary and Poland, and the only South American country with comparable data, Chile.

Source: Adapted from UNESCO Institute for Lifelong Learning (2009). Global Report on Adult Learning and Education. http://uil.unesco.org/fileadmin/keydocuments/AdultEducation/en/GRALE_en.pdf

This historic study provided a baseline to measure adult participation in the United States for decades since. During the 1961–1962 study period, it was estimated that 22% of American adults engaged in learning and that their learning was practical and skill-oriented in its focus. Johnstone and Rivera offered a profile of the adult learner: "The adult education participant is just as often a woman as a man, is typically under forty, has completed high school or more, enjoys an above-average income, works full-time and most often in a white-collar occupation, is married and has children, lives in an urbanized area but more likely in a suburb than large city, and is found in all parts of the country, but more frequently in the West than in other regions" (p. 8).

While the rate of participation has grown from Johnstone and Rivera's 1965 estimate of 22% to 44% in 2005 (U.S. Department of Education, NCES, 2007), the descriptive profile of the typical participant has remained fairly constant. As with all previous participation studies, educational level predicts participation (U.S. Department of Education, NCES, 2007). Non-high school completers participated 22.1% of the time as compared to 62.5% of those possessing a bachelor's degree. Employment status and occupation of adults also impacted participation. Adults working for pay during the survey period were more likely to participate than those not working (51.7% versus 25.5%). Adults working in professional or managerial roles were most likely to participate (70.2%) as compared to occupations such as service, sales, or support occupations (48.3%) and trade occupations (34%). Work-related courses were the most common (27%), followed by personal interest courses (21%) (U.S. Department of Education, NCES, 2007). Ginsberg and Wlodkowski (2010) revisited adult participation data to develop a 21st century understanding of participation and access:

> The sheer numbers [of adult participation in formal learning] are startling: mega transnational universities such as the University of Phoenix with adult student enrollments well beyond 350,000; online students in distance programs totaling nearly 1.5 million as of 2006 and tripling from 483,113 in 2002 (Romano, 2006); more than 360 colleges and universities offering accelerated programs created especially for working adults (Commission for Accelerated Programs, 2008); and an estimated 90 million adults participating in formal and informal education including basic education, English-language learning, workplace learning, and personal development classes (Paulson & Boeke, 2006). (p. 25)

Further, though the field is awaiting an up-to-date participation study to confirm the above trends, it is highly likely that now "more than 50% of all adults in the U.S. between the ages of 25 and 55 [are] involved in some form of adult education" (Ginsberg & Wlodkowski, 2010, p. 25).

Settings Where Learning Occurs

This book is devoted to what we know about *how* adults learn and in subsequent chapters we explore different theories, models, concepts and insights into the phenomenon of learning. All learning takes place in a social context and it is this context that we have been exploring in this opening chapter. We have already looked at the larger socioeconomic context and the adult learner's life context which differs from that of children. Now we turn to the settings where learning occurs, and conclude with brief descriptions of the concepts of lifelong learning and the learning society.

Learning settings are most often divided into formal, nonformal and informal settings (Coombs, Prosser, & Ahmed, 1973). While this is not a perfect typology and there are instances of overlap and intersection, it is a framework that resonates with most adult learners' and adult educators' experiences. Briefly, formal learning settings are those sponsored by educational institutions, whereas nonformal settings are organized learning opportunities sponsored by institutions, agencies, and community-based groups whose primary mission is other than educational. Informal learning activities are embedded in one's everyday life.

If asked about their learning, most adults will refer to a formal classroom situation. Indeed, we have been so conditioned to thinking of learning as something that takes place in an educational institution that our learning at work or in our everyday life does not seem to count as part of our learning. Formal learning sites are equated with educational bureaucracies going from preschool to post-graduate studies. In adult education we would include adult basic education programs, adult high schools, English as a Second Language programs, or professional training programs. We also think of the growing numbers of adults in post-secondary educational institutions. In fact, it has been estimated that adults aged twenty-five years and older account for 36% of students enrolled in four-year colleges and universities (Sandmann, 2010). In a provocative article on "post-traditional learners" Soares (2013) makes the point that "today traditional students represent only about 15 percent of current undergraduates. They attend four-year colleges and live on campus. The remaining 85 percent, or about 15 million undergraduates, are a diverse group that includes adult learners, employees who study, low-income students, commuters, and student parents. Unpacking this 85 percent a little further, . . . 43 percent of all undergraduates attend community colleges. And, adult learners make up as much as 60 percent of all community college students" (p. 6).

In contrast to formal learning organized by educational institutions, nonformal learning is sponsored by organizations, agencies, and institutions whose primary mission is not education, though education might be a secondary mission employed to carry out the main reason for existence. Think for a moment about a training session you attended at work, or a study group at your local library, or even a two-hour clinic on "How to lay floor tile" sponsored by the nearby home improvement store. These are all examples of nonformal education. Educational opportunities sponsored by business and industry, indeed, all workplace training and educational programs are in the service of the business, and education is a secondary concern. So too, is the case for religious (churches, mosques, synagogues), cultural (museums, art galleries), health (hospitals, Red Cross), and recreational (parks, sports associations) organizations' sponsorship of educational programs.

Nonformal learning is further distinguished from formal learning by the activities typically being short-term, voluntary, often occurring in public places. There is usually a curriculum and often a facilitator, but both of these components are quite flexible. While it is much harder to gather enrollment figures for nonformal sites of learning, it is widely assumed that most adults are engaged in learning in these venues—it is just that most adults do not recognize these as learning events. Taylor (2012), who has studied nonformal learning, especially that which takes place in public places like museums, parks, and consumer education sites, comments that it is "mind-boggling to begin to try to make sense of the level of participation" (p. 6), when you consider, for example, just cultural institutions alone where:

> Millions of adults can be found gathering every day in libraries, parks, zoos, aquariums, and museums across North America. For example, each year more than 287 million people visit the 391 units of parks, monuments, national recreation areas, battlefields, wild and scenic rivers, and seashores of the national parks in the United States (National Park Service, 2007). During these visits, many adults often meet a park interpreter and participate in local nonformal education programs, such as a trail tour of park vegetation and wildlife, a discussion on land management practices, or a hands-on exploration of the geology in the park. (p. 5)

If it is hard to estimate participation in nonformal adult learning, it is impossible to do so when speaking of informal learning, the third form of learning proposed by Coombs (1985). By its very definition as "the spontaneous, unstructured learning that goes on daily in the home and neighborhood, behind the school and on the playing field, in the workplace, marketplace, library and museum, and through the various mass media" (p. 92), informal learning is by far the most prevalent of the three forms of learning in the Coombs typology. Illeris (2004a) calls it "everyday learning" because it "takes place in all the private and non-organised contexts of everyday life" (p. 151). Because it is so embedded in our lives, to recognize "everyday learning" as learning we do have to stop and think about it as learning. For example, most of us have encountered a health problem that has sent us to the Internet, the library, and health professionals to learn all we can about this problem, its cause, treatment, and perhaps lifestyle changes required to cope with it. Relocating to a new area requires us to learn about housing, transportation, and community resources. Think about your workplace. Interacting with coworkers at lunch, in the break room, informally at your desk, perhaps on the company's intranet, often involves learning. And presumably most Internet searches are by people wanting to learn something. The magnitude of this type of informal learning is astounding, given for example, that in 2010 there were 88 billion searches a month on Google (www.searchengineland .com). Informal learning is endless, boundary-less, and ubiquitous in our lives. And as King (2010) points out, in this fast-paced world where "knowledge is increasing at lightning speed, . . . formal learning is inadequate to meet these lifelong learning needs: people do not have time to enroll in formal classes at every new life stage and for every decision they must make" (p. 421). She goes on to note that the "virtual and digital ages" of today "have opened new possibilities as adults can engage in learning outside the constraints of time and place" (p. 422).

Indeed, research on informal learning points to how widespread and embedded it is in our lives. A study of Canadian adult learners, for example, found that 90% were engaged in informal learning activities (Livingstone, 2002). And although billions are spent each year on formal training in the workplace, it has been estimated that upwards of 70% of learning in the workplace takes place informally (Kim, Hagedorn, Williamson, & Chapman, 2004; Kleiner, Carver, Hagedorn, & Chapman, 2005). Just what constitutes informal learning in the workplace and how to access it has been the topic of lively discussion in the literature. Billett (2002) recommends rejecting the notion of "informal learning" as it actually constrains our understanding of how learning occurs through work, a process he conceptualizes as "inter-dependent between the individual and the social practice" (abstract). Sawchuk (2008), in a comprehensive review of theories and research on informal learning and work, comes to a different conclusion, suggesting that we think of formal and informal learning as a continuum, rather than as dichotomous categories.

Informal learning often includes several other types of learning. Self-directed learning, an area of research and theory-building in adult education (see Chapter 4) is considered to be largely informal, although one can certainly choose to take a class as part of a self-directed learning project. And if one regards self-directed learning projects as a form of informal learning, there is substantial research suggesting that "upwards of 90 percent of adults are engaged in hundreds of hours of informal learning" (Merriam, Caffarella, & Baumgartner, 2007, p. 35). Other conceptions of informal learning include incidental learning which has been defined as an accidental by-product of doing something else. "Incidental learning happens outside the learner's conscious awareness, while informal learning involves a conscious effort on the learner's part such as learning how to play the guitar or taking a self-guided tour of a museum" (Taylor, 2012, p. 14). In incidental learning, one becomes aware that "some learning has taken place" after engaging in some experience (Marsick & Watkins, 1990, p. 4). For example, say you are on your way to a meeting and you need to quickly make a copy of a handout. The copy machine jams and you rush to get someone to help you. This person fixes the problem but in so doing, tells you what was wrong and what to do if it happens again. You learned something as a by-product of doing something else. This is incidental learning. Finally, tacit learning—that which occurs at a subconscious level, but which we regularly draw upon in negotiating our daily lives—is perhaps the most subtle form of informal learning. We know, for example, not to bring up particular topics in the presence of certain coworkers or family members; this is tacit knowledge.

Informal learning is indeed most difficult to capture and understand. Some interesting theorizing in this area is being done by Bennett (2012) who has proposed a four-part model of informal learning. Three parts we are familiar with—self-directed, incidental, and tacit learning. She adds a fourth component, integrative learning which she defines as "*a learning process that combines intentional nonconscious processing of tacit knowledge with conscious access to learning products and mental images*" (p. 28; italics in original). She explains how integrative learning might occur:

> Integrative learning may be responsible for creative insight, intuitive leaps, and moments of sudden understanding. Because implicit processing deals with memory fragments, images, and sensory data, it would not occur in a linear and rational fashion . . . For example, adults who are working on a problem—that is they have identified an important learning gap they intend to fill, but have gone as far as they can with conscious thought—may find the solution when they turn their attention *away* from the problem so that integrative learning takes over. This might happen during sleep or exercise and activities that distract the conscious mind so that implicit processing can occur. (p. 28)

Before we conclude this section on learning contexts, we thought it would be useful to briefly mention the notion of the "learning society" which is part of the global concept of "lifelong learning." The learning society (or in some places, learning regions, communities, cities, towns or villages) is a place-bound application of the concept of lifelong learning designed to promote economic, social and cultural development, often with the goal of competing globally (Walters, 2005). China, with its growing social class stratification for example, has instituted a countrywide learning society program designed to maintain and foster a "harmonious" society (Chang, 2010). Of course all types of learning—formal, nonformal, and informal—are fostered by and take place in learning cities.

Learning societies is one manifestation of the concept of lifelong learning. By the early 1990s, lifelong learning had supplanted the earlier concept of lifelong education. As Hasan (2012) explains, "the word 'education' was replaced by 'learning', to signal an emphasis on the learner, the learning processes and outcomes, as opposed to a focus on imparting education" (p. 472). UNESCO and OECD took the lead in conceptualizing the concept and "coverage was extended to all purposeful learning activity" across the lifespan, and "learning activities in all settings (OECD, 2009), from formal education to informal and non-formal learning" (pp. 472–473). Indeed, the notion that lifelong learning should not only be lifelong, from cradle to grave, but "'lifewide'—recognizing the interplay of informal, non-formal and formal learning in different life domains—and 'life deep'—incorporating the religious, moral, ethical and social dimensions that shape human expression—have led to richer and more pluralistic interpretations of the scope and possibilities of learning throughout the lifecourse" (Aspin, Evan, Chapman, & Bagnall, 2012, p. liii).

A number of international organizations and countries have adopted the concept of lifelong learning as an overarching concept to guide policy, research, and learning programs. While the United States has no official policy on lifelong learning, the concept is framing some of our thinking and writing particularly in the field of adult education. In the United States at least, lifelong learning is used usually in reference to adults and the need to continue learning past formal schooling. Often this application results in an emphasis on learning to meet labor market expectations or as a rationale for mandatory continuing education. As Crowther (2012) writes, "There are few educators who would disagree with the principle that lifelong learning is a good thing, but the important questions are about the types of learning that the concept promotes, the life that it encourages us to lead, who benefits from this and the nature of the society that it upholds" (p. 801).

Chapter Summary

With this discussion of lifelong learning and the learning settings of formal, nonformal, and informal, we bring this chapter on the context of adult learning to a close. We know from research studies and our own personal experiences that adults are extensively engaged in learning whether or not this learning is formally recognized. Finally, this learning is firmly embedded in the greater social context characterized by globalization, the knowledge society, technology, and changing demographics.

Linking Theory and Practice: Activities and Resources

1. Describe a learning activity you have been recently engaged in. To what extent did the activity relate to the global context? Did your learning involve technology? For example, if you attended a session on "planting a resource-friendly garden" sponsored by the local botanical garden, did climate change or water preservation come up as topics? Did you become familiar with the botanical garden's website? Use the Internet to find out more about certain plants and shrubs?

2. With regard to changing demographics, informally survey your immediate community for learning opportunities designed for immigrants, English language learners, or older adult learners. Have these opportunities increased over the last five years? What about participation?

3. Consider the institution of higher education where you are perhaps taking a course in which you are using this textbook on adult learning. What proportion of students is over the age of 25 across the institution? In this program? In this course? What are the other demographic characteristics that describe these adult students?

4. Take any topic of interest to you. Describe the nature of the setting, the curriculum, and the instruction if this topic were explored in a formal setting, a nonformal setting, or an informal setting.

5. Keep a log of your activities over the period of a week. Which ones involved informal learning?

6. Springer has just published a two-volume handbook on lifelong learning. The 55 chapters are divided into four sections on (1) History,

Theory, and Philosophy; (2) The Policy Challenge; (3) Programmes and Practices; and (4) A Critical Stocktaking. Aspin, D. N., Chapman, J. Evans, K. & Bagnall, R. (Eds.). (2012). *Second International Handbook of Lifelong Learning, Parts 1 & 2*, New York: Springer.

7. Reports and Web Links:
   a. UNESCO's Institute for Lifelong Learning (UIL) "promotes lifelong learning policy and practice with a focus on adult learning and education, especially literacy and nonformal education and alternative learning opportunities for marginalized and disadvantaged groups" (http://uil.unesco.org). Both the UIL and OECD (Organisation for Economic Co-operation and Development) (www.oecd.org) have numerous documents on adult education and lifelong learning.
   b. For interesting information and videos on globalization see the websites on the "miniature earth" (http://www.miniature-earth.com) or one of the many "Did you know?" sites (Google "Did you know videos" for multiple websites). Also, there are numerous short YouTube videos on globalization such as one that uses Friedman's work (http://www.youtube.com/watch?v=hg5EerKh0L4).
   c. See the National Center for Education Statistics (NCES) National Household Education Surveys Program of 2005—the most recent report detailing adult education participation in the U.S. http://nces.ed.gov/pubs2006/2006077.pdf

Chapter Highlights

- Globalization is the movement of goods, services, people, and culture across national boundaries. The intensity and speed of this movement characterizes globalization today.
- The knowledge society wherein knowledge and education are commodities of value has eclipsed the industrial society where labor and machines were of greatest value. Both globalization and the knowledge society are powered by communication technologies and the Internet.
- Changing demographics, particularly with reference to cultural and ethnic diversity and an aging population characterize most societies today.

- Due to their position in the social context and in the life cycle, the adult learner has qualitatively different learning needs and interests from children.
- Learning takes place in formal and nonformal settings, and informally as part of an adult's everyday life.
- Lifelong learning is an overarching concept often applied to adults to capture the all-encompassing nature of learning in adulthood.

CHAPTER TWO

TRADITIONAL LEARNING THEORIES

Think about building a home. First you map out where the home will sit on the lot, then you lay the foundation, followed by framing in the structure, raising walls, and adding a roof. So before we build this house of adult learning, we will first examine the foundation upon which the rest of the structure sits. We begin by exploring the notion of learning itself, then review several theories of learning and show how these theories have informed the growing body of knowledge about *adult* learning.

What Is Learning?

Human beings would not have survived without learning and even today there is the recognition that learning is a basic human endeavor, one that is truly lifelong. The study of learning and what it means to know used to be a philosophical undertaking rather than the arena of psychology or education. The West drew from Aristotle and Plato while for much of Asia, Confucius defined the nature of learning. The nature of knowledge and how we know and learn were topics of philosophical debate and analysis. Aristotle, for example, believed that knowing was a sensory experience, that is, we come to know through our five senses, whereas for Plato knowing involved introspection (Hergenhahn & Olson, 2005). Confucius, however, defined learning as a moral and ethical endeavor with the goal of becoming "fully human" (Kee, 2007, p. 159).

While for centuries philosophers explored the nature of knowledge and what it meant to know, it was not until the late nineteenth century that learning was investigated "scientifically"; that is, psychologists in Europe and North America began to systematically study learning by conducting laboratory experiments and observing behavior. And perhaps because of the focus on behavior, learning first became defined as a *change in behavior*. But, as many have pointed out, one can learn something such as an attitude or an emotion without any accompanying overt behavior change (Hill, 2002). A more nuanced definition of learning is "a change in human disposition or capacity that persists over a period of time and is not simply ascribable to processes of growth" (Gagne, 1985, p. 2). Now learning is thought to be both a process, as in "I am learning to use my new iPhone," or "I am learning to cope with diabetes," and an outcome, as in "I have figured out how to use my iPhone." Further, learning can emphasize the cognitive as in gaining knowledge of something, psychomotor as in learning a new physical skill, or affective, having to do with emotions and attitudes.

To explore the multidimensionality of learning a bit more, think about something you have recently learned. Did you study the motor vehicle manual in preparation to take the test to get your driver's license? That would be cognitive learning. Or maybe you practiced some new plays in coaching your daughter's soccer team, primarily a psychomotor learning activity, or you assisted a loved one to get help for an addiction and in so doing learned how to deal with your own emotional response. These are all examples of learning. Learning theories, which we now turn to, are more comprehensive explanations of human learning.

Learning Theories

Nothing is so practical as a good theory, the saying goes. What this means with regard to learning theory is that the theory provides an explanation of how learning occurs as well as being suggestive as to how such an explanation translates into practice. Learning theories, then, are explanations of what happens when learning takes place. Unfortunately there is little consensus as to which orientations are considered "theories" or how many theories there are. Further, different writers divide and label the knowledge base using different criteria. Gross (1999), echoing Reese and

Overton (1970), groups theories according to either a mechanistic or an organic worldview. Gredler (1997) discusses seven contemporary "perspectives." Even adult educators vary in their classifications of learning theory. Garrison and Archer (2000) discuss three orientations—behaviorist, cognitive, and "integrative," which considers the interaction between the environment and the learner. Illeris (2004b) draws from a number of learning theorists under three general "dimensions" of learning—cognitive, psychodynamic, and social-societal.

Given the lack of consensus as to how many and which perspectives are learning theories, we have chosen to discuss five orientations that offer different explanations of learning and which also have ready application to adult learning (Merriam, Caffarella, & Baumgartner, 2007). Beginning with the earliest scientifically developed learning theory, behaviorism, these five orientations/perspectives/theories are presented in somewhat chronological order. The five orientations are behaviorist, humanist, cognitivist, social cognitivist, and constructivist. These five are considered traditional learning theories and are foundational to what we have come to understand about adult learning.

Behaviorism—Learning Is a Change in Behavior

One of the most famous experiments of all time involved a dog, a bell, and some food—known as Pavlov's dog experiment. Back in the 1890s, the Russian psychologist Ivan Pavlov discovered that if he rang a bell whenever he fed the dog in his laboratory, eventually, just by ringing the bell, the dog would salivate as if food had been presented. This is a conditioned reflex, a precursor to the 20th century theory of behaviorism.

Founded by Watson in the 1920s and developed into a comprehensive theory by Skinner and others, behaviorists believe that human behavior is the result of the arrangement of particular stimuli in the environment. If this behavior is reinforced or rewarded, it is likely to continue; if it is not reinforced it is likely to disappear. Thus what one learns is a response to particular stimuli arranged in the environment for the purpose of bringing about learning. Further, observable behavior, not internal mental processes or emotional feelings, determines whether learning has occurred. Learning for behaviorists is defined as a change in observable behavior. Skinner (1971) in particular felt that a behavioral approach to education was crucial for the survival of human beings and societies. By arranging the environment to bring about desired behavior, he thought we could control how people behave and thus develop a better society. Consistent with a behaviorist perspective, Skinner (1971) made the case that personal freedom is an illusion—personal freedom "is the avoidance of or escape from the so-called 'aversive' features of the environment" (p. 42).

Edward L. Thorndike, a contemporary of Watson, has been called "perhaps the greatest learning theorist of all time" (Hergenhahn & Olson, 2005, p. 54). Thorndike studied many aspects of learning theory and educational practice including intelligence testing, transfer of learning, environmental versus innate causes of behavior, and how to measure the quality of life. He and his colleagues were the first to systematically study adult learners and published the first book on this topic in 1928 titled *Adult Learning* (Thorndike, Bregman, Tilton, & Woodyard, 1928). Their research seems rather quaint now, but nearly one hundred years ago it was considered groundbreaking. Basically interested in the question of whether adults could learn and whether there was a decline in learning ability as people age, they presented various memory and learning tasks to people between the ages of fourteen and fifty. They concluded that "teachers of adults of age twenty-five to forty-five should expect them to learn at nearly the same rate and in nearly the same manner as they would have learned the same thing at twenty" (pp. 178–179). Later research that considered previous education along with age and eliminated time pressure, found that adults up to age seventy did as well as younger adults (Lorge, 1944).

The key components of a behaviorist approach to learning are part of our everyday vocabulary. For example, we might "reward" ourselves with a special purchase when we reach a particular weight-loss goal, we "reinforce" our children's good behavior with a compliment (and ignore bad behavior so as to not reinforce it), and we use behavioral objectives in our instruction, objectives that specify the conditions under which behavior will be performed and the criteria for judging that behavior.

Not only are behavioral principles integrated into K–12 curriculum and instruction, behaviorism is also alive and well in adult education practice. Adult educators often use behavioral objectives to specify particular learning outcomes, and the notions of competency-based curricula, instructional design models, and some program-planning models are behaviorist in nature. What has become known as evidence-based practice wherein quantifiable, systematic, and observable "outcomes" are used as markers of learning and in turn used to structure learning activities is a behavioristic-oriented model permeating adult basic education (ABE) and continuing professional education especially in the areas of health and medicine (Das, Malick, & Khan, 2008).

Behaviorism is particularly evident in adult career and technical education, business and industry, and the military. Much of adult vocational education is focused on identifying skills needed for specific occupations, teaching those skills from basic to expert levels, and then requiring learners to demonstrate certain levels of competency in performing those skills. Whether learning to be an auto mechanic or a chef, one begins as a novice learning and practicing the basic skills before progressing to higher skill levels. Some countries, such as Australia, Singapore, and the United Kingdom, have national skill qualification programs across manufacturing and service sectors of their economies. In business and industry and the military, the emphasis for many is on performance improvement, training, and behavioral change. Sleezer, Conti, and Nolan (2003) note that human resource development professionals "who rely on behaviorism . . . emphasize rewards, the stimuli that learners receive from the environment, [and] the systematic observation of behavior" (p. 26).

Finally Mackeracher (2004) points out that behaviorism permeates our lives as learners through (1) instructional technology "encompassing the development of sound educational resources such as instructional manuals, self-instructed learning modules . . . and so on"; (2) programmed learning modules and computer-based training programs "to assist learners to acquire and master skilled behavior"; (3) programs designed to modify behavior, "such as assertiveness training and anger management"; and (4) biofeedback programs "designed to help the learner change behaviours, such as those that cause high blood pressure" (p. 213).

Behaviorism is so embedded in our daily lives and our practice as educators that we may not even acknowledge its presence. And we certainly do not mean to imply that all educators subscribe to behaviorism's learning principles at the expense of other approaches. However, as reflective practitioners it is important to recognize the role of feedback, the nature of reinforcement, learning objectives, and behavior modification in structuring learning activities for adults. Further, Roessger (2012) has suggested that the field of adult education needs to revisit behaviorism as "the current monolithic understanding of behaviourism is inaccurate and unjustly applied to Skinner's philosophy. As a result, educators and learners are denied effective and valuable practical applications" (p. 17). At the same time, behavioristic principles have been soundly criticized as too mechanistic and too controlling. With regard to curriculum design and instruction in adult education, there is a concern that too slavish adherence to behaviorism's principles ignores the complexity of the human being in the learning process. We now turn to a very different orientation to learning which most challenges the assumptions underlying behaviorism, that of humanism.

Humanism—Learning Is About the Development of the Person

It would be difficult to find a perspective more different from behaviorism than humanistic psychology. To highlight the difference between these two perspectives, picture yourself attending a workshop or training event that your employer has mandated that you "need." You are not the least bit interested in this topic, or you already know the content, or you foresee no need to ever know the content. Material is delivered by the instructor and at the end you will be asked to demonstrate how much you "learned" by taking a multiple-choice exam. In contrast to this rather behavioristic model, you discover that you rather enjoy cooking. You find it relaxing and creative and you feel a sense of accomplishment and pride when you share your dishes with friends. You decide you would like to learn more about a particular cuisine and you plan how you would like to learn this new cuisine. You might take a class, read a book, hire an expert, or experiment on your own. You would decide when you have learned what you want to know. This more self-directed model, lodged in a humanistic worldview, evolved as a contrast to what was seen as the mechanistic and impersonal nature of learning predetermined by the teacher arranging the environment to elicit certain behavior. Called the "third force," humanistic psychology rejected both behaviorism and Freudian psychology, which presented behavior as determined by the subconscious mind.

Originally drawing from the philosophy of humanism, by the 1950s humanistic psychologists such as Maslow and Rogers in particular, had firmly established this alternative perspective on human nature and learning. Underpinning this perspective is the assumption that human beings have the potential for growth and development and that people are free to make choices and determine their behavior. In contrast to external, overt behavior, the spotlight in this orientation is on the whole person including body, mind, and spirit, and the potential of humans for growth and development. The goal of learning for Maslow (1970) is self-actualization, whereas for Rogers (1983) it is to become a fully functioning person.

Few symbols are as famous for this perspective as Maslow's triangle depicting human motivation as a hierarchy of needs. At the base of the triangle are the basic physiological needs for survival such as hunger and thirst, needs which must be addressed before moving to the next level, that of safety needs. Here one has to feel safe and secure before attending to the next levels of belonging and love, self-esteem, and finally, the need for self-actualization. This need for self-actualization pertains to what a person's full potential is and realizing that potential. Maslow (1954) describes self-actualization as "the desire to become more and more what one is, to become everything that one is capable of becoming" (p. 92). What one is capable of becoming is specific to each individual. For example, one individual may have the strong desire to become an ideal parent, "in another it may be expressed athletically, and in still another it may be expressed in painting pictures, or in inventions" (p. 92). As mentioned before, in order to reach a clear understanding of this level of need one must first not only achieve the previous needs of physiological, safety, love, and esteem, but also master these needs. While this hierarchy is not without its critics, its emphasis on motivation translates well into an educational milieu. The focus is on the inner person, that person's needs, desires, and wants and how these require attending to in any learning encounter.

An even stronger influence in establishing humanistic psychology as a learning theory, especially for adult educators, was Carl Rogers. From his client-centered therapy approach, he is credited with establishing a "student-centered" versus teacher-centered approach to learning. In this approach the teacher is a *facilitator* of self-directed learning rather than a dispenser of knowledge. Rogers' understanding of learning can be found in his 1983 book *Freedom to Learn for the 80s* where he defines learning in terms of five principles. Significant learning, according to Rogers,

> *has a quality of personal involvement*—the whole person in both feeling and cognitive aspects being in the learning event. It is *self-initiated*. Even when the impetus or stimulus comes from outside, the sense of discovery, of reaching out, of grasping and comprehending, comes from within. *It is pervasive.* It makes a difference in the behavior, the attitudes, perhaps even the personality of the learner. *It is evaluated by the learner.* She knows whether it is meeting her need, whether it leads toward what she *wants* to know, whether it illuminates the dark area of ignorance she is experiencing. The locus of evaluation, we might say, resides definitely in the learner. *Its essence is meaning.* When such learning takes place, the element of meaning to the learner is built into the whole experience. (italics in original, Rogers, 1983, p. 20)

Finally, over forty years ago Rogers (1969) articulated the very contemporary notion that in this high-speed globalized world what is really crucial for survival is that we all become lifelong learners. He wrote that an educated person is one "who has learned how to learn . . . how to adapt and change" and realizes "that no knowledge is secure, that only the process of seeking knowledge gives a basis for security" (p. 104).

Humanistic learning theory has had a profound effect on adult learning theory. The three major adult learning theories (or models, as some call them) of andragogy, self-directed learning, and transformative learning all have roots in humanistic psychology. Malcolm Knowles's writings on self-directed learning, groups, and andragogy in particular, are firmly lodged in humanistic principles. The assumptions of andragogy (see Chapter 3)—for example, that the adult learner becomes more independent and self-directed, is internally motivated, and can use experience as a resource for learning—all suggest the adult's capacity to grow, develop, and learn—and participate in making decisions about his or her own learning.

Self-directed learning (see Chapter 4), a second major thrust in adult learning research and theory, is also firmly grounded in humanistic psychology. The focus is on adults directing their own learning with the goal of self-development in mind. Further, the role of educators in self-directed learning "is to act as facilitators, or guides as opposed to content experts" (Caffarella, 1993, p. 26). Finally, the third major adult learning theory to have some connection to humanistic tenets is Mezirow's theory of transformative learning (see Chapter 5). Key to his theory is the notion of personal development, that is, through transformative learning experiences our perspective becomes more inclusive, open and permeable. The process is in fact, "the central process of adult development" (Mezirow, 1991, p. 155).

Cognitivism—Learning Is a Mental Process

Humanistic psychologists were not the only ones to challenge behaviorists' theories of learning. *Gestalt* (a German word meaning pattern or shape) psychologists found behaviorists' explanations too simple, too mechanized, and too dependent on observable behavior. Known as cognitivist or information-processing, this theory represented a shift in the locus of learning from the environment (behaviorists), or the whole person (humanists), to the learner's mental processes. A common metaphor for this approach is the computer with its input, throughput, and output and in fact this is where the "information processing" label originated.

The mind sees patterns, they felt, and uses prior knowledge to process new information. "The human mind," according to cognitivists, "is not simply a passive exchange-terminal system where the stimuli arrive and the appropriate response leaves. Rather, the thinking person interprets sensations and gives meaning to the events that impinge upon his consciousness" (Grippin & Peters, 1984, p. 76). Cognitivists focus on insight (the moment when a solution to a problem becomes clear), information processing, problem solving, memory, and the brain. Given the broad sweep of this particular orientation to learning, it is difficult to single out a particular theorist or set of research most prominent in informing adult learning. However, a brief look at three areas of research would seem to have relevance for adult educators—cognitive development, memory, and instructional design theories.

The ability to process information is related to one's cognitive structure. Piaget (1972) is considered a pioneer in this area and his four-stage model of cognitive development provided the basis for theory development with adults. In his model the human being moves from the infancy stage of a sensory-motor response to stimuli, to the early childhood stage of being able to represent concrete objects in symbols and words (called "preoperational"), to understanding concepts and relationships of middle childhood (concrete operational), to being able to reason hypothetically and think abstractly called formal operational. There have been a number of critiques of Piaget's theory, the most serious of which is with the invariate nature of his model. Some feel that adults can move among the stages and the context may well determine which level of thinking is most appropriate (Knight & Sutton, 2004).

Building on this theory, neo-Piagetian scholars have suggested there is evidence of postformal thought in which one goes beyond problem solving and instead thinks creatively to perhaps reformulate the problem itself—or "problem-finding" (Arlin, 1975; Sinnott, 1998/2010). Piaget inspired research on cognitive development and several of these models have entered the adult learning knowledge base. Perry (1999) proposed a nine-position model of cognitive development from his research with male college students. However, recent research suggests that his model may not account for cultural differences (Zhang, 2004). Building on Piaget, King and Kitchener developed a seven-stage model of reflective judgment (1994, 2002), and Kohlberg (1981) focused on moral development. In 1986 Belenky, Clinchy, Goldberger, and Tarule published *Women's Ways of Knowing* in which they identified five "positions" of women's cognitive development ranging from silence to constructed knowledge. Yet others dismiss the notion of stages or positions of cognitive development and concentrate on the development of dialectical thinking where one recognizes the contradictions, paradoxes, and ambiguities of modern life and lives within that recognition. Whether one believes cognition is a developmental or dialectic process is directly linked to one's view of how information is processed.

Research on memory is also central to the cognitivist perspective. "When learning occurs, information is input from the environment, processed and stored in memory, and output in the form of some learned capability" (Driscoll, 2005, p. 74). This processing is dependent upon memory—sensory, short-term, and long-term memory. The process begins as we take in information from the environment via our senses. For example, knowing I am planning a trip to Italy, a friend of mine introduces me to a friend of hers who has just returned from there. I hear her name and I see what she looks like; through hearing and vision her name and an image of her enters my memory system. Within seconds this information is lost (if I don't want to remember it) or if I want to remember it I "process" it and it enters my short-term memory. This processing involves sorting and filing the data in some manner as to "remember" it. I might "file" her name along with other information I have collected regarding my future trip to Italy. Or I might visualize a map of Italy but instead of writing "Italy" on the map, I instead place this woman's name on the map. This processing in short-term memory leads to it being stored in long-term memory. Sometime later I retrieve her name from the storage of my long-term memory. (See Chapter 9 for more on memory.)

This is of course a very simplified version of the role of memory in cognitive processing. However, it is a central component of understanding cognitive or information processing learning theory and, as we come to learn more about memory and aging, it is particularly relevant to adult learning. For example, declining acuity in hearing and vision may impact sensory memory. (If, in the previous example, I did not hear her name, it cannot be registered into my working memory). Research with older adults also suggests that as people age they appear to become less efficient at both processing information into long-term memory, and retrieving material from long-term memory storage (Bjorklund, 2011). This research is by no means conclusive, however, and many factors such as personal interest and good instructional techniques may well mitigate any memory and aging deficits.

In addition to cognitive development and memory, theories of instruction intersect with cognitive theory. We briefly review the main contributions of Ausubel, Gagne, and Bloom to better understand information processing as a learning theory. Ausubel (1967) proposed a theory of meaningful learning as that learning which can connect with concepts already in a person's cognitive structure. "This cognitive structure is made up of sets of ideas that are organized hierarchically and by theme" (Driscoll, 2005, p. 117). Rote learning, on the other hand, is soon forgotten as it does not relate to a person's cognitive structure. To connect new knowledge to one's cognitive structure, Ausubel suggested the use of advance organizers. "Advance organizers are relevant and inclusive introductory materials, provided in advance of the learning materials, that serve to 'bridge the gap between what the learner already knows and what he needs to know before he can meaningfully learn the task at hand' (Ausubel et al., 1998, pp. 171–172)" (Driscoll, p. 138).

Information processing theory is the foundation for Gagne's instructional design theory (Gagne, 1985). His theory is rather complex and includes a taxonomy of learning outcomes (for example, intellectual, affective, and motor skills), learning conditions for attaining the outcomes, and nine "events" of instruction. His theories are still used today, especially in the planning of instruction from a cognitivist theory perspective. Recently Gagne's nine events of instruction were suggested for planning educational programs on genetic cancer risk for African American communities (Kendall, Kendall, Catts, Radford, & Dasch, 2007). For example, the first condition, "gain attention" could be addressed by presenting "a culturally relevant family history," or by presenting "a surprising fact about cancer genetic risk and the African American community" (p. 284). Transfer, the ninth condition, could be facilitated by following up with the same group some time after the program's conclusion.

Finally, most have heard of Bloom's taxonomy of cognitive outcomes (Bloom, 1956). He is also credited with identifying three types of learning outcomes—cognitive, affective, and psychomotor. His taxonomy is used for curriculum planning and developing learning objectives. At the lowest level of Bloom's six-level taxonomy is knowledge—the remembering of specific facts or concepts. The next level is comprehension, which is understanding the material, followed by application, analysis, synthesis, and evaluation. Critics have suggested that these six "outcomes" may not be hierarchical, or that synthesis is a higher level skill than evaluation, or that while the first three are hierarchical, the last three are parallel (Anderson & Krathwohl, 2001). Most agree, however, that the higher level skills require more cognitive flexibility.

Clearly, cognitive learning theory explains a lot about how we use the brain and our senses to process information. For adult educators, the work in cognitive development, memory, and instructional design theory can be used to facilitate learning and plan instruction with adults.

Social Cognitive Theory—Learning Is Social and Context Bound

While *social* cognitive theory is sometimes included as a subset of cognitive learning theory, we feel the social dimension to understanding how learning occurs is particularly important and relevant to adult learning and so we present it separately. "Social cognitive learning theory highlights the idea that much human learning occurs in a social environment. By observing others, people acquire knowledge, rules, skills, strategies, beliefs, and attitudes. Individuals also learn about the usefulness and appropriateness of behaviors by observing models and the consequences of modeled behaviors, and they act in accordance with their beliefs concerning the expected outcomes of actions" (Schunk, 1996, p. 102). So not only do we cognitively process information as we learn, we also observe others and model their behavior. These observations are also "processed" and often physically replicated.

Social cognitive theory draws from both behaviorism and cognitive theory in the following manner. Some theorists felt that observation and imitation of behavior were not enough for learning to occur; this behavior had to be reinforced for learning to occur (Hergenhahn & Olson, 2005). Bandura (1976), the major theorist for this perspective, focused on the cognitive processes involved in observation and maintained that "persons can regulate their own behavior to some extent by visualizing self-generated consequences" (p. 392). But for Bandura, the cognitive component of learning was only part of the picture. He felt behavior was a function of the interaction of the person with the environment. He pictured his model of learning as a triangle in which learning, the person, and the environment are interactive and reciprocal (Bandura, 1986).

The addition of a social dimension to learning theory models resonates well with what we have come to know about adult learning. Adults learn social roles by observing and modeling others. For example, learning to be a parent of a newborn often involves observing how friends have managed. Further, mentoring is a process that offers adult learners models to observe and has been much written about in the adult learning literature (Daloz, 2012; Mullen, 2005). A variation of mentoring is cognitive apprenticeships (see Chapter 6) wherein the mentor or instructor models how to think about whatever is being learned. For example, a medical student might model how her instructor reasons through a diagnosis, or a novice gardener might model a master gardener in arranging plants in a garden for maximum growth. Finally, Gibson (2004) suggests that social cognitive theory is relevant to the workplace where on-the-job training and behavior modeling can assist in socializing employees to the workplace.

Constructivism—Learning Is Creating Meaning from Experience

Constructivism is less a single theory of learning than a collection of perspectives all of which share the common assumption that learning is how people make sense of their experience—learning is the construction of meaning from experience. Driscoll (2005) contrasts this view with behaviorists and cognitivists: "Behaviorists define desired learning goals independent of any learner and then proceed to arrange reinforcement contingencies that are presumed to be effective with any learner; only the type of reinforcer is assumed to vary according to the individual. Although information processing theorists put mind back into the learning equation, they, too, appear to assume that knowledge is 'out there' to be transferred into the learner. The computer metaphor itself suggests that knowledge is input to be processed and stored by learners" (p. 387).

In contrast, constructivists see knowledge as "constructed by learners as they attempt to make sense of their experiences. Learners, therefore, are not empty vessels waiting to be filled, but rather active organisms seeking meaning" (Driscoll, 2005, p. 387). Constructivists draw from a number of well-known theorists including Piaget, Dewey, and Vygotsky. From Piaget comes his theory of cognitive development wherein our cognitive structure changes as we mature, allowing us to construct meaning at more sophisticated levels (reviewed above under cognitivism). Dewey's notion (1938) of experience is that it is "a transaction taking place between an individual and what, at the time, constitutes his environment" (p. 41). This experience then, is the basis for "genuine education." Vygotsky (1978) drew attention to the very important role of the sociocultural context in how people construct meaning from experience. He pointed out that this process is a social process mediated through a culture's symbols and language. As a result of these and other theorists' contributions to constructivism, a continuum has emerged with a more psychological orientation on one end drawing from Piaget, to what is called social constructivism on the other end drawing more heavily from Vygotsky.

Constructivism is foundational to understanding much of adult learning theory and practice. As Candy (1991) observed, "teaching and learning, *especially for adults*, is a process of negotiation, involving the construction and exchange of personally relevant and viable meanings" (italics in original, p. 275). Indeed, aspects of constructivism, especially the social construction of knowledge are central to self-directed learning, transformational learning, experiential learning, reflective practice, situated cognition, and communities of practice.

A closer look at situated cognition or contextual learning (see Chapter 6) as it is sometimes referred to, reveals the constructivist nature of this theory. Situated cognition posits that learning occurs in context, that is, our learning is situation specific, and in fact the nature of the context structures the learning. But this learning is also social and mediated through the use of tools (either physical such as computers, maps, books, or psychological/cultural such as language). Workplace learning is very "situated" for example, as employees learn their job using the tools of that environment in social interaction with others. As another example, Sharan, who lived for a year in Asia learned how to shop in the outdoor night market by interacting with the merchants and other shoppers (social interaction), in conjunction with using the local language and currency to buy fruits and vegetables (tools).

Understanding learning from a constructivist, situated cognition perspective has led to suggestions for maximizing learning in this manner in an instructional setting. Learning in context is emphasized in cognitive apprenticeships wherein the thinking process is modeled and supported for new learners; communities of practice where members share and learn from each other (Wenger, 1998), making learning as "authentic" as possible through field trips, case studies, and service learning; and problem-based learning. Brooks and Brooks (1999) discuss a dozen strategies instructors can use as "mediators of students and environments, not simply as givers of information and managers of behavior" (p. 102). Several of these strategies, such as encouraging dialogue with the teacher and each other and building on what students already know about a concept before presenting their own ideas and theories, are quite congruent with what we know about maximizing adult learning. Finally, Brandon and All (2010) make a persuasive case for a constructivist perspective in nursing education: "The essential role of nurse faculty is to engender active-learning processes in settings where nursing is taught: the classroom, the skills laboratory, and the clinical environment" (p. 91).

Chapter Summary

Beginning with the earliest learning theory, behaviorism, we have presented five learning theories in roughly the order of their appearance in the psychological and educational literature. Behaviorism, humanism, cognitivism, social cognitivism, and constructivism are foundational to understanding current thinking about adult learning. We have linked each of these to adult learning theory and practice and will continue to reference them as we explore theories and research specific to adult learning in more depth in the following chapters. A useful summary of the five orientations along with a suggested activity can be seen in Exhibit 2.1. Other applications of some of these orientations can be found in Walters's (2009) discussion of adult environmental education, and Wang and Sarbo's (2004) model of how adult educators need to adapt their philosophy and roles to facilitate transformative learning.

Linking Theory and Practice: Activities and Resources

1. As can be seen in Exhibit 2.1, Taylor, Marienau, and Fiddler (2000) have applied the five orientations to learning to thinking about our roles as adult educators. Study the Exhibit and determine which orientation or orientations best "fit" your perspective on learning. For example, if you believe that the locus of learning is stimuli in the external environment, then your orientation to learning is predominantly behaviorist. If you identify the purpose of education as becoming self-actualized and autonomous, then you have a humanist orientation. They point out that our orientations are often a mix of these perspectives: "In our own practice, we three find that whatever our philosophical starting point, we actually move frequently and fluidly among them, as circumstances warrant. One of our own adult programs, for example, stresses self-directed learning within a competency-based outcomes framework. At the same time, it focuses on constructing meaning from experience and developing metacognitive skills toward becoming life-long learners" (p. 359).

2. Another assessment tool that students might find helpful in identifying one's orientation to learning is Zinn's Philosophy of Adult

EXHIBIT 2.1 RELATIONSHIPS OF DIMENSIONS OF TEACHING AND ORIENTATION TO LEARNING

When Your Belief That the Locus of Learning Is	*Your Orientation to Learning Is Predominantly*
Stimuli in external environment	Behaviorist
Internal cognitive structuring	Cognitivist
Affective and cognitive needs	Humanist
Interaction of person, behavior, and environment	Social learning
Internal construction of reality by individual	Constructivist

When You Identify the Purpose of Education as	*Your Orientation to Learning Is Predominantly*
Producing change in desired direction	Behaviorist
Develop capacity and skills to learn better	Cognitivist
Becoming self-actualized, autonomous	Humanist
Modeling new roles and behavior	Social learning
Constructing knowledge	Constructivist

When You View Your Role as a Teacher Is to	*Your Orientation to Learning Is Predominantly*
Arrange environment to elicit desired response	Behaviorist
Structure content of learning activity	Cognitivist
Facilitate development of the whole person	Humanist
Model and guide new roles and behavior	Social learning
Facilitate learners' negotiation of meaning	Constructivist

When Your View of the Learning Process Is	*Your Orientation to Learning Is Predominantly*
Changes in behavior	Behaviorist
Internal mental process	Cognitivist
A personal act of fulfill potential	Humanist
Interaction with and observation of others in a social context	Social learning
Construction of meaning from experience	Constructivist

When Your Efforts with Adults Are	*Your Orientation to Learning Is Predominantly*
Toward meeting behavioral objectives	Behaviorist
Competency-based	Behaviorist
Toward skill development and training	Behaviorist
Toward cognitive development	Cognitivist
Learning how to learn	Cognitivist
Correlating with intelligence, learning, and memory with age	Cognitivist
Framed by andragogy	Humanist
Toward self-directed learning	Humanist and Constructivist
Toward socialization and social roles	Cognitivist
Framed by mentoring	Social Learning
Orientation to the locus of control	Social learning
Framed by experiential learning	Constructivist
Toward perspective transformation	Constructivist
Toward reflective practice	Constructivist

Source: Taylor, Marienau, & Fiddler (2000), adapted from Merriam and Caffarella (1999).

Education Inventory (PAEI) (Zinn, 1990). Based on the philosophical orientations of Behavioral Adult Education, Liberal Arts Adult Education, Progressive Adult Education, Humanistic Adult Education, and Radical Adult Education, PAEI asks respondents to indicate how much they agree with various statements about how people learn best, and their preferred teaching methods. This self-scoring inventory is helpful in reflecting upon and identifying one's personal beliefs and values about adult education practice. Typically, the PAEI reveals a primary orientation or a combination of two orientations is also common (such as progressive and humanistic). The PAEI is available free online at http://www25.brinkster.com/educ605/paei_howtouse.htm (though you do have to create an account). It is also available in Zinn (1990).

3. An activity that we have used in our own instruction to highlight the underlying principles and differences among the five learning theories is to divide students into five groups representing each of the five theories (a small class could divide into three or four orientations). Each group is to design a three-hour workshop for returning adult students on the topic of "How to Balance Work, Family, and Student Life." Each group is to use an *exaggerated v*ersion of their particular theory. For example, behaviorists might test for correct responses to learned material and "reward" participants with a certificate or some other reinforcement; humanists might invite participants to determine their own learning needs; social cognitivists might bring in students who have successfully balanced family, work, and student roles as models or mentors to workshop participants. As each group presents their plan for the workshop, other participants are asked to point out how congruent the plan is with the particular learning theory (or how it deviates if it does).

4. In a variation of the graduate student workshop above, Allen (2007) reports on a similar application of adult learning theory to leadership development programming. Using behaviorism, cognitivism, social learning theory and constructivism, Allen suggests learning strategies and activities for leadership development that are congruent with each of these theories. For example, in a behaviorist orientation, immediate feedback for new behaviors is important and program developers might also link the learning to "some form of prestige or desirable outcome. For instance, a promotion, a degree, a certificate or some other reward will motivate learners to incorporate and internalize new behaviors" (Allen, 2007, p. 29). Similarly, students could be encouraged to apply two or three theories to their own field of practice as Rostami and Khadjooi (2010) did in contrasting behaviorism and humanism in medical education.

5. Yet another activity for working with these learning theory orientations would be to ask yourself or your students to think about a time when they learned something new. Perhaps they learned a new software program for work, or how to install a ceiling fan, or studied French in anticipation of a visit to Paris, or investigated what shrubbery might grow best in their yard. How did they learn this? Did they have some instruction, did they read about it, experiment, or watch someone else do it? Tracing back through the learning experience will reveal what theory or combination of theoretical orientations best captures how the learning occurred.

Chapter Highlights

- Learning is a complex behavior that can involve how we think (cognitive), feel (affective), or do something (psychomotor).
- Behaviorism emphasizes skills and overt behavior, while a humanistic learning theory focuses on the inner person. Andragogy, self-directed learning, and transformative learning have roots in humanistic learning theory.
- Cognitive learning theory is about how the brain processes information; social cognitive theory includes learning through observing, modeling, and mentoring.
- Constructivist learning theory is not only about how we mechanically process information, but how we make *meaning* of that information, meaning which is shaped by our sociocultural context.

CHAPTER THREE

ANDRAGOGY: THE ART AND SCIENCE OF HELPING ADULTS LEARN

Scenario 1: One of the worst adult learning experiences I had was when I signed up for a six-week community education course on "How to Figure Your Own Income Taxes." The room was too small for the number of people who had signed up and we were forced to sit in rows in small desk chairs. After taking attendance the instructor sat on the teacher's desk and talked non-stop for three hours about the new tax codes and new regulations. She never asked us why we had signed up, what we wanted to learn, or what questions we had. I decided to give it one more try. The second week she again sat on the desk and talked about tax issues related to retirement (although no one appeared to be of retirement age), and how to deal with operating a business out of your home. I left and never returned. (Sharan)

Scenario 2: A memorable worst experience for me was attending a week-long training on diversity staffing sponsored by a nationally prominent human resource management society. Participants sat for the entire week being lectured at by a parade of prominent white males (for example, vice presidents of staffing and diversity at Fortune 500 corporations). It seems the importance of recruiting and retaining a diverse staff was lost on the program planners. Not only was the importance of diverse staffing not modeled by the presenters, but also the issue of diversity was addressed in the most cursory fashion. In addition to poor role modeling, the pedagogy was instructor-centered. There were no opportunities to compare notes with other human resource managers about their staffing challenges. The instructors never sought feedback on whether the participants' needs were being met. Participants struggled to stay awake and were visibly checking their watches, shifting in their seats, and not paying attention. (Laura)

Scenario 3: One of the best adult learning experiences was the time I was invited to accompany a South African friend to her wine-tasting class. This particular session involved some wine-tasting but also a review for an exam the following week. We were seated at long tables and each person was given four food samples (beef jerky, cheese, salty crackers and chocolate) and asked to rate which of the five wines went best with each food sample. By a show of hands she recorded our "answers" into a 4'×5' chart on the blackboard. While the wines that were best with certain foods clustered in the appropriate boxes, there were some "votes" in every box. She made the point that while there may be a "preferred" coupling, wine preference is individual and there was nothing "wrong" with our votes. She then reviewed for the test by throwing out questions to the group from the material, and further indicated what was important to know for the test and what could be ignored. (Sharan)

Scenario 4: A favorite learning experience was spending a week learning the theories behind the Learning Organization at MIT under the guidance of Peter Senge. Although there were 100 participants, there were multiple opportunities for engagement. All learners sat in a very comfortable leather executive chair on wheels that was adjustable for comfort. There were no tables, allowing learners to quickly move into new groups. Each day began with a silent meditation and was varied with brief lectures, simulations, embodiment exercises, games, themed meals, movies, application exercises, and opportunities for individual and group reflection. Learners had opportunities to meet and work with different learners and were challenged to "think outside the box." The sessions were visually compelling with art displayed throughout the training room, inspirational quotes, music during breaks, and toys to play with. Not only was the experience highly engaging, but also very educational. I still refer back to my journal from that session, almost 20 years later! (Laura)

The preceding scenarios highlight differences between good and bad adult learning experiences. In the tax class and staffing training, not only was the physical setting uncomfortable, the instructors had no idea what the needs of the learners were. Sharan, for example, wanted to go through the form line by line, learning which figures go where. Laura wanted to learn what other staffing managers were doing in their practice and how to recruit and retain a diverse workforce. Further, instructors lectured nonstop, never asking questions, or giving opportunities to interact with other participants. In contrast, the wine-tasting event and learning organization workshop fully engaged the participants through a variety of activities, valued the participants' contributions, and enabled participants to learn from each other as well as gain personal expertise. Creating good learning experiences for adults is what andragogy is all about. In this chapter we explain where andragogy came from, its underlying assumptions about the adult learner, some critiques, and finally, how it is being applied in practice.

Before Andragogy

Human beings have always engaged in learning—learning to survive, learning to live in a social group, learning to understand the meaning of our experiences. And interestingly, "all the great teachers of ancient times were teachers of adults, not children" (Ozuah, 2005, p. 84). Savicevic (2008) points out that "Plato's Academy and Aristotle's Lyceum were adult education institutions" (p. 366) and that these teachers as well as Chinese, Hebrew, and Christian educators used dialogue, parables, and what today we would call problem-based learning activities with adults. It was not until monasteries in the seventh century established schools for children that the term "pedagogy" came into use. Pedagogy, Knowles (1973) tells us, "spread to the secular schools of Europe and America and, unfortunately, was much later applied even to the education of adults" (p. 42). Nevertheless, the seeds of an approach to adult learning as being different from pedagogy can be found with scholars of antiquity.

While we have stories of these ancient adult educators, there was no systematic investigation of learning until the late 19th and early 20th centuries. Behavioral and social scientists from Pavlov and Skinner to Piaget, Freud, and humanists Maslow and Rogers used the investigative tools of their day to try to understand the nature of learning. It is from them and others that we have what we call "traditional" learning theories. Behaviorism, humanism, cognitivism, social cognitivism, and constructivism are five traditional learning theories that we reviewed in the previous chapter in this book. *Adult Learning* by Thorndike et al. in 1928 was the first publication from this period to report on "scientific" studies with adult learners rather than animals or children.

Aside from Thorndike's work, much of the writing on adult learning in the early decades of the 20th century was social philosophy oriented. Lindeman, in his classic *The Meaning of Adult Education in the United States*, first published in 1926, the same year of the founding of American Association for Adult Education, wrote about the dual purpose of adult education, that of changing individuals and changing society. He also identified the learner's experience as "the resource of highest value in adult education" and "the adult learner's living textbook" (1926/1961, pp. 9–10). Further, Lindeman proposed that adult learning be built around "needs and interests" which are embedded in an adult's situation—"his work, his recreation, his family life, his community life . . . Adult education begins at this point" (pp. 8–9). Interestingly, Lindeman who used the term "andragogy" in an article in 1926, and in *The Meaning of Adult Education*, presented it as a method for teaching adults (Henschke, 2011). Knowles was apparently unaware of this early usage of the term.

Until the 1970s, adult educators relied on Lindeman and other social philosophers and on behavioral and cognitive research in learning, memory, and intelligence for understanding and designing instruction for adult learners. Knowles (1984) himself talks about his unease teaching adults in the 1930s and 1940s: "I tried to find a book that would tell me how to conduct a program of this sort, and I couldn't find one. So I sought out people who were directing adult education programs . . . and formed an advisory council to give me guidance" (p. 2). Lindeman and his book "enlightened me about the unique characteristics of adults as learners and the need for methods and techniques for helping them learn" (Knowles, 1984, p. 3). He sums up this period between the 1930s and 1970s: "It is interesting to me now, in retrospect, that although there was general agreement among adult educators that adults are different from youth as learners, there was no comprehensive theory about these differences. The literature was largely philosophical and anecdotal" (Knowles, 1984, pp. 3–4).

Only gradually did resources on adult learners and adult learning begin to appear which helped move the field towards identifying how learning in adulthood was distinguishable from learning in childhood. Two were particularly important because they were based on research with adult learners. Houle's *The Inquiring Mind*, published in 1961, reported on a study of 22 adult learners and their motivations for learning. He found some were goal-oriented in that they had clear-cut objectives in their learning, some were activity-oriented where the primary motivation was human interaction, and others were learning-oriented wherein the adults seek knowledge for knowledge's sake. The other research-based study was Tough's *The Adult's Learning Projects* (1971). Building on Houle's work in this study of the learning projects of 66 people, Tough is credited with beginning a line of inquiry still viable today—that of self-directed learning. He found that self-directed learners often spend hundreds of hours on their learning project, a project which they plan, implement, and evaluate on their own.

In 1967 Yugoslavian adult educator Dusan Savicevic attended one of Knowles's workshops on adult learning and introduced him to the term "andragogy," a term widely used in Europe "to provide a label for the growing body of knowledge and technology in regard to adult learning" (Knowles, 1984, p. 6). Knowles first wrote about andragogy in an article published in 1968, and by 1970 had published the first edition of *The Modern Practice of Adult Education: Andragogy Versus Pedagogy*. In a recent article, Savicevic (2008) seems ambivalent about Knowles' popularization of andragogy. He says Knowles "reduced andragogy to a prescription, recipes for teachers' behavior in the process of education and learning" (Savicevic, 2008, p. 374). Savicevic also writes that through his writing and lectures, Knowles enabled the term to "become rooted in the American professional literature" and that "his contribution to dissemination of andragogical ideas throughout the USA is huge" and "the history of andragogy will put him on a meritorious place in the development of the scientific discipline" (Savicevic, 2008, p. 375).

In any case, andragogy as promoted by Knowles is considered the first systematic formulation laying out the differences between children and adult learners. Andragogy contributed to the development of the field of adult education at a time when adult educators were struggling to establish their own identity separate from childhood education. Andragogy helped "professionalize" the field of adult education by establishing a knowledge base unique to adult learners.

Assumptions About Adult Learners

"A new label and a new technology" of adult learning is how Knowles introduced andragogy to American educators in 1968 (p. 351). Pedagogy comes from the "Greek word 'paid,' meaning child (plus 'agogus' meaning leader of). So, literally, pedagogy means the art and science of teaching children," (Knowles, 1973, p. 42–43) while andragogy comes from the Greek word *aner*, meaning man, so andragogy refers to helping *adults* learn (Knowles, 1973). Of course having a term to differentiate adult learning from pedagogy was not enough to establish a robust theory of adult learning. It is at this point that Knowles drew heavily from Lindeman's ideas regarding adult learning being situation-motivated, and experience-centered. Knowles (1973) was perhaps less concerned with a definition of andragogy than with "differentiating between the *assumptions* about learners that have traditionally been made by those who practice pedagogy in contrast to the assumptions made in andragogy" (p. 43, italics in original). In introducing andragogy, Knowles (1980) proposed the following four assumptions:

1. As a person matures, his or her self-concept moves from that of a dependent personality toward one of a self-directing human being.
2. An adult accumulates a growing reservoir of experience, which is a rich resource for learning.
3. The readiness of an adult to learn is closely related to the developmental tasks of his or her social role.
4. There is a change in time perspective as people mature—from future application of knowledge to immediacy of application. Thus, an adult is more problem centered than subject centered in learning (pp. 44–45).

A fifth and sixth assumption appeared in later publications:

5. Adults are mostly driven by internal motivation, rather than external motivators (Knowles & Associates, 1984).
6. Adults need to know the reason for learning something (Knowles, 1984).

Each of these assumptions has implications for program design and instruction. While a pedagogical model emphasizes content—content determined, organized, delivered, and evaluated by the teacher—an andragogical model emphasizes process. In this model, the facilitator sets a climate for learning that physically and psychologically respects adult learners and then involves the learners in the planning, delivery and evaluation of their own learning (Knowles, 1984). Following is a more detailed discussion of each of the assumptions underlying andragogy and their application to practice.

The Learner's Self-Concept

This first assumption posits that as people mature they become more independent and self-directing. An infant, for example, is totally dependent on others for survival. Children slowly learn to do things for themselves, but are still rather dependent on adults for most aspects of their lives. The teen years bring more independence and by young adulthood people are expected be responsible for their own lives.

This difference in self-concept between a child and an adult is reflected in how we often encounter a child or an adult. We ask children how old they are or what grade they are in at school because it is assumed that their primary role in life is that of full-time student. With an adult we are much more likely to ask about their family, work, or community engagement—reflecting the adult roles of being independent, contributing members of society. Because adults see themselves as independent and self-directing, there develops "a deep psychological need to be perceived by others, and treated by others, as capable of taking responsibility for ourselves" and if "others are imposing their wills on us without our participating in making decisions affecting us, we experience a feeling, often subconsciously, of resentment and resistance" (Knowles, 1984, p. 9).

This "resentment and resistance" is what happens when an instructor uses pedagogical strategies with adult learners. Adults who make decisions on a daily basis with regard to family, work, and community life suddenly find they have no voice in what and how they learn something. Knowles points out that this is a "special problem" for adult educators because even though most adults are self-directing in major areas of their lives, "the minute they walk into a situation labeled 'education,' 'training,' or any of their synonyms, they hark back to their conditioning in school, assume a role of dependency, and demand to be taught. However, if they really are treated like children, this conditioned expectation conflicts with their much deeper psychological need to be self-directing" (Knowles, 1984, p. 9). This dependency in a learning situation needs to be addressed gradually, working with adults in ways that allow for increased self-direction in their learning.

The fact that adult learners can be presumed to have a more independent self-concept than a child and therefore be more self-directed in their learning does not imply that all adults are always self-directing and can plan their own learning, or that all children are always dependent learners. Even Knowles (1984) eventually conceded that there are situations where an adult encountering a new area of learning will of necessity be more dependent on a teacher and, similarly, children who are naturally curious and "very self-directing in their learning *outside of school* . . . could also be more self-directed in school" (p. 13, italics in original).

What does this assumption that adult learners have independent self-concepts and can be self-directed in their learning imply for educational programs for adults? There are several important implications. First, with regard to what Knowles called "climate setting" in his process model of instruction, it is important that the physical environment be comfortable and adult-oriented. Second, there should be a psychological climate of mutual respect and trust and an atmosphere of collaboration. In this kind of atmosphere where adults are respected as adults, participants can contribute to planning the content of the course and in so doing, engage in self-directing their own learning. If we go back to the "worst" learning experiences described at the beginning of this chapter, none of these factors were present—the physical and psychological climate of the room was far from adult-oriented and the needs of the learners were never considered in the planning of the course.

This first assumption underlying Knowles' promotion of andragogy converged with Houle's typology (1961) of adult learners and Tough's research (1971) on adult learning projects. In particular, Tough's finding that upwards of 90% of adults engaged in self-directed learning launched an entirely new program of research and theory-building in self-directed learning. Knowles contributed to this line of research with a book published on self-directed learning in 1975. (See Chapter 4 in this volume).

Experience

The second assumption of andragogy is that an adult's accumulated life experiences are a "rich resource" for learning. Clearly, as one ages one has a variety of life experiences which can be drawn on in a learning situation, but which also stimulate the need for learning. Lindeman (1926/1961) recognized this when he wrote that an adult's life situations "with respect to his work, his recreation, his family life, his community life" are what initiate learning. Rather than beginning with an established curriculum, "subject matter is brought into the situation, is put to work, when needed" (p. 8).

The important role of experience in learning is well documented in the literature on learning. Cognitive psychologists such as Piaget, Bruner, and Ausubel strongly acknowledge the role of experience in a person's ability to process information (see Chapter 2). Developmental psychologists and educators also see development as the processing of life experiences. Erik Erikson's famous eight-stage theory of psycho-social development (1963) is a good example. At each stage of life from infancy to old age, one deals with a central issue important to development. The adult issues are all connected to adult life experiences such as dealing with intimacy in young adulthood or generativity (caring for others) in middle age.

The link between learning and development is perhaps most clearly obvious in the work of psychologist and educator, Robert Havighurst. In

1952 he published *Developmental Tasks and Education* where he laid out developmental tasks to be accomplished at each life stage, such as finding a mate and getting started in an occupation in young adulthood. These "life situations" as Lindeman might have called them, presented what Havighurst termed *the teachable moment* (Havighurst, 1952/1972). For example, the "teachable moment" to learn about parenting is when one has young children, or to learn about retirement when one is bringing fulltime work life to a close. Knowles (1980) acknowledged that these developmental tasks created "'a readiness to learn' which at its peak presents a 'teachable moment'" (p. 51).

An adult accumulates life experience just by engaging in the roles of adult life. This life experience is what makes each individual unique, for no two life trajectories are exactly the same. Experience thus is integral to an adult's identity, or self-concept. Knowles, Holton, and Swanson (2011) explain: "Young children derive their self-identity largely from external definers—who their parents, brothers, sisters, and extended families are; where they live; and what churches and schools they attend. As they mature, they increasingly define themselves in terms of the experiences they have had. To children, experience is something that happens to them; to adults, their experience is who they are. The implication of this fact for adult education is that in any situation in which the participants' experiences are ignored or devalued, adults will perceive this as rejecting not only their experience, but rejecting themselves as persons" (p. 65). Because adults are who they are largely due to their accumulated life experiences, rejecting or ignoring their experiences is threatening to their independent self-concept, the first assumption of andragogy. The self-concept and life experience assumptions further intersect when one considers the number and variety of life experiences of the typical adult. The implication is that a group of adult learners is likely to be quite different from a group of children. Because of this variety, not only is it imperative to make use of these experiences in learning, it is also important for adults to take control of their learning and become independent, self-directed learners. This is yet another point wherein the first and second assumptions intersect.

The nature of life experience in adult learning also has its downside. Adults can become dogmatic and closed-minded about learning something new because their prior knowledge and experience has worked for them in the past and they see no need to learn something else. Or, a traumatic life experience might function as a barrier to learning (Merriam,

Mott, & Lee, 1996), nor does the amount of experience necessarily equate with the quality of experience. At the same time, some children may have had a range and depth of experience more intense and powerful than that of some adults.

Life experience as a resource for learning has been applied to adult education practice in a number of ways. It is often seen as a starting place in instruction with adults, that is, a facilitator can *begin* with an adult student's experiences and then assist the learner to connect those experiences with new concepts, theories and experiences. For example, in the vignette of the wine-tasting event presented in the opening of this chapter, the facilitator asked everyone to experience the taste of each wine with several foods and evaluate which wine went best with which food. This collective experience formed the basis for instruction about the properties of each wine. Discussion, role play, simulations, field experiences, problem-based learning, case studies, and projects of all sorts enable learners to draw on their life experiences as resources for learning.

Finally, this connection between life experience and learning is at the heart of a number of theoretical frameworks explaining learning and in particular, adult learning. From Dewey's classic, *Experience and Education* (1938), to Kolb's experiential learning cycle (1984), to Schön's notion of reflective practice (1983), to communities of practice where participants' experiences form the basis for learning (Fenwick, 2003), the learner's experiences are front and center. (For more on experiential learning, see Chapter 6.)

Readiness to Learn

This assumption that an adult's learning agenda is closely related to developmental tasks and social roles of adult life is closely connected to the previous assumption on life experiences being a resource for learning. The main emphasis in this assumption is that the *social roles* of adulthood create a need for learning. As mentioned earlier, the child's main social role in life is that of "student." Much of the learning of children is subject-centered and in preparation for future learning—learning the alphabet so they can read, learning basic math so they can move on to algebra, and so on. Adults, on the other hand, are engaged in multiple social roles of worker, spouse, parent, community member. The demands of each of these roles also change as we age. A young adult may be preparing for work or experimenting with various career options, whereas a middle-aged adult may be managing or supervising other workers or looking to change careers; and the older adult may be trying to figure out how to stay up to date to keep a job, or to plan for retirement.

Readiness to learn can be seen as intersecting with the "teachable moment" mentioned above. Adult social roles create the teachable moment and entire adult education programs can be planned around these needs. Forrest and Peterson (2006) give an example from management education: "A newly promoted manager may have had little interest in learning about giving performance feedback when holding a nonmanagement position. However, such an individual can be eager to learn such information because the knowledge has relevance once the individual is promoted to a management position" (p. 119).

Although all social roles and changes in these roles throughout the life span present myriad opportunities for learning, the social role of "worker" has been shown to be the predominate reason adults engage in formal learning activities. When adults in national surveys are asked for their reasons for participation in formal adult education activities, 85–90% of those surveyed cite career- or job-related reasons for participation (Merriam, Caffarella, & Baumgartner, 2007). However, these studies focus on formal programs sponsored by educational institutions, businesses and industry. Even more prevalent than learning in formal settings is the learning which is embedded in everyday life—called informal or nonformal learning. While considered to be more prevalent, this kind of learning is more difficult to capture. However, studies of informal learning and self-directed learning (see Chapter 4) indicate that personal development related to social roles other than the role of worker is a strong motivating factor.

Though it seems obvious that readiness to learn is related to an adult's development and social roles, much of this learning, especially that in formal settings, rather than responding to an immediate need, emphasizes preparation for future roles. The "trick" for adult educators is to create the readiness for learning through instructional techniques that are experiential in nature. For example, using a natural disaster much in the news can be a real-life stimulus for learning about community organization, or disaster relief management. Industry downsizing can lead to learning activities focusing on updating employee skills or career development activities. Knowles (1973) discussed how this could be done with professional preparation: "It is my observation that a good deal of professional education is totally out of phase with the students' readiness to learn. For example, . . . the new social work student needs to have some direct experience with clients with problems before he is ready to learn about public welfare legislation and policy, case work principles and techniques, theory and practice of administration, concepts of community organization, group work, and research methods. He'll be ready to inquire into these areas of content as he confronts problems to which they are relevant" (p. 47).

Problem-Centered Orientation

Let us imagine that you, the reader, have just been diagnosed with a serious health problem such as cancer. You want to find out about this form of cancer, what the treatment options are, where to get the best care, what you can do in terms of diet and exercise to maximize your chances of survival. You consult with health care professionals, family, friends, and go on the Internet to learn all you can. You might even attend a cancer self-help group. Your learning is problem-centered; *your* cancer diagnosis is the problem. It is not subject-centered, that is, you are not interested in learning about cancer in general, and you would not have investigated this topic at all if it had not become a problem for you. Further, you are interested in immediate application—what you can learn to apply to your situation now, not later. This is the essence of the fourth assumption—that adults are problem-centered, not subject-centered, and desire immediate, not postponed application of the knowledge learned.

The fourth assumption of andragogy is of course logically related to the previous three. Basically, most adults are motivated to learn in order to deal with an issue or problem of immediate concern. Often these issues are related to their social roles which are intertwined with their life experiences. Again, as with the other three assumptions above, there are a couple of caveats to consider here. First, some adults learn for the sheer joy of learning, for the sense of accomplishment in learning something outside one's comfort zone, and not to deal with an immediate problem. At the other end of the continuum, not all learning in childhood needs to be subject-centered with postponed application. Service learning which engages students in real issues in their community is very problem-centered.

Nevertheless, adult learning more often than not is problem-centered with a desire for immediate application. Most continuing education programs and community-based nonformal offerings are of this nature. An interesting example are Taylor's studies (2005; 2012) of learning activities offered by home-improvement stores. These stores offer short sessions on topics related to problems that arise for home owners such as fixing a leaky faucet or laying floor tile.

Problem-centered learning is preferred by adults because it is more engaging and lends itself to immediate application, which in turn solidifies the learning. Indeed, this is the rationale behind some forms of professional preparation such as problem-based learning in medical training and just-in-time teaching in management education. Here students tackle a real-world business problem with an organization as their "client" (Watson & Temkin, 2000). Finally, professional graduate education has become open to students engaging in action research where they and their organization define a real problem to study, design and implement a solution, and evaluate the solution.

Internal Motivation

In light of the above four assumptions, it is no surprise that the most potent motivators for adults to learn are internal rather than external. In other words, increased job satisfaction with one's work, enhanced self-esteem, improved quality of life and personal fulfillment lead adults to learn beyond what might be required by some agency or institution. An adult is free to choose to learn, which is quite a bit different from pre-adult learning where others determine what the student needs to know.

Andragogy is firmly rooted in humanistic psychology as this assumption about internal motivation demonstrates. As we explored in the previous chapter on traditional learning theories, humanistic psychology and, in particular, the work of Maslow and Rogers underpin much of andragogy, especially being intrinsically motivated to learn. From this perspective, human nature is intrinsically good, and human beings are free to choose how they behave and what they want to learn. There is also present the potential for growth and development and in Maslow's term, self-actualization (1970). Adults are internally motivated and self-actualization is the goal of learning. Rogers (1969) also felt learning needed to be self-initiated and that the goal was to develop a "fully-functioning person." Indeed, internal motivation along with the other assumptions of andragogy place this theory squarely in a humanistic framework where the individual is at the center of the learning transaction, where self-direction and independence are valued, and where learning leads to personal growth and fulfillment.

Of course not all adult learning is internally motivated. There are times when our employer requires us to participate in particular workplace training programs, when a degree or certificate is required to engage in certain activities or professional work, or when an educational program is mandated by a governmental or social agency (for example, to retain our driver's license or access unemployment benefits). Even in these situations, efforts by the facilitator to link the content to the needs and interests of the learners might result in participants becoming more internally motivated.

The Need to Know

Adults want to know why they need to learn something and how what they learn will apply to their immediate situation. This assumption goes hand in hand with the above assumption on intrinsic motivation. If adults can see why it is important to learn something *before* they begin a learning activity, their motivation is that much stronger. Of course, much of one's "need to know" arises from encountering life situations and developmental changes in social roles. For example, a childless adult has no "need to know" about raising children. However, this certainly could become a need should this adult decide to raise a child. A person caught up in a company merger may find herself out of a job; now she has a need to know how to prepare a résumé and compete in the job market. One who becomes a caretaker for a family member with a newly diagnosed disease has a great need to know about the disease and how best to care for the affected person. It is clear in these examples that these adults need to know this information and that the knowledge will have immediate application.

As with the other assumptions, there are situations where learning is mandated or where the learning is in preparation for some future application. These situations present a challenge to the adult educator who cannot rely on the learners' internal motivation and need to know to become fully engaged. Knowles et al. (2011) address this situation in a business environment:

> The first task of the facilitator of learning is to help the learners become aware of the "*need to know*." At the very least, facilitators can make an intellectual case for the value of the learning in improving the effectiveness of the learners' performance or the quality of their lives. Even more potent tools for raising the level of awareness of the need to know are real or simulated experiences in which the learners discover for themselves the gaps between where they are now and where they want to be. Personnel appraisal systems, job rotation, exposure to role models, and diagnostic performance assessments are examples of such tools. (p. 63)

In summary, these six assumptions make up the andragogical model of adult learning. It is based in a mostly humanist philosophy wherein the individual is central, internally motivated and self-directed, and engages in learning for self-fulfillment, problem solving, and greater competency in life roles. The instructor's role is to facilitate rather than dominate the learning. We can see the contrast between pedagogy and andragogy by returning to the scenarios at the opening of this chapter. The income tax class and the week-long seminar on diverse staffing were 100% teacher-directed with no recognition of, let alone accounting for, the adult students' needs and interests. By contrast, the wine-tasting course and the learning organization workshop placed the participants' interests and needs front and center and the facilitators used strategies to engage the participants in their own learning.

Andragogy Today

Andragogy came into use first in Europe then in North America in the mid-twentieth century as the profession of adult education took shape. Andragogy enabled adult educators to claim a knowledge base by identifying what was unique about adult learners. Today the term *andragogy* is used in a number of ways in Central and Eastern European countries. There are some academic departments of andragogy, and some places where andragogy and pedagogy are subdivisions under education (Savicevic, 1991, 2008). In other countries andragogy is equivalent to the North American term *adult education*, signifying a professional field of practice. In North America, andragogy is primarily presented as a way of differentiating adult learners from children.

In a few years it will be half a century since Knowles first introduced andragogy to North America. The fact that andragogy is studied in all academic programs preparing people to work in adult education and human resource development, that research continues to be conducted, and that practitioners continue to find ways to apply it to their fields of practice speaks to its durability and utility in planning and implementing programs with adult learners. The appeal of andragogy is that educators who encounter it can readily relate the assumptions to their *own* learning and in so doing, transition to planning meaningful instruction for adults. But as Henschke (2011) points out, there is no consensus as to whether andragogy is a theory, a philosophy, a teaching description, a scientific discipline, a mechanical tool or technique, or a strategy to help adults learn.

Despite its intuitive appeal to practitioners working with adults in all settings from literacy programs to leisure activities to continuing professional education, to higher education, to business and industry, scholars of andragogy have critiqued it from a number of positions. An early question was whether andragogy was a theory of adult learning; Knowles (1989) ceased calling it a theory and instead called it "a model of assumptions about learning or a conceptual framework that serves as a basis for an emergent theory" (p. 112). While most can accept that andragogy is a model of assumptions about adult learners that can guide practice, a second question is whether the assumptions are true for adults only and not children. When Knowles first presented it in his 1970 book *Modern Practice of Adult Education*, the subtitle was *Andragogy Versus Pedagogy*. After educators pointed out that the assumptions did not necessarily apply to all adults and that some children could be self-directed in their learning, Knowles revised the subtitle in the 1980 edition of the book to *From Pedagogy to Andragogy*. He proposed thinking of andragogy as one end of a continuum; that is, there was a range between being totally teacher-directed as in pedagogy, to being totally student-directed as in andragogy. It depended on the situation; that is, sometimes adults know so little about the subject that the teacher by necessity takes the lead; conversely, some young people are capable of being self-directed depending on their experience with and knowledge of the content area.

While most are content to acknowledge that andragogy describes what adult learners are like most of the time, the actual research in support of these assumptions is mixed at best. Each assumption seems to be somewhat situation-dependent as we pointed out in the discussion above. For example, there are times when adults are externally pressured to learn something and not at all intrinsically motivated, or adults sometimes learn something for the sheer joy of learning and not because they "need" to learn it or have a problem to solve. Some studies find support for some assumptions, others are inconclusive. Rachal's review (2002) of eighteen experimental or quasi-experimental theses and dissertations of andragogy reported a mix of results in support of andragogy. He attributes the ambiguous findings to a number of factors that need to be addressed in order for future research to establish the validity of andragogy for adult learners. For example, participation in the learning activity should be voluntary, objectives and instruction should be collaboratively determined, and learners should be adults and not traditional college-age participants. Rachal also points out that assessing the effectiveness of andragogy is hindered by the fact that tests and grades are anathema to andragogy which assumes adults are capable of self-evaluating their own learning.

Some researchers feel that the way to assess the validity of andragogy is through the development and use of a valid and reliable instrument. Taylor and Kroth (2009) suggest using a panel of experts to develop a Likert-style questionnaire based on the six assumptions. They feel that an instrument that can evaluate how these assumptions are being incorporated into instruction would help "overcome the major criticism that has plagued [andragogy] for the last 30 years: Finding empirical data" (Taylor & Kroth, 2009, p. 10). Holton, Wilson, and Bates (2009) have addressed this challenge by developing a survey instrument to assess the effects of andragogical principles and design elements on learner satisfaction and outcomes. They report that their initial testing of the instrument with a convenience sample of graduate students "holds promise for advancing research on andragogy" (p. 169).

For many, the most problematic issue with andragogy is its unquestioning focus on the individual adult learner who is insulated from the world, fully in control of his or her own learning. As Pratt (1993) points out, the learner operates "as if he or she has risen above the web of social structures." Andragogy "does not acknowledge the vast influence of these structures on the formation of the person's identity and ways of interpreting the world" (p. 18). Our identity, what roles we engage in as adults, what we desire to learn and how we prefer to learn are all shaped by the culture and society in which we live. In reviewing a number of studies with foreign-born learners, for example, Lee (2003) noted that "the adults from whom [Knowles] drew andragogical assumptions . . . were overrepresented by privileged individuals, who were primarily White, male, educated, and from middle-class backgrounds—a population that was not unlike himself." In so doing, "Knowles overgeneralized the characteristics of this population . . . and silenced those [who] were less privileged, whose values and experiences were often ignored in educational settings" (Lee, 2003, p. 15). An even more pointed critique of andragogy's context-free orientation is from Sandlin (2005), who states that an educational context is never value-free or apolitical, that all learners do not look and learn the same, that race, gender, class, and culture all influence learning.

Chapter Summary

Despite the lack of research documenting the assumptions of andragogy, and despite the criticism that it ignores the sociocultural context of learn-

ing, andragogy continues to be a major theory/model/approach to understanding and planning instruction for adult learners. For those new to
adult education, the assumptions about adult learners make intuitive
sense and the instructional practices that go along with them acknowledge
the experience and needs of many adult learners. Knowles (1984)
compiled 36 case examples of andragogy being applied in practice in the
fields of business and government, postsecondary education, professional education, health education, religious education, K–12, and reme-
dial education. From these 36 cases, he draws several lessons about applying
andragogy to practice: it is flexible and the whole or parts can be applied,
climate setting is the most common and easiest starting point, both teachers and learners need to be oriented to an andragogical approach, and
that many practitioners "have found imaginative ways to adapt to traditional systems without sacrificing the essence of the andragogical model"
(Knowles, 1984, p. 419). Finally, recent publications attest to the continued
wide applicability of andragogy to numerous settings including agriculture
(Gharibpanah & Zamani, 2011), nursing (Riggs, 2010), e-learning (Muirhead, 2007), engineering (Winter, McAuliffe, Hargreaves, & Chadwick,
2009), criminal justice (Birzer, 2004), management (Forrest & Peterson,
2006), and human resource development (Holton, Wilson, & Bates, 2009;
Knowles, Holton, & Swanson, 2011).

Linking Theory and Practice: Activities and Resources

1. A good starting point for engaging with andragogy is for you, the
   reader, to examine your own learning as an adult. You can do this by
   recalling a good and bad learning experience as we did with the
   vignettes at the beginning of this chapter. Write out a short narrative
   description of each, then stand back and compare the two incidents.
   What was different? What assumptions of andragogy were present in
   the good experience and absent in the bad experience? What could
   have been done to turn the bad experience into a good one? We have
   found this to be a good student activity also.
2. A second activity would be to inventory your own or your students'
   orientation to learning, whether it is more pedagogical or andragogical.
   There are several instruments available (see a review of these by Holton,
   Wilson, and Bates, 2009), but the one that we have had experience
   with is Conti's Principles of Adult Learning Scale (PALS). This 44-item
   instrument assesses the extent to which your teaching style is more
   learner-centered than teacher-centered, and thus more andragogical

(1991). The PALS assesses your knowledge of learner-centered instructional activities, climate-setting, relating learning to real life problems and experience, and the extent to which students are encouraged to participate in planning and evaluation. The PALS is available in Conti, 2004.

3. An entertaining activity to engage students in understanding andragogy would be to view the movie, *Renaissance Man.* Danny DeVito plays an unemployed marketing executive hired to teach army boot camp recruits English comprehension skills. In the process, DeVito discovers how to engage the recruits in their own learning through the enactment of a Shakespeare play. He stumbles upon andragogical principles which viewers of the movie will be able to readily identify.

4. Take a topic that you are thinking about teaching that has traditionally been taught in a teacher-centered, lecture format mode. How can you redesign the course to employ some if not all of the six assumptions of andragogy?

5. Finally, for those of you interested in more resources on andragogy, John Henschke of Lindenwood University has made many of his and other authors' writing on andragogy available at www.lindenwood.edu/education/andragogy. Likewise, German professor Jost Reischmann maintains a website on andragogy at www.andragogy.net.

Chapter Highlights

- Andragogy, promoted by Malcolm Knowles, is the first model of learning to identify characteristics of *adult* learners.
- Adult learners are characterized by an independent self-concept, a reservoir of experience, the developmental tasks of adult social roles, desire for immediate application, internal motivation, and the need to know.
- Because of its validity in identifying adult learner characteristics, andragogy is popular with educators and trainers of adults in all types of instructional settings.
- Due to these very same characteristics, definitive research on andragogy is difficult to do and inconclusive in results.

CHAPTER FOUR

SELF-DIRECTED LEARNING

When was the last time you attempted to learn a new skill, tackle a home improvement project, address a life issue, or make a personal change? Take a moment and recall an example. What was the project? How did you learn? What resources did you use? How did you know you were making progress? How did you evaluate it? Are you continuing to work on it? Chances are, your project was self-directed learning (SDL) if you: intentionally sought the learning, planned your learning, took responsibility, controlled your learning, and evaluated the outcome. Your learning might have been short term, lasting several hours, or a continuous, perhaps lifelong project. For example, Laura recently took on pottery making as a self-directed learning project. She intentionally sought to learn the art she had so long appreciated. She planned her learning, which included taking pottery classes. She took responsibility not only for attending the classes, but also for making time to work in the studio and study different clay techniques. She is still learning, so it is probably too soon to evaluate the outcome, but her hope is for beautiful, functional pottery, placing this learning project in the continuous, lifelong category.

If you identified one or more SDL projects for yourself, you are in good company. Tough (1971) found that 90% of the 66 adults in his study were engaged in at least one learning project and that 70% of all learning projects were planned by the learners themselves. Subsequent studies have confirmed that upwards of 90% of adults are engaged in some sort of informal learning project (Livingstone, 1999; 2002). Knowles (1975) believed that we become increasingly self-directed as we mature (see Chapter 3), and that SDL is a hallmark of adult learning. At the heart of SDL is the notion that *the learner takes control* of his or her own learning; that is, the learner decides what and how to learn. SDL does not necessarily mean you are sitting in a room all alone, learning something; indeed, you might decide to take a class as Laura did in the pottery example, consult with others, or find materials through the Internet to support your learning. The key is that the learner takes responsibility, that is, *self-directs* what and how something is learned.

You may be thinking it is obvious that we continually learn. Indeed this type of informal, self-directed learning characterizes adulthood and shapes us as individuals. Sometimes SDL is taken for granted as a key learning process, given shallow meaning of little more than self-study (Silen & Uhlin, 2008). Tough (1967), building on work by Houle (1961), provided the first comprehensive model of SDL, initially calling it "self-teaching." SDL is sometimes used interchangeably with independent learning, autonomous learning, self-study, learning projects, self-teaching, and self-education (Leach, 2005; Rager, 2006), and several authors have provided reviews and analyses of SDL (Brockett, et al., 2000; Brockett & Hiemstra, 1991; Caffarella, 1993; Garrison, 1997; Long, 1998; Merriam, Caffarella, & Baumgartner, 2007). Although it is thought that all adults have the capacity to be self-directed learners, the willingness, motivation and/or life circumstances to be self-directed vary.

This chapter begins with reviewing the nature of self-directed learning in adulthood, including definitions of SDL, the goals of self-directed learning, myths of SDL, and approaches to SDL as a process and attribute. Also addressed are contexts, assessment, critiques, and strategies for engaging in SDL.

The Nature of Self-Directed Learning

In this section of the chapter we review self-directed learning from three perspectives. First are definitions of SDL that frame it both as a method of organizing instruction and as a personal attribute; second, we review the goals of SDL ranging from gaining new knowledge to inspiring social action and change. Finally, examining some of the myths of SDL will help to further clarify what this type of learning is all about.

Defining SDL

SDL which has been researched, theorized, and practiced for over 50 years (Brockett & Hiemstra, 1991, 2012; Candy, 1991; Houle, 1961; Knowles, 1975; Tough, 1967, 1971, 1978) has been described both as a personal attribute (that is, a person can be very self-directed and autonomous in their learning), or as a process (that is, a way of organizing instruction). SDL as a personal attribute refers to an individual predisposition toward this type of learning, and comfort with autonomy in the learning process. SDL as a process is an approach to learning that is controlled by the learner. Knowles is well-known for his definition of the process of SDL "in which individuals take the initiative, with or without the help of others, in diagnosing their learning needs, formulating learning goals, identifying human and material resources for learning, choosing and implementing appropriate learning strategies, and evaluating those learning outcomes" (1975, p. 18). Knowles (1975) also delineated a six-step process which could form the basis of a learning contract for learners and instructors to follow in planning self-directed learning. The six steps are: (1) climate setting, that is, creating an atmosphere of mutual respect and support; (2) diagnosing learning needs; (3) formulating learning goals; (4) identifying human and material resources for learning; (5) choosing and implementing appropriate learning strategies; and (6) evaluating learning outcomes.

Tough (1978) studied SDL from the perspective of learning projects which he defined as deliberate efforts to build knowledge, develop skill or make changes, efforts that took a minimum of seven hours. He also outlined a process similar to that of Knowles. Learners move through a series of steps that have to do with first deciding what to learn, then what resources they need (time? money? materials?), where to learn, and how to maintain the motivation for learning. The steps also involve setting goals and timetables, determining the pace, and assessing the current level of knowledge and skill. Self-directed learners also evaluate their learning to determine what might be hindering their learning and adjust accordingly.

Clardy (2000) interviewed 56 adult workers and identified four *types* of SDL projects: induced, synergistic, voluntary, and scanning. *Induced* SDL occurs when learning is mandated by an authority. You have no mastery of the material (indeed, you may have no knowledge at all) and would be considered "unconsciously incompetent" in the area. For instance, imagine you have been diagnosed with high blood pressure and your doctor directs you to lower it. Now you need to take steps to learn about the condition and change your health behaviors. Before you were diagnosed, you had no knowledge about how to manage your blood pressure, making you "unconsciously incompetent." *Synergistic* SDL is not mandated learning, but instead optional and inspired by the opportunity to take advantage of a learning situation made available by another person. You would be "consciously incompetent" in these situations. Continuing with the high blood pressure example, imagine that you are now aware of your management options and meet another person who has managed the condition well for some time who offers you access to her library of books and resources to learn more. *Voluntary* SDL occurs when learning something helps you achieve a goal. This type of learning is not motivated or validated by a higher authority and you are "consciously competent" in knowing what you need to do in order to attain your goal. Say you have made progress in managing your blood pressure and you decide to commit to lowering it even further as a preventive health measure. You embark on a learning journey that includes new cooking methods and an exercise regimen. Finally, Clardy's last category, *Scanning* SDL, is an ongoing process of searching for new learning. Now that you have your blood pressure well managed, you are constantly on the lookout for new studies and information on the condition. Or, keeping up to date in your field would be another example of Scanning SDL. As an adult educator, you are always seeking new ideas, teaching techniques, and ways of better reaching your learners.

Goals of SDL

Caffarella (2000) suggested that there were four goals likely to motivate learners to engage in SDL. The first is the *aspiration to gain knowledge or develop skill*—say you want to learn to speak Spanish. Another is to *become more self-directed in learning*. This might mean that after you take some Spanish classes, you are ready to strike out on your own by watching Spanish speaking television shows, traveling to Spanish speaking countries, or conversing with Spanish speakers. SDL can also *inspire transformational learning* when critical reflection is a component of the process. One transformation that an acquaintance of Laura's had during an educational trip to Costa Rica was the opportunity to meet an independent coffee farmer. She learned that the only way these farmers can support their families is to bypass large corporations and sell their beans directly to the premium market. The insight changed how she views her coffee and other purchases. Finally, SDL can be *emancipatory*, supporting social justice and political action—moving beyond the realm of individual learning. In this case, the Costa Rican traveler might decide to become politically active to support small farms or protest corporate exploitation.

Myths of SDL

Though adults have always continued to learn, it wasn't until the late 1960s that adult educators and researchers began systematically attending to adult learning. Andragogy (see Chapter 3) and self-directed learning were the two earliest and most robust conceptualizations of the nature and characteristics of adult learning. While andragogy identified assumptions or characteristics of adult learners, self-directed learning is more about the process involved when adults engage in their own learning. SDL immediately resonated with adult educators and researchers, producing a burgeoning body of writings, publications and applications. Along with the growing body of research and writing a number of misconceptions or, as Brockett (1994) calls them, *myths* of SDL evolved which sometimes cloud new learners' understanding of this type of learning. We thought it would be helpful to look at these myths and their refutation by Brockett. Six of the myths relate to the learners themselves and their activities. Myth 1, *SDL is an all-or-nothing concept*, is the mistaken notion that you either are a self-directed learner or you are not. In reality, every learner is different, possessing varying levels of self-directedness. It is more accurate to view SDL as a continuum, "a characteristic that exists, to a greater or lesser degree, in all persons and in all learning situations" (Brockett & Hiemstra, 1991, p. 11). Myth 2, *Self-direction implies learning in isolation*, is an incorrect stereotype that places the learner in seclusion from other learners. Although learners may engage in periods of intense, individualized learning, their learning will be enhanced by sharing it with others and inquiring with other adults or instructors about their questions, insights, and reflections. Myth 3, *SDL is the best approach for adults*, can cause problems if the unique needs and goals of learners are not taken into account when structuring learning activities. As with any approach, we must be realistic about the limitations of SDL and use it appropriately. Myth 4, *SDL is limited primarily to white, middle-class adults*, suggests that this learning method reflects the dominant culture. Although this is one of the main critiques of SDL, Brockett notes that there are examples of SDL across diverse social groups and societies outside North America and Western Europe. Myth 5, *SDL is not worth the time required to make it work*, depends on a cost-benefit analysis of the learning goals versus the time and resources available. It is true that not all learning can be best accomplished using SDL. Investing in SDL preparation, learning needs diagnosis, determination of a learning plan, and learning assessment engages the learner in a very meaningful way that is likely to result in deeper learning than teacher-directed approaches, making it worth the time. Myth 6, *SDL activities are limited primarily to reading and writing*, overlooks the informal nature of learning and that many skills cannot be learned from books such as improving a golf swing, speaking a language, building a deck, or training a dog. SDL works best when it is experiential, that is, lodged in the adult's life context (see Chapter 6).

The remaining four myths focus more on teachers, pedagogy, and institutions. Myth 7, *facilitating self-direction is an easy way out for teachers*, is one of the most pervasive myths, according to Brockett (1994). Helping learners be self-directed requires educators to take a very active, individualized approach with learners to communicate the process and support the development of their SDL plan. Learners come to SDL with different needs and capabilities, making facilitating it as demanding as—if not more demanding than—traditional teaching. Myth 8, *SDL is limited primarily to those settings where freedom and democracy prevail*, assumes ideal conditions must exist for SDL to occur. Yet, SDL certainly occurs in very controlling social and educational environments. Think of the SDL engaged in by protesters in the Arab Spring revolutions or by women and girls who continued their learning in hiding under Taliban rule in Afghanistan. Myth 9, *self-direction is just another adult education fad*, can be debunked just on the longevity of SDL as a theory and practice in adult education for over 50 years. Myth 10, *SDL will erode the quality of institutional programs*, has not emerged when learners are given greater control over learning. The only risk to quality is when SDL is poorly administered.

The Process of Self-Directed Learning

Since Tough and Knowles's groundbreaking work in SDL, many others have contributed to our understanding of this form of adult learning. For example, Spear (1988) and Spear and Mocker (1984) questioned the step-by-step linear processes outlined by Knowles and Tough. Spear and Mocker interviewed 78 self-directed learners who had less than high school completion about their experiences and concluded that SDL preplanning is uncommon. Rather, SDL is mediated by opportunities learners find in their own environments, past or new knowledge, and chance occurrences, and that all SDL projects have elements of these factors. Spear and Mocker call the influence of the immediate environment the "organizing circumstance," that is, "self-directed learners, rather than preplanning their learning projects, tend to select a course from limited alternatives which occur fortuitously within their environment, and which structures their learning projects" (p. 4). Spear did not believe that self-directed learning projects occurred in linear lock-step formation, but that the learning spiraled between several sets of activities or clusters which would eventually meld into a coherent whole. For instance, while searching in the library for information on a particular topic, a student discovers a new concept. Deciding to pursue the issue further, she searches the Internet and finds a virtual community on the topic. From interacting with that community, new insights and understandings of the topic evolve. Eventually, the woman exploring the new idea in cyberspace discovers an interesting way to tie her new learning to her ongoing research. As another example, David is engaged in a learning project to landscape his yard. He reads about which plants will do well in the climate where he lives and draws up a plan for his yard. At a neighborhood block party he overhears a conversation about the problem of deer eating his neighbors' flowers. In joining the discussion he learns that they particularly like certain plants and flowers. He then consults with a cooperative extension agent as to what plants to avoid and which would be "safe" to plant. Some time after the landscaping has been completed however, he discovers deer are still going after some of his flowers. He then searches the Internet, consults with neighbors and others about which deer repellants actually work. In Spear's model (1988), both the student's and David's learning projects have spiraled from one cluster of activity to another; that is, circumstances have organized their learning. How has your own environment, knowledge, and chance encounters affected your SDL experiences?

Brockett and Hiemstra (1991) developed their Personal Responsibility Orientation (PRO) model of self-direction in learning that accounts for instructional methods (or process) as well as personality attributes of the learner. Stockdale and Brockett (2010) tested a 25-item Personal Responsibility Orientation to Self-Direction in Learning Scale (PRO-SDLS) and found the instrument to be highly reliable in measuring SDL among college students. The *instructional process* involves the learner taking the primary responsibility for planning, implementing, and evaluating learning. For instance, you might want to learn how to sail. You decide to ask your neighbor, an expert sailor, to teach you. A clear evaluation of your learning will be whether you learn to effectively sail on your own. Another person may serve as an educational agent, one who should be skilled at providing resources or in facilitating the learning. In this example, it would be your neighbor. The *personal attributes* aspect of SDL in this model depends on the learner's propensity to be self-directed in learning and take responsibility for it. In other words, if you were not determined to learn sailing and willing to manage the process, you would not do it. Brockett and Hiemstra also emphasize that SDL is affected by the context in which it occurs. Your learning context in this sailing example might be affected by the sailboat you are using, weather, your relationship with your neighbor, available funds, or proximity to water and access to a boat.

Recently Brockett and Hiemstra (2012) updated their PRO model in response to confusion over some of the terminology. They explain that the term "personal responsibility" created confusion noting that it has become "politically co-opted" by the political right in the United States by "blaming the victim for their circumstances in life because they did not take responsibility to avoid getting into their difficulties" (p. 158). They also attempted to address critiques that their model was too humanistic, ignored social and cultural influences, and did not fully address meta-cognitive learning. In response, they propose the Person, Process, Context (PPC) model as an intersecting dynamic between the *person* (personal characteristics such as creativity, critical reflection, enthusiasm; life experience; life satisfaction; motivation; previous education; resilience; and self-concept), *process* (the teaching-learning transaction including facilitation, learning skills, learning styles; planning, organizing, and evaluating abilities; teaching styles; and technological skills), and *context* (the environmental and sociopolitical climate such as culture, power, learning environment, finances, gender, learning climate, organizational policies, political milieu, race, and sexual orientation).

Building on Knowles' definition of SDL, Garrison (1997) suggested that SDL was affected by self-management, self-monitoring of the knowledge construction process, and intrinsic and extrinsic motivation. Self-management situates the learner within the social context and is the degree to which the learner assumes control of the environment so that she can meet her goals. Self-management involves using learning materials and sustaining communication to build collaborative understanding. For instance, the person who is learning to sail takes advantage of her environment (resources) and the people in it (her neighbor) to test and confirm her learning. Self-monitoring and motivation are the cognitive aspects of the model. Self-monitoring is the learner's ability to gauge her cognitive and metacognitive processes, in many ways like double-loop (reflecting on assumptions) and triple-loop (reflecting on the learning itself) learning

(Argyris, 1991). Self-monitoring is also closely associated with reflective practice and critical thinking. The sailor might draw on her previous boating experiences and knowledge to learn how to sail, as well as critique her own learning process as she attempted navigating the boat. Motivation is what drives the learner to engage in SDL. The sailor may have been motivated by spending time with her neighbor, or watching as others enjoy sailing, or hearing from a friend about how much fun sailing is.

In a popular application of SDL, Grow (1991, 1994) proposed an instructional model that is based on Hersey and Blanchard's (1988) stages of Situational Leadership. Grow's model describes how educators can help learners be more self-directed in their learning and has four stages as shown in Table 4.1. In this model, problems occur when the instructor is not meeting the stage of the learner. It is the role of the educator to continually monitor and customize the learning to meet the individual. For example, if the learner is not at all self-directed, as might be the case in learning something totally new and unfamiliar, the educator's role has to be more directive, perhaps employing a lecture and immediate feedback. At the other end of the continuum is a learner who is very self-directed, in which case the educator's role is more of a consultant and resource person, one who fosters independent learning projects and discovery learning. Can you recall a match or mismatch that affected your own SDL? How did it affect you as a learner? As an educator? Which of these models best describes your SDL? Why?

SDL as a Personal Attribute

Much of the focus on SDL has been on the process, yet just as much is concerned with SDL as a learner attribute (Guglielmino, 1977). Knowles (1975) thought of self-directedness as a growing preference with age and as an outcome of learner maturity. Further, the propensity to be self-directed is one of the major assumptions of andragogy outlined by Knowles (see Chapter 3). Brockett and Hiemstra (1991) are also proponents of the learner taking responsibility for learning and suggest SDL is positively associated with high self-efficacy. This means that the more responsibility you take for your learning, the more confident you are in doing so. Per the sailing example above, you might start with sailing a sunfish and then build confidence to try a catamaran or larger boat next. Research to understand SDL as an attribute has examined learning style, education level, life satisfaction, and readiness; however, clear conclusions about defining attributes are elusive (Merriam, Caffarella, & Baumgartner, 2007).

TABLE 4.1 GROW'S SELF-DIRECTED LEARNING STAGES

Stage	Learner Status	Educator Role	Teaching Strategies for Stage

1	Dependent
	Lacking
	  self-direction
		Authority
		Direct learning
		Coach
		Teacher-centered
			Providing introductory material
			Giving few choices
			Lecturing—subject centered
			Drilling
			Helping the learner see the immediate
			  connection between concepts and
			  application
			Giving immediate feedback
			Tutoring

2	Interested
	Confident
		Motivator
		Guide
			Inspiring learning
			Helping learner set goals
			Assisting with development of learning
			  strategies
			Lecturing inspirationally with guided
			  discussion
			Applying the basics in an interesting way
			Providing close supervision

3	Involved
	Engaged as
	  self-directed
	  learners
	Possess knowledge
	  and self-efficacy
	  for SDL
		Facilitator
		Partner
			Applying the material
			Facilitating discussion
			Applying learning to real problems
			Group projects or presentations
			Encouraging critical thinking
			Providing learning strategies
			Collaborative learning

4	Self-directed
	  learner
	Able to plan,
	  execute, and
	  evaluate
	  learning
		Consultant
		Delegator
		Mentor
			Encouraging independent projects and
			  learner-led discussions
			Learning through discovery
			Offering expertise, consulting, and
			  monitoring as needed
			Providing autonomy
			Building in opportunities for learners to
			  share their learning with each other
			Focus on both the process and product
			  of learning
			Service learning
			Coaching

Source: Adapted from Grow, 1991, 1994.

The Oddi Continuing Learning Inventory (OCLI) and the Self-Directed Learning Readiness Scale (SDLRS) are used extensively to measure learners' tendency toward self-direction. The OCLI is a 24-question scale that measures self-directedness as a personality trait (Oddi, 1986; Oddi, Ellis, & Roberson, 1990). The more widely used SDLRS was developed by Guglielimino (1977) and measures *readiness* to engage in SDL. According to Guglielimino, SDL is a blend of attitudes, values and abilities that predispose learners' capacity for SDL. Psychological qualities contributing to readiness include initiative, independence, learning persistence, responsibility taking, self-discipline, curiosity, independence in and enjoyment of learning, goal setting, and a problem-solving orientation. Think about your own characteristics according to this list. How self-directed do you think you are? To test your own readiness, refer to the links under the "resources for self-directed study" at the end of this chapter. The SDLRS has been heavily relied on; however, it is criticized by Stockdale and Brockett (2010) as used in empirical studies without revision, and in spite of challenges to its validity. Still, it is the most widely used instrument in SDL research (Merriam, Caffarella, & Baumgartner, 2007).

Self-Directed Learning in Various Contexts

SDL has been described as both a process and an attribute. The importance of context—the psychological, social, political, cultural, and economic environment—in learning is also being more widely discussed because we may be more comfortable and capable of SDL in an area or environment where we have some experience (Candy, 1991). The importance of context in learning has dominated adult education scholarship for the past twenty years. Understanding how aspects of learner characteristics such as age, gender, race, or socioeconomic status play out within a learning environment is important for us to appreciate as both learners and educators. For example, an African American man is interested in learning how to use a new software system, so he attends a continuing education class offered at a community college. All of the other learners are white and they treat him as if he is invisible. His sense of self-efficacy and motivation to return to that context will likely be low and even his motivation to learn the software may be diminished. On the other hand, imagine he returns to the class the following week. This time, the learners are a different mix and an effort is made to include him and value his knowledge and experience. His learning experience becomes very different—this time in the same environment, but with different individuals. SDL learning contexts are many such as personal, professional, organizational, educational, and online environments. This section considers SDL in these settings.

Self-directed learning can occur across a range of contexts for a variety of reasons. The context of one's personal life generates much of our learning. You may want to learn how to cook a new dish, understand a medical condition, improve your parenting skills, or gain a promotion. You initiate a learning program to meet your learning needs. For example, Rager examined how a diagnosis of breast cancer (2004) and prostate cancer (2006) shaped patients' self-directed learning. Roberson and Merriam (2005) shed light on how SDL is used to navigate life changes in older adulthood. They interviewed 10 rural older adults about their SDL and found that they used it to negotiate life transitions, in particular those related to late-life family transitions such as becoming a grandparent, and loss, such as having to leave one's family home or death of a spouse or others close to them. Their findings also point to the importance of understanding how an adult's position in the lifespan intersects with and shapes learning needs. Wilson and Halford (2008) examined the process of change in self-directed couple relationship education. Fifty-nine couples completed a self-directed program that included a DVD and guidebook with telephone-based coaching sessions with a professional relationship educator. Couples completed a mean of 96% of the learning tasks and implemented a wide-range of self-change with continued implementation of learning strategies at a six-month follow-up interview. They concluded that SDL is an effective approach for couple education.

SDL is also becoming a prominent feature of continuing professional education in many fields including physical therapy (Musolino, 2006), dental education (ADEA Commission on Change and Innovation in Dental Education et al., 2007), veterinary and medical education (Raidal & Volet, 2009), pharmacy education (Huynh et al., 2009), and library science (Quinney, Smith, & Galbraith, 2010). These professions recognize the need for continuous, lifelong learning and are attempting to build it into the curriculum. Perceiving a generational technology gap in the skills of its librarians and users, for example, the Library at Brigham Young University implemented a self-directed training program to improve the technology skills of librarians as well as develop their lifelong learning skills (Quinney, Smith, & Galbraith). Librarians engaged in a self-paced exploration of new technologies of their choice independently for 15 minutes per day. Ninety-six librarians participated, 66 of whom reached or exceeded the learning goals upon an exit survey. Material resources, feedback, and small instructor-led groups were provided. Learners' preferred learning strategies were small, instructor-led groups and self-learning through books and articles.

Self-directed training is also used in business and organizational settings as a strategy for competing in a globalizing, changing environment.

As Oh and Park (2012) state, "with rapidly continuing changes in organizations and globalization, it is important for organizations to support workers by promoting SDL which is more adaptable and responsive to change (Lee, 2001)" (Oh & Park, 2012, p. 269). Self-directed learning is also used in areas such as sales force training (Artis & Harris, 2007), human resource development (Ellinger, 2004), and industry (Smith, Sadler-Smith, Robertson, & Wakefield, 2007). Artis and Harris (2007) propose that sales managers can use SDL to supplement traditional training and improve salespeople's performance. Smith et al. drew on an Australian national research project to interview learning and development mangers across a variety of organizations and industries to assess the feasibility of developing self-directedness among employees within the work context. They found that managers responsible for facilitating learning and leaders had a positive disposition toward developing SDL and identified strategies to help foster it within work settings.

Higher education is yet another site where SDL has taken hold. Long common in adult education programs, it is now used in service learning projects (Butin, 2010), and problem-based education (PBL), especially in medical education (Silen & Uhlin, 2008). Integrating SDL into higher education can be challenging as evidenced by Raidal and Volet (2009), who examined 128 preclinical students' disposition toward social and self-directed learning (key elements in problem-based and case-based learning used in medical training). They found the students preferred external teacher regulation and individual forms of learning—a mismatch with the type of learning required in practice. They concluded that guiding students towards greater learning autonomy needed for social and self-directed learning is imperative for continuous lifelong learning post-graduation. Musolino (2006) examined how physical therapy students and new graduates assessed themselves and developed a conceptual model of how her participants engaged in self-assessment. Her findings have implications for both SDL as an attribute and as affected by context. She found that one of the ways self-assessment occurs is through self-learning and that it is largely affected by psychosocial values.

SDL in online contexts is a growing phenomenon with implications for both the learning process and learner attributes (Song & Hill, 2007). Known as Virtual Learning Environments (VLEs), these contexts for learning include online training or e-learning, and are gaining popularity for convenience and cost efficiency in both education and business (Simmering, Posey, & Piccoli, 2009). Chu and Tsai (2009) surveyed 541 Taiwanese adults enrolled in adult education institutes to measure their preference for VLEs. A key finding was that self-directed learning readiness was a strong factor in predicting preferences for online learning environments, particularly when dealing with highly intellectual challenges. The higher the SDL readiness, the higher the need for constructing ideas, solving problems, and creating learning activities on the Internet. One of the problems with VLEs is the lack of direction from the instructor. Self-directed learning is almost assumed for this type of learning, which can leave some learners lost and frustrated. If we are to pursue online SDL, we need new ways of understanding and facilitating it. Song and Hill contend that existing frameworks focus primarily on SDL as a process and as personal attributes but in face-to-face settings. They posit that current models may not account well for the online context of learning.

Building on arguments that SDL is not well researched in specific contexts, Song and Hill (2007) propose a framework that considers the process of SDL in an online context. Their framework is based on the learner's SDL process that includes personal attributes and comfort with autonomous processes, which are situated within a learning context that is well designed and supported by instructors and peers. Recent findings have shown that the role of both the instructor and other learners in online learning are important (Simmering, Posey, & Piccoli, 2009). Simmering, Posey, and Piccoli surveyed 190 students to measure their motivation, computer self-efficacy, and learning. Not surprisingly, Internet usage prior to the online learning was positively related to learning. Contrary to what they expected, computer self-efficacy (self-perception of computer abilities) was not related to initial motivation to learn, nor was it related to learning in the online class.

Assessing Self-Directed Learning

Assessment Strategies for Self-Directed Learning, by Costa and Kallick (2004), is chock-full of strategies. Self-assessment begins with goals that are appropriate and attainable. Effective self-directed learners have a sense of responsibility for their learning goals, set criteria for their learning, and are able to modify their process based on feedback and self-knowledge. They identify the attributes of self-directed learners as self-managing, self-monitoring, and self-modifying and suggest that the key to self-directed learning is to become effective at self-assessing the learning. Table 4.2 presents their criteria for assessing effective SDL for both educators and learners. For example, with regard to self-managing your SDL, you could draw from

TABLE 4.2 COSTA AND KALLICK'S CRITERIA FOR
SELF-DIRECTED LEARNER ASSESSMENT

Self-Managing	Self-Monitoring	Self-Modifying
Draws from prior knowledge, sensory data, and intuition to guide, hone, and refine actions	Seeks perspectives beyond self and others to develop thoughtful responses	Explores choice points between self-assertion and integration with others
Displays internal locus of control	Generates new and innovative ideas and problem-solving strategies	Seeks feedback from appropriate sources for improved performance
Thoughtfully plans and initiates actions	Pursues ambiguities and possibilities to create new meanings	Reflects on and learns from experience
Manages time effectively	Manages self in relation to group	Continues to learn new skills and strategies
Produces new knowledge through own research and experimentation	Is aware of what is known and not known and develops strategies to fill in the gaps	Thoughtfully receives feedback and acts on it
Uses clear and precise language	Evaluates, corrects, and adjusts to work to improve its quality	
Balances solitude and togetherness, action and reflection, and personal and professional growth		
Displays a sense of humor		

Source: Adapted from: Costa, A. L., & Kallick, B. (2004). *Assessment strategies for self-directed learning*, pp. 86–87. Thousand Oaks, CA: Corwin Press/Sage.

prior knowledge to manage your learning as well as organize your time effectively. For self-monitoring your learning you might ask others to share their perspectives on your project. For self-modifying your SDL, you might seek feedback from others, reflect on your performance, and adjust your SDL accordingly. Costa and Kallick not only describe what makes an individual effective at self-direction, but also how SDL can be cultivated in other people and organizations. Costa and Kallick (2004) also have a self-assessment (pp. 93–95) if you are interested in evaluating your own SDL competency further.

Highlights of the Costa and Kallick (2004) assessment strategies include: holding conferences with peers or the instructor to reflect on learning goals, monitor progress, and adjust as needed. You may want to create a set of reflective questions for these conferences such as: "What is working well with your project?" "What is not going well?" "What has surprised you?" "What adjustments do you need to make?" Costa and Kallick are also advocates of creating reflection worksheets that give learners guided questions to consider individually as they assess their learning. They also recommend making checklists of key steps or competencies related to the overall learning task and offer several examples. We often assign self-directed learning projects in our courses and have found it helpful to build in opportunities to report on progress both informally during class as well as in reflective papers. These reports have been effective at helping students assess and adjust their projects. Portfolios, a collection of the learner's work, are also effective for both project documentation and assessment. When using portfolios, we recommend dedicating class time to portfolio sharing in small groups. This has proven a valuable exercise as learners compare notes on their learning journeys.

Costa and Kallick (2004) identify factors that deter and diminish SDL, such as there being too much dependency on the instructor. This might occur when the instructor has all the answers or does not push learners to find their own answers. When learners have an unclear vision for their projects, it can also be difficult to focus and sustain them. We have effectively used learning contracts with students when they plan SDL projects and they are very useful for ensuring clear goal setting and accountability in the process (See Exhibit 4.1 at the end of this chapter for an example). SDL projects will also suffer from instructors who try to overcontrol and micromanage the process. It is key for us as instructors to step back and support the risk taking, mistakes, and uncertainty that such projects engender for both learners and instructors. We have also found it important to role model the self-directed learning process in ourselves. When one of us assigns a SDL project, she also engages in one, reporting on her progress to show that it is OK when a learning project stalls or takes an unexpected turn.

Critiques of Self-Directed Learning

Although SDL has been embraced by many, it is not without its problems. First, the assumption that all adults desire self-direction in their learning is problematic on developmental, technical, economic, and cultural levels. Developmentally, not all adults are desirous or capable of SDL. Readiness to engage in SDL varies among learners. We need to recognize and be sensitive to the varying levels of readiness to engage in SDL and customize learning accordingly. Brookfield (1984) raises concerns about our ability to facilitate SDL's goal setting, instructional design, and evaluation without questioning the validity or worth of it as compared to other options. Not all adult learners have the means to engage in SDL pursuits, and some cultures may be averse to relying on such learning techniques.

Brookfield (1984) suggests that SDL describes how the dominant majority learns and may ignore important aspects of culture and context. For example, SDL tends to be a Western teaching method that may be culturally at odds with some learners. "Confucius asserted that students would need a competent teacher to guide them and believed students would better spend their time absorbing structured ideas than thinking independently (Confucius, 479 BC). In contrast, the ultimate goal of Western-style universities is creating self-directed, self-motivated, independent learners who are able to critique and direct their own work with critical thinking and rational judgment" (Lee, 2012, p. 395). Wang and Farmer (2008) surveyed Chinese instructors of adults and found that they favored teaching lower thinking skills associated with the first three levels of Bloom's Taxonomy (knowledge, comprehension, and application), confirming their hypothesis that Chinese education features a teacher-centered, information-based, test-driven instructional format. Yet, when Chinese learners matriculate into Western universities, professors may expect them to acculturate immediately to learning processes (including SDL) that are very new and possibly threatening to their expectations of how they should behave in an educational context. Educators' sensitivity to learners from non-Western cultures is very important if we hope to effectively support and facilitate learning.

An important question for us to consider is whether SDL remains a relevant, robust area of research. Recent adult education texts have omitted the topic (Drago-Severson, 2009; Foley, 2004; Merriam, 2008; Merriam, Courtenay, & Cervero, 2006; Merriam & Grace, 2011). Although SDL receives 10 mentions in the 2010 *Handbook of Adult and Continuing Education*, the topic does not even warrant a chapter in this 40-chapter volume published once a decade to provide an assessment of the field (Kasworm, Rose, & Ross-Gordon, 2010). Does this omission mean that we have exhausted the subject? Conner, Carter, Dieffenderfer, and Brockett (2009) analyzed the citations of the SDL literature from 1980–2008 and concluded that the current state of the research is strong. Also, a website (www.sdlglobal.com), journal (*International Journal of Self-Directed Learning*), and an annual conference in existence for over 25 years attests to SDL's continued relevance in understanding adult learning.

Yet, longevity alone is not synonymous with relevance and innovation. Long (2009) classifies five foci of SDL research as (1) measurement as an individual variable; (2) within institutional settings; (3) via electronic media; (4) in relation to self-efficacy, self-esteem, and performance; and (5) in terms of volition and autonomy. Based on our review of the literature for this book, only SDL in virtual learning environments is relatively undeveloped. Brockett (2009) advocates for more study of the foundations of SDL, new measures of self-directedness, new research methods including phenomenology and critical theory, and connecting SDL to other fields to build a richer understanding of it. These suggestions seem a good starting point for future explorations of SDL.

Chapter Summary

Self-directed learning is a primary process and defining characteristic of many adult learners. This chapter opened with defining SDL, described the goals of self-directed learning in adulthood, explored myths about SDL, examined SDL as a process and an attribute, considered the context where SDL occurs, discussed SDL assessment, and raised critiques. Given our fast-changing environment, it is no longer possible to learn everything we need to know in formal preparatory education; therefore, one of our most important roles as adult educators is to support self-directed learning. Building our own knowledge and skill in this area allows us to foster SDL in others. Finally, we turn our focus to SDL teaching and learning applications.

Linking Theory and Practice: Activities and Resources

1. List your learning experiences over the past year. Categorize them (individual learning projects, classes, workshops, and so forth). See if you can tally the number of SDL projects you engaged in and how many hours you spent on them. What patterns do you notice? What do you do particularly well? What do you need help with?
2. Using Grow's instructional model (see Table 4.1), design *four* different instructional plans in your area of expertise that address each level of student comfort with SDL (dependent, interested, involved, SDL learner).
3. Embark on an individual change project:

   > Select a personal change that you think is important to achieve over the next few weeks or months. The change can be work related or personal, such as improving your listening or eating more healthfully. It should be something you have energy to devote some time to changing.

Identify:

The change goal

Why it is important to you

Specific strategies you will use to achieve your goal

How you will appraise and measure your progress

Track your progress weekly and adjust accordingly.

4. Develop an annual SDL plan; update it on a regular basis.
5. Schedule regular self-learning retreats to either work on your SDL project or reflect on your learning.
6. Build service learning as SDL projects into your syllabus or your learning experience.
7. Use learning contracts to encourage SDL (see Exhibit 4.1).
8. Consider SDL in virtual learning environments (VLEs). What are strategies you could incorporate so that the learner does not feel abandoned and adrift? This issue will be discussed more in Chapter 10, Adult Learning in the Digital Age.
9. Resources and Web Links
   a. International Society for Self-Directed Learning
      http://www.oltraining.com/SDLwebsite/indexSDL.php
   b. SDLRS
      http://www.guglielmino734.com/
   c. Infed Self-Directed Learning
      http://www.infed.org/biblio/b-selfdr.htm
   d. Hiemstra's Home Page
      http://www-distance.syr.edu/distancenew.html
   e. International Journal of Self-Directed Learning
      http://www.oltraining.com/SDLwebsite/journals.php
   f. See Loyens, S.M.M., Magda, J., & Rikers, R.M.J. P. (2008). Self-directed learning in problem-based learning and its relationship with self-regulated learning. *Educational Psychology Review, 20,* 411–427, for a literature review comparing self-directed learning, problem-based learning, and self-regulated learning.

Chapter Highlights

- Self-directed learning involves planning, organizing, controlling, and assessing your individual learning in a process initially described by Tough as "self-teaching."

- Self-directed learning is not necessarily a solitary activity. You may elect to consult with peers, experts, or instructors during the quest. You may even enroll in a class.
- SDL is both a process of instruction as well as an attribute of the learner.
- Self-directed learning can be integrated into highly structured, formal, controlled learning environments through activities and assignments.
- In formal settings, SDL requires active involvement of the instructor to guide the learners in identifying goals and strategies, and in assessing their own learning.
- Learners exhibit varying degrees of self-directedness along a continuum from high dependency on the instructor to independent SDL that may rely on the instructor as a consultant or mentor.
- Self-directed learning helps adults learn in personal, professional, organizational, educational, and online contexts.

Exhibit 4.1: Independent Study Learning Contract

This worksheet is to help you plan your independent study. You should provide a typewritten paper or electronic copy to (name of instructor).

Your project should be aligned with the amount of time and effort you would put forth in a typical graduate class. A general guideline is that each credit requires 15 hours of "contact" (time you would spend in class) and usually about twice that amount outside the class contact hours. Thus, one credit of independent study would be equivalent to about 45 hours of work. Your learning contract should be aligned with a typical course workload, based on the number of credits you are taking. Terms of the contract will be negotiated between us.

General Information

Name:	Semester Enrolled:
Contact Information:	Number of Credits:

Contract

1. Describe the overall title and focus of the learning project
2. Outline the objectives or learning outcomes you hope to achieve for the project
3. Describe the activities you will engage in to achieve these objectives:
   a. Time frame and duration of the project
   b. Where will it take place
   c. What will you do
   d. And so forth
4. List the resources and materials (books, articles, and so on) you expect to use in the pursuit of these objectives.
5. Anticipate the number of meetings you would like to have with me for planning and advisement.
6. Explain the basis upon which you expect to be graded. What products will you turn in as a basis for a grade?

_____

Student's Signature   Date

_____

Professor's Signature   Date

CHAPTER FIVE

TRANSFORMATIVE LEARNING

In a mesmerizing story of transformation published nearly 100 years ago, Franz Kafka's *The Metamorphosis* (1915) tells the story of Gregor Samsa, who awakes one morning to find himself changed into a giant insect. Although, of course, the physical change has taken place in his imagination, it functions to capture the longer process of his metamorphosis from a human being, brother, and son, to a worker bee whose existence has become bug-like, scuttling to and from work as the sole support for his freeloading, unemployed family.

While Gregor Samsa's transformation is not something we would want to emulate, it is a dramatic metaphor for what we are talking about when we speak of transformation and the learning that brings about a transformation. Simply defined, "transformational learning shapes people; they are different afterward, in ways both they and others can recognize" (Clark, 1993, p. 47). Transformative or transformational learning (terms used interchangeably in the literature) has become the most studied and written about adult learning theory since Knowles proposed andragogy in the 1970s (see Chapter 3). In fact transformative learning has "replaced andragogy as the dominant educational philosophy of adult education, offering teaching practices grounded in empirical research and supported by sound theoretical assumptions" (Taylor, 2008, p. 12). Perhaps because transformative learning is considered to be a form of learning engaged in by adults, not children, "transformative learning theory has brought a new and exciting identity to the field of adult education" (Cranton & Taylor, 2012, p.16).

As testimony to its central place in adult learning theory, there are hundreds of articles and chapters and dozens of books, the most recent being the 600-page *The Handbook of Transformative Learning* (2012), a journal devoted to this type of learning (*Journal of Transformative Education*), and biannual international conferences on transformative learning. In just one setting, that of higher education for example, Kasworm and Bowles (2012) report reviewing 250 published reports of research grounded in the theoretical framework of transformative learning. Given the plethora of resources and approaches to transformative learning theory, we have been challenged to figure out how to capture, in one short chapter, the essence of this theory. To that end, we have organized the chapter into the following sections—what is transformative learning (TL), promoting and evaluating TL, and unresolved issues in TL.

What Is Transformative Learning?

Given the vast array of definitions, frameworks, and theories of transformative learning, some organizational scheme is needed for summarizing this material. We could proceed historically which is loosely what Gunnlaugson (2008) does with his division of the literature into "first" and "second wave" theories. The first wave centers on Mezirow's groundbreaking work and includes Mezirow's own refinements as well as research building on, and critiquing his theory. The second wave includes those who depart from Mezirow's rationalistic perspective and expand transformative learning to include holistic, extrarational, and integrative perspectives. Dirkx (1998) proposed four lenses for understanding transformative learning— emancipatory, cognitive, developmental, and spiritual-integrative, and Taylor (2008) suggested that Mezirow's psychocritical approach could be augmented by neurobiological, cultural-spiritual, race-centric and planetary conceptions. For this chapter we have chosen a more recent organizing scheme which seems to include all the various perspectives. Cranton's three-part framework (in press) consists of the cognitive perspective, beyond rational, and social change.

The Cognitive Perspective

We can think of learning as both a verb—I am learning about this theory— and a noun—I have acquired knowledge (more learning) about this theory. This is similar to how Kegan differentiates between "informational learning," that learning that adds to "*what* we know," and is cumulative, and transformational learning—learning that "changes . . . *how* we know" (Kegan, 2000, p. 49, italics in original). While much of adult learning is additive—we know more about many things as we move through life, there is that occasional, often dramatic life experience that causes us to stop and examine how we think about something. Hearing you have a life-threatening disease, being the first in your family to earn an advanced degree, winning a lottery, or being caught in random violence all may lead to questioning some of our assumptions about ourselves and the world. The transformative learning process is then set in motion, a "process by which we transform our taken-for-granted frames of reference (meaning schemes, habits of mind, mindsets) to make them more inclusive, discriminating, open, emotionally capable of change, and reflective so that they may generate beliefs and opinions that will prove more true or justified to guide actions" (Mezirow, 2000, p. 8).

Transformative learning is essentially a learning process of making meaning of one's experience. Mezirow (1978) who first articulated transformative learning as a cognitive, rational process, studied the experiences of women who returned to school to prepare for jobs. He found that this experience of returning to school caused them to examine their assumptions about who they were and how they were products of sociocultural expectations of women at that time. Mezirow (1991) describes the transformative learning process as follows: "Transformative learning involves an enhanced level of awareness of the context of one's beliefs and feelings, a critique of their assumptions and particularly premises, an assessment of alternative perspectives, a decision to negate an old perspective in favor of a new one or to make a synthesis of old and new, an ability to take action based upon the new perspective, and a desire to fit the new perspective into the broader context of one's life" (p. 161).

Mezirow's early description (1978) of transformational learning included a 10-step process beginning with what he called "a disorienting dilemma." A disorienting dilemma is brought about when a significant personal life event precipitates a crisis in our lives such as the death of a loved one, being a victim of a crime, or losing your job. Subsequent research suggests that while a disorienting dilemma is most easily identified as triggering the process, there can also be an accumulation of experiences over time that eventually come together to foster a transformation. For example, after numerous incidents of sexist treatment in the workplace, a woman employee begins to question her assumptions about equality in the workplace—this questioning, or self-examination is the second step in the process followed by the third step of critically assessing the assumptions which one has been living with *prior* to the initiation of this process (that is, that men and women are treated equally in the workplace). Next steps include "recognition that one's discontent and the process of transformation are shared" (there are other women who have experienced sexist treatment and want to do something about it); "exploration of options for new roles, relationships, and actions," and "planning a course of action" (Mezirow, 1991, p. 22), as in forming a women's network, bringing sexist practices to the attention of management, and so on. The remaining four steps include "acquiring knowledge and skills for implementing one's plans," trying out new roles which includes "building competence and self-confidence in new roles and relationships," (p. 22) and finally, reintegrating the new perspective into one's life.

Since the first presentation of his theory in the late 1970s, Mezirow has refined and expanded his theory taking into account theoretical critiques and empirical research (for an excellent review of the evolution of Mezirow's theory, see Baumgartner, 2012). He also clarified the notion of reflection saying it could involve "*content reflection*—reflection on *what* we perceive, think, feel, or act upon. *Process reflection* is an examination of *how* we perform these functions of perceiving, thinking, feeling, or acting" (Mezirow, 1991, pp. 107–108, emphasis in original). *Premise reflection* is going deeper, asking "*why* we perceive, think, feel, or act as we do" (p. 108). Premise reflection is the only one of the three that leads to a perspective transformation. If we take the preceding example of the woman employee who experienced sexism in the workplace, content reflection might be her thinking about an incident in a meeting where her suggestions were ignored by her male coworkers. She might ask herself, "What just happened in that meeting?" Process reflection might be her asking herself if she had been ignored perhaps because the wording of her suggestions had been unclear or confusing. Premise reflection would involve asking *why* her suggestions had been ignored. Was it because the suggestions were made by a woman? Such a question has the potential to set in motion a perspective change about the role of women in the workplace.

In light of a growing body of research on his theory, Mezirow has acknowledged that emotions, intuition, context, and relationships play a role in the transformational learning process, although still secondary to the critical cognitive aspects (Baumgartner, 2012). He also clarified his view on the relationship of perspective transformation to social action. Action itself, the final component of the process, can be in terms of "immediate action, delayed action or reasoned reaffirmation of an existing pattern of action" (Mezirow, 2000, p. 24). Social action is not the goal of transformative learning; rather, personal transformation "leads to alliances with others of like mind" which can lead to social action (1992, p. 252).

Beyond Rational

As discussed, Mezirow's theory of transformative learning is, at its core, a rational, critical, cognitive process that requires thinking, reflection, questioning, and examination of one's assumptions and beliefs. Others have placed the unconscious, emotions, relationships, culture, spirit, aesthetics, and ecology at the center of the process. We now turn to a few of these conceptualizations.

In stark contrast to what some consider to be Mezirow's overly rational process, Dirkx (2012a) sees transformative learning as emotional "soul work." Drawing from Jungian psychology and Boyd and Myers' notion (1988) of transformation as centered in the emotional, inner unconscious world of the human psyche, Dirkx understands the work of transformative learning as accessing the unconscious world and incorporating it into our conscious being, our ego. This is done by way of attending to our emotions: "It is the ego that comes to represent or mirror conscious content of the psyche. For us to become conscious or aware of unconscious content in our lives, it must be represented in some manner in the ego. Insights or epiphanies are examples of the ego making conscious connections with psychic content that was previously unconscious. Such experiences are usually associated with a surge of psychic energy or emotion, such as surprise, enthusiasm, excitement, or . . . anger" (p. 118).

Dirkx (2001) points out that these emotions are present in any learning experience, even in online contexts. They are present whenever we feel joyful, bored, angry, intimidated, pleased, or excited. Attending to these emotions, which he calls "messengers of the soul," rather than ignoring them can make our learning more powerful, perhaps transformative. Dealing with these emotions is what Dirkx calls soul work or the imaginal method. But rather than analyzing and dissecting these emotions and feelings, he suggests we "imaginatively elaborate their meaning in our lives" (p. 69). In attending to and elaborating "these feelings and emotions, the nature of the image behind them may begin to emerge. As we recognize, name, and work with these images, we move toward a deeper, more conscious connection with these aspects of ourselves" (p. 69). In the example of the woman employee being ignored in a meeting with male colleagues, her visceral response—perhaps feeling angry, puzzled, rejected—would be attended to, brought into consciousness, and examined as to why she had felt this way. Dirkx (2012a) is careful to point out that "soul work" is not meant to replace the "more analytic, reflective, and rational processes that have been associated with transformative learning. Rather, it is intended to provide a more holistic and integrated way of framing the meaning-making that occurs in contemporary contexts for adult learning" (p. 127). (For a recent discussion of some of the issues underlying this extrarational perspective of transformative learning, see Kucukaydin and Cranton, 2013).

There are a number of other "beyond rational" approaches to transformative learning. Charaniya (2012), for example, draws from the expansive literature on spirituality and culture and explores what it means to engage in cultural-spiritual transformation. She sees a three-part process that begins when someone's cultural or spiritual identity is challenged by some experience or contradiction between beliefs and practice. One's cultural or spiritual identity "is then expanded through engagement with experiences that are intellectual, relational, and reflective. Finally, the culmination is a clearer or more pronounced understanding of self and of one's role in the world" (p. 231). What makes this kind of transformation different from Mezirow's is in terms of process and outcome. The process is not limited to rational discourse but relies heavily on engaging in "an ongoing, cyclical smorgasbord of opportunities to dialogue, share stories, explore symbols, and learn from each other" (p. 238). What changes is one's own identity as a cultural or spiritual being, and how one now sees the world and his or her role in the world. Let us say, for example, that you have been brought up in a culture and religion to believe that marriage is a sacred covenant that lasts until death, that the woman's role is to serve her husband and raise a family. However, your husband becomes abusive and you fear for yourself and your children. You see a television show about abused women and you may even go to a women's shelter where you hear about other women's experiences. You find yourself rethinking and changing your beliefs about marriage and women's roles.

In a very expansive vision of transformative learning as planetary and ecological, O'Sullivan (2012) would have us move beyond the dysfunctional political, economic, and technical Western world to a view that "recognizes the interconnectedness among universe, planet, natural environment, human community, and personal world" (Taylor, 2008, p. 9). "We live on a planet, not on a globe," he writes. "We are one species living on a planet called Earth, and all living and vital energies come out of this organic cosmological context" (O'Sullivan, 2012, p. 169). The "deep" transformation that he is calling for involves thinking holistically, "in terms of webs and circles rather than hierarchies" (p. 174). This kind of perspective transformation allows us to see how severe drought in India, melting ice fields in Greenland, or coal mines in Britain are all in some ways linked to the overall health of our planet. Such a change in perspective leads to actions we might take in preserving our planet. Other ways of facilitating a transformation of this sort is to attend to the wisdom of women, the feminine (even in men), the wisdom of indigenous, aboriginal peoples, and the spiritual nature of human beings. "Our spirituality should open us to differences and to the 'inscape,' the inner mysteries of life" (p. 175).

For all of these "beyond rational" conceptions of transformative learning, there are suggested instructional strategies for fostering, or perhaps more realistically, making space for these types of transformations to occur. The use of art, literature, music, drama, dialogue, storytelling, journaling, or group work will be discussed in more detail in the next section of this chapter.

Social Change

Transformative learning can also be viewed from a social change perspective, or as Taylor (2008) calls it, a social-emancipatory perspective. Here the goal is to challenge and transform oppressive structures in society. In order to do this, according to the chief spokesperson for this perspective, Brazilian educator Paulo Freire, people need to first become aware of power and oppression in their own lives, and then work to change these structures. This is about transformation at both the individual and social levels. In Freire's view these processes are inseparable.

In numerous writings, most famously *Pedagogy of the Oppressed* (1970/2000), Freire discusses some of the major components of this transformative process. The process begins with the individual, who in dialogue with other learners and facilitators (coinvestigators) propose concerns about their daily lives. These concerns or themes are discussed, examined and reflected upon, with the ultimate goal of taking action to change oppressive and disenfranchising practices and structures. Freire calls this process conscientization, where through dialogue and critical reflection, participants move from a fatalistic, passive acceptance of their situation, to realizing they can have some influence, to critical consciousness. "Here one achieves an in-depth understanding of the forces that shape one's life space, and becomes an active agent in constructing a different, more just reality" (Merriam, Caffarella, & Baumgartner, 2007, p. 141). Freire's work was anchored in working with illiterate Brazilian farmers whose life situation was the starting point for learning to read. By being able to "name" the world around them, they in turn began questioning the way things were, leading eventually to becoming an agent of change.

Critical theory, which Mezirow draws from in his transformational learning theory, has added to the notion that transformative learning is about examining dominant ideologies with the goal of changing social inequities. As mentioned earlier in this chapter, Mezirow was criticized for neglecting social change in his theory. His response was to say that individual transformation was his focus and a necessary precursor to aligning with other like-minded people to effect social change. Brookfield (2012a) discusses this relationship of critical theory to transformational learning: "As a body of work, critical theory has a transformative, metamorphosing impulse, so its connection to transformative learning seems natural and obvious . . . The kind of transformative learning that is endemic to critical theory is learning how to create the cooperative and collective structures, systems, and processes necessary for democratic socialism (Brookfield & Holst, 2010; Gramsci, 1971; Horkheimer, 1995) . . . Critical theory's focus on how adults learn to challenge dominant ideology, uncover power, and contest hegemony is crucial for scholars of transformative learning to consider if transformative learning is to avoid sliding into an unproblematized focus on the self" (pp. 131–132).

Although many adult educators recognize that transformative learning can, and perhaps should be seen as a social change process, it is a lot more difficult to understand and document this process than transformations at the individual level. Most reports of transformative learning at the social level are case studies of community-based development programs. Mejiuni's (2012) analysis of five community-based transformational education programs from different parts of the world revealed several "enablers of transformative learning" at the social level (p. 310). First, participants in these programs had a "deep personal experience" of marginalization or abuse that became the focus of change, such as female factory workers in South Africa being subjected to humiliating strip searchers (p. 311). Instructional methods such as dialogue and facilitators as coparticipants in the process were also important. Other "enablers" were participants coming to see how their personal experiences fit into the larger social, political, and cultural context, and how the "bonding and unity forged during educational interactions contributed to transformative learning and also served as the basis for social action" (p. 313). Mejiuni also identifies several issues with studying transformative learning at the social level such as whether the transformations are permanent, possible unanticipated consequences of participation in these activities, and the problems with self-examination and dialogue in collectivist cultures.

In summary, transformative learning is about change and change can be at the individual as well as social level. The models reviewed here can be loosely grouped as to whether the focus and process is seen as largely cognitive, of which Mezirow is considered the chief architect, beyond rational, involving subconscious, emotional, spiritual and planetary versions of transformation, or social action which positions transformative learning as a means of addressing societal inequities and oppression.

Sites of Transformative Learning

Transformative learning has been promoted and studied in a myriad of contexts ranging from individuals to classrooms to organizations, to workplaces and communities. Transformative learning begins with the individual, which is the first "site" we explore here. Other sites are the classroom and online, the workplace, and one's community. Within these sites transformative learning can be engaged in through self-directed, experiential, or formal activities.

Individual

From the above review of the development and various conceptualizations of transformative learning, it is clear that the individual learner is at the heart of the process. It is the learner herself or himself whose attention turns to questioning and examining long-held assumptions about the self and the world in which one lives. Even if changing society is the ultimate goal as in the social change perspective of Freire and other activists, the process begins with individuals questioning and ultimately altering the way they see themselves in the world. As Freire (1970/2000) writes in *Pedagogy of the Oppressed*, social transformation begins with individuals: "The point of departure of the movement lies in the people themselves. But since people do not exist apart from the world, apart from reality, the movement must begin with the human-world relationship. Accordingly, the point of departure must always be with men and women in the 'here and now,' which constitutes the situation within which they are submerged, from which they emerge, and in which they intervene. Only by starting from this situation—which determines their perception of it—can they begin to move" (pp. 72–73).

As learners ourselves and as educators engaged in facilitating learning in a myriad of settings and institutions, most of our efforts are focused on learning subject matter or skills. Some learning is about change in perspective usually at the individual level, but sometimes with an added goal of changing an organization or society itself. Before reviewing some specific instructional and evaluation strategies for transformative learning, we look a little more closely at several sites where transformative learning has been studied—the classroom and online, the workplace, and in the community.

Classroom and Online

As a site for learning, classrooms of adult students can be found everywhere including colleges and universities, online, in corporate training centers, in churches, museums, or community agencies. We think of these classrooms as institutionally sponsored formal learning environments with a planned curriculum and an educator who structures the learning activities. There is usually some assessment, outcome, or closure to the experience. Students are there to learn something, and rarely is it to change their perspectives of themselves. But perspective transformations do sometimes happen, and there are some educators who actively engage in practices to promote this type of learning along with their other content-based learning objectives.

The most studied classroom setting is in higher education. As mentioned earlier, Kasworm and Bowles (2012) reviewed some 250 published reports on transformative learning in credit and noncredit higher education settings. The authors note that higher education is a natural site for transformative learning to occur because "ideally, higher education offers an *invitation* to think, to be, and to act in new and enhanced ways . . . These learning environments sometimes challenge individuals to move beyond their comfort zone of the known, of self and others" (p. 389, italics in original).

An array of activities and strategies has been used to foster transformative learning in higher education. Gravett and Petersen (2009) for example, employed what they called "dialogic teaching"—"a reciprocal communicative educational relationship, with participants (educators and learners) exploring, thinking, inquiring, and reasoning together" (p. 101) in a faculty development workshop in South Africa. In other studies facilitators employed other strategies such as mentoring (Mandell & Herman, 2009), experiential learning (Deeley, 2010), and use of art forms (Butterwick & Lawrence, 2009), to foster the possibility of transformative learning taking place. Kasworm and Bowles (2012) summarize the literature in higher education: "Transformative learning represented a learner or environmental process focused on learner change in perspective, worldview, and/or sense of self. This change or transformation was most often based in a self-reported shift from previously held beliefs and assumptions about self and world. For some of these studies, the predominant focus was on the learner experience of openness and engagement toward change; other studies considered the role of specific intervention through educational programs, instructors, and facilitators, or of specific instructional experiences supporting or triggering aspects of a transformative learning process" (p. 389).

Most institutions of higher education have some component of their instruction online, and there are a growing number where online is the sole site of instruction. Indeed, much of informal adult learning today takes place online (see Chapter 10). What of transformative learning in this context? At first glance it would seem to not be possible to actively promote this type of learning online. However, Dirkx and Smith (2009) make a convincing case for its possibility if certain design and pedagogical strategies are employed. They draw from their experience with teaching an online course in adult learning, identifying the following six design and instructional strategies that appeared to foster "deep" or transformative learning: "(1) use of messy, ill-structured practice-based problems as the central pedagogical focus; (2) interactive and collaborative learning; (3) use of consensus group writing teams; (4) individual and team debriefings; (5) reflective activities; and (6) journal writing" (p. 60).

The online environment is still a relatively new site for promoting and studying transformative learning. Smith's review (2012) of the literature in this area turned up "only one empirical study that examined the topic of fostering transformative learning" (p. 409), though there were numerous studies of using transformative learning as *one* of several lens for understanding students' online experiences. And while there is a scarcity of rigorous research studies assessing this type of learning in an online environment, there are numerous books, articles and reports suggesting how the technology and pedagogical strategies can be merged to foster this type of learning (for a review of these resources see Smith, 2012).

Workplace

Whether preparing for work, looking for work, or actually working, adults spend much of their lives in work-related activities. The workplace is a major context for both formal and informal/incidental learning. Though not often intentionally planned for, the workplace can also be a site for transformative learning. And in some scholars' thinking, the way to address some of the rigidity, inequities, and oppressive practices in the workplace is through first getting workers to critically examine their role, perhaps inadvertent, in perpetuating such practices. With critical reflection at the heart of the process, the enormity of the task of doing this regarding one's role as a worker and of the workplace itself is daunting. As Brookfield (2009) notes, "Encouraging the practice of critical reflection seems at best highly problematic, at worst doomed to failure, if critical reflection is defined . . . as the process by which people learn to challenge dominant ideologies of capitalism, white supremacy, homophobia, and patriarchy and how hegemony encourages workers to collude in their own oppression. Few working as educators or process consultants are hired to root out hegemony and challenge capitalism, since such projects are directly in opposition to the interests of boards of directors and shareholders" (p. 127). What Brookfield and others hope to do is to open up the possibility of improving the workplace by getting people to question and reflect on the practices of the workplace and their role in these activities and practices. For example, instead of accepting the dismissive "That is just the way things are done around here," something as simple as asking *why* something is done the way it is can begin the process. In instructional activities related to work and the workplace, some suggested strategies for engaging in critical reflection possibly leading to transformative learning are modeling and peer learning (Brookfield, 2009), storytelling and dialogue (Tyler, 2009), coaching (Fisher-Yoshida, 2009), and action learning conversations (Marsick & Maltbia, 2009).

Transformative learning in the workplace has some similarities and differences with transformative *organizational* change. Both are change processes but as is the focus in this chapter, transformative learning is usually about individual change, whereas transformative organizational change is "typically focused on system-wide, instrumental goals" (Watkins, Marsick, & Faller, 2012, p. 375). The two foci can of course be brought together as the change process for an organization involves individuals and "individuals who are transformed make changes in the environment that enable others to likewise transform and together act on the environment to move toward desired goals" (p. 376). Critical human resource development (HRD) emerged in the 2000s with the goal of transforming HRD theory and practice (Bierema, 2010; Stewart, Rigg, & Trehan, 2006). Traditional HRD tends to privilege management and shareholder interests over workers and other stakeholder interests. Both transformative learning and organizational change are applicable to critical HRD as it is concerned with individual, group, organization, and system transformation.

Community

Finally, a community itself can be the site for transformative learning. This site was mentioned above in our explanation of the social action goal of this type of learning. Community activists and social activists in the tradition of Highlander Folk School, the Women's and Civil Rights Movements, PETA, and environmental activist groups, seek a transformation at the community or societal level. Though it is presumed that individuals in these activities have undergone perspective transformations, their goal is to effect change in the larger socio-political context. Cranton (in press) addresses this tension between individual and social change: "Organizations and societies and cultures may change, but they do not learn in the way that people learn . . . Some of this [individual] learning is inner-oriented and personal (but still always within a social context), and other times this learning maybe about social injustice, unveiling oppression, social action, and so forth, but it is the individual who is transforming his or her perspectives on social issues. Transformative learning involves action, so when a person transforms a perspective related to social issues, that person acts on the transformed perspective. And there we join individual transformation and social action" (in press).

Through an exploration of sites of transformative learning including the self, the classroom, online, the workplace, and the community, we have uncovered more about the process itself as well as identified some of the strategies used to foster this type of learning. Next we turn to a more detailed discussion of how to promote and evaluate transformative learning.

Promoting and Evaluating Transformative Learning

Mezirow (2000) has stated that the goal of adult education itself is "to help adults realize their potential for becoming more liberated, socially responsible, and autonomous learners—that is, to make more informed choices by becoming more critically reflective as 'dialogic thinkers' (Basseches, 1984) in their engagement in a given social context" (p. 30). Facilitating transformative learning is central for those of us who share his vision of the goal of adult education. While we have already alluded to a number of specific instructional strategies in our discussion of the theory and sites of transformative learning, and there are numerous strategies discussed in the literature (see especially Cranton, 2006; and Mezirow, Taylor, & Associates, 2009), in this section we suggest several underlying components of instruction necessary to facilitate transformative learning.

First, the importance of critical reflection cannot be overlooked. Although some suggest a transformation of perspective can occur through noncognitive means such as a spiritual or intense emotional experience, in an instructional setting the tools at our disposal are to model and enable students to examine and critically assess their assumptions about themselves, the world, and their place in the world. Brookfield (2012b) has written extensively about how to actually engage students in this process (see also Chapter 11 of this book).

In addition to fostering transformative learning from the cognitive strategy of critical reflection, many other writers have suggested this type of learning can be evoked through nonrational media such as storytelling (Clark, 2012), embodied knowing, intuitive and affective, emotional and spiritual experiences. While these are more challenging to prepare for, most who write about nonrational forms of transformative learning suggest using music, poetry, art, photography, literature, dreams, drama, fiction, and film to stimulate this type of learning. Lawrence (2012b) sees artistic expression of a means of provoking transformative learning at both the individual and community levels. Because "art is a universal language," she writes, "witnessing art created by others can provoke community awareness and incite action to create positive change" (p. 479). We are reminded of the artworks created by the famous World War II "comfort women"—young women who had been kidnapped by the Japanese and used as sex slaves by Japanese servicemen. This atrocious practice first came to light in the 1990s aided by the women expressing their long-suffering burden through drawings and paintings. This traveling art exhibit helped galvanize a worldwide protest movement aimed at raising awareness of women's suffering during war and of calling on Japan to renounce their role in this practice (Hye-Jin, 2000).

Cutting across the research on fostering transformative learning in practice is the theme of dialogue or discourse and social interaction. It can be recalled that an important component of Mezirow's 10-step process is engaging in dialogue with the self and with others. Mezirow (2000) even presents "ideal" conditions for this dialogue or discourse, realizing that these conditions "are never fully realized in practice" (p. 14). "Discourse," he writes, "is not a war or a debate; it is a conscientious effort to find agreement, to build a new understanding" (Mezirow, 1996, p. 170). For those who advocate nonrational, artistic means of bringing about transformative learning, dialogue and supportive relationships are important components of the process (Dirkx, 2012a; Lawrence, 2012b) as it is for those working with groups (Schapiro, Wasserman, & Gallegos, 2012) or in community and international settings (Mejiuni, 2012). Mejiuni in fact recommends fostering "alternative discourses or counter-discourses to the ones offered and generally agreed on in the groups and communities to which participants belong" (p. 317).

Finally, a theme that spans accounts of fostering transformative learning is the idea that instructors need to create space in which this type of learning might occur. While most adult educators value fostering critical reflection, it is far less common for educators to have as their primary goal effecting perspective transformations among their adult learners. Rather, this might be an outcome for some students as they go about learning the course's prescribed content. For this to occur, however, there must be space for students to reflect, discuss, and engage in activities that draw upon their life experiences. Such a space is safe, open, supportive, and in Vella's words, "sacred" (2000), where each can listen to others' experiences without judgment.

While there are many pedagogical strategies that adult educators can employ to foster transformative learning, there is much less in the literature about how to evaluate this type of learning. This is an important question for both theory and practice. Newman (2012a), for example, recently startled the adult education world with an essay questioning the very existence of transformative learning. In his view the theory has become "all things to all people" (p. 49) and is unsubstantiated, ambiguous, and unwieldy. He proposes that "we strike the phrase *transformative learning* from the educational lexicon altogether" and instead talk about "*good learning*" (p. 51, italics in original). One of his main reasons for doubting its existence is that "transformations can only be verified by the learners themselves" (p. 39). Even in telling their "stories" of transformation, stories "contain invention as well as record" (p. 40).

So how do we verify the existence of transformative learning in either a research or a practice setting? The most common strategy is the use of interviews in which learners are asked to tell their stories of change. It might be recalled that Mezirow (1978) developed his theory primarily from interviews with women returning to school. From across these women's stories, Mezirow derived a common learning process involving changes in the way these women saw themselves and their role in the world. Dozens and perhaps hundreds of studies of transformative learning using interviews and other qualitative data collection strategies have expanded his original theory. These strategies include narratives/stories, case studies, use of video, and "participant writing in journals, student writings, photography, and portfolios" (Taylor & Snyder, 2012, p. 39).

Evaluating whether transformative learning has taken place in an instructional setting, and if so, what the nature of that transformation is, presents challenges similar to assessing the phenomenon in a research setting. Often in fact, these settings overlap when the research study *is* about an instructional program designed to foster transformative learning. Cranton and Hoggan (2012) review various evaluation strategies that might be used in either setting including self-evaluation, interviews, narratives, observations, surveys, checklists, journals, metaphor analysis, conceptual mapping, and arts-based techniques. They caution that we "need to think deeply about how and when we can and should evaluate transformative learning" (p. 532). The knowledge gained from a transformative learning experience is emancipatory, that is, freeing and empowering rather than instrumental (knowledge about observable, material things) or communicative (knowledge about social interaction). Emancipatory knowledge involves critical reflection and challenging the status quo. Of this type of knowledge Cranton and Hoggan write: "Emancipatory knowledge cannot be predetermined, predicted, or set up as an objective for a course. Educators can create the environment and conditions that may foster transformative learning, but they cannot make it happen. Yet it can be evaluated, and it is evaluated in some way every time a researcher determines the extent to which transformative learning has occurred in a particular setting, context, or program and every time an educator realizes that some of her students have experienced a major shift in their perspectives on themselves or the world around them" (p. 531).

By its very nature, transformative learning is hard to capture, plan for, or evaluate. However, despite Newman's critique (2012a), many educators and researchers have resonated with the power of this type of learning to change the way people see the world, and perhaps to change for the better, some of the oppressive and constraining structures in society. If we believe this is an important goal for adult education, the challenge is how to both facilitate this kind of learning, and then to evaluate its outcomes.

Concluding Thoughts, Unresolved Issues

There is little doubt that today transformative learning holds center stage in adult learning theory research and practice. And we have come a long way in conceptualizing and studying this type of learning since Mezirow published his initial study nearly 40 years ago. What we would like to do here as we bring this chapter to a close is to present some of the issues about this theory that are challenging researchers and practitioners alike. Engaging with these issues will perhaps bring an even more robust understanding of transformative learning to our field.

First, however, we would like to look a little more closely at the most serious challenge yet to the entire theory of transformative learning. Michael Newman (2012a) published an article in *Adult Education Quarterly* titled "Calling Transformative Learning into Question: Some Mutinous Thoughts." Expressing what some other critics have suggested—that it seems as though the label of transformative learning is being applied to all kinds of learning, Newman questions whether transformative learning is really a different "kind" of learning, or just a difference in degree. He writes, "But any learning effectively done involves reassessment and growth. The learner recognizes that she or he knows something new, that she or he could not perform a certain task and now can, or that she or he has a new viewpoint" (p. 40). This is not new, he argues, but merely what we have come to understand learning to be—a change in knowledge, skills or attitudes. He critiques several aspects of the theory including the fact that it fails to differentiate between identity and consciousness, whether the learning is a finite or "flowing" experience, whether ideal conditions of discourse exist, whether mobilization is necessary, and the "unproblematic" inclusion of spirituality in the discourse of transformative learning.

Newman's article has generated a lively debate with responses by Cranton and Kasl (2012) and Dirkx (2012b), and finally a rejoinder from Newman (2012b) to their critiques. His critics acknowledge some of his concerns but also point out that he relied heavily on Mezirow's early work, ignoring more recent understandings of transformative learning. No one is expecting transformative learning to go away and the debate has been healthy in further clarifying aspects of this theory. At this point we would like to turn to a brief discussion of some issues still under discussion.

With regard to the theory itself, there is still some question as to *what* is being transformed in this type of learning. Is it one's identity? Is it our consciousness? Is it our actions in the world? Is it the social context in which we live? There are different answers to this question depending on which theoretical framework you are working from (rational-critical; beyond rational; social action). Perhaps also there are different answers to "what" transforms depending on one's sociocultural framework. Ntseane (2012) discusses the African perspective on transformative learning and finds that communality and interdependence are valued over individual and autonomous learning. There is also an emphasis on the "unity of spirit, mind, and body as well as emotions instead of a focus on cognitive qualities" (p. 285). Mejiuni's (2012) review of five community-based transformative programs from Africa, Europe, and South America echoes Ntseane's points about social and cultural context defining the nature of the learning and what is actually transformed. Further, Kokkos (2012) in a review of European publications on transformative learning found that European writers tend not to use transformative learning as the main focus of their work; rather, "they tend to adopt its elements in order to assign further depth and argumentation in the elaboration of issues on which they intensively work" (p. 295). Further, transformative learning theory "does not have concrete roots in the conceptual formation of the European adult educators" (p. 297), and finally, Freire's work on critical pedagogy and other "elements of critical thinking and social dimensions of learning" (p. 297) are more prevalent than Mezirow's conception.

Not only does "what" is transformed remain unclear, but so do the boundaries of transformation. Here again the individual versus the social focus comes into play. Certainly individuals have to have a transformative experience before social change is possible. But can groups change? Can an organization be transformed? And is societal change merely the cumulative efforts of numerous individuals, or something organic in and of itself? And how can such transformations be documented? While individuals can tell us they have had a transformative learning experience, how do we assess a group or societal level transformation? Further, if we as educators "recognize transformative learning as a worthwhile goal of teaching adults," how do we know this goal has been accomplished? Its assessment in an educational context is still quite problematic, and as yet, "little is known about its impact on traditional measures of education (grades, test scores, performance)" (Taylor, 2012, p. 15).

Other questions about the transformation process itself have to do with whether there is a somewhat linear process with a clear end point (taking action on a transformed perspective) as suggested by Mezirow's 10-step model, or more of what Charaniya (2012) calls "an ongoing, cyclical smorgasbord" (p. 238) of experiences. Are transformations permanent? Mezirow (1991) says unequivocally that transformations are permanent: "The transformative learning process is irreversible . . . we do not regress to levels of less understanding" (p. 152), but we do hear of people who have come to renounce previous perspectives. In a fascinating study of transformative learning, Wilner and Dubouloz (2011, 2012) use Ed Husain's autobiography, *The Islamist* (2007), to show how he came to transform his perspective from a moderate, Moslem Londoner to a radical Islamist internalizing rationales that legitimized violent behavior. While the article focuses on this transformation which took several years, we learn that he later rejected this persona, reverting back to a more moderate stance. There is also little in the literature addressing the permanence of social-level transformations.

Mezirow (2000) claims that this type of learning leads to a perspective that is "more inclusive, discriminating, open, emotionally capable of change and reflective" (p. 8). However, what of Ed Husain's transformation into a violent radical Islamist? What of transformations that lead to more constricted, perhaps violence-condoning perspectives? Merriam, Mott, and Lee's 1996 study of transformative learning from a traumatic or negative life event suggests that one may end up with a transformed, yet more constricted perspective. For example, one woman in their study who was the victim of an attempted kidnapping by a person she (erroneously) thought was a minority, now held an admittedly racist perspective. In her interview she said: "'So I [developed] this incredible fear of minorities . . . and that is still with me today . . . I also probably have a greater bias toward minorities than I did before'" (Merriam, Mott, & Lee, 1996, p. 15). Are perspective transformations only in one direction toward a more "inclusive" and "open" perspective?

Yet another issue, and perhaps the most important of all, are the ethical issues involved in transformative learning. As educators, do we engage in facilitating transformative learning, regardless of where that leads? In the case of Ed Husain, what is an educator's role in enabling his perspective transformation to a violent jihadist? And what about the consequences of fostering transformative learning at the individual or societal level? For example, abused women may be led to transform their perspective from one of helpless victim to empowered individual, but what happens if they return to their abuser? And one can only imagine the retribution of repressive governments on communities who have challenged corrupt governing practices.

From a transformative learning perspective, adult educators are change agents. This is a very challenging role as few of us are trained to handle the discomfort, angst and conflict that often accompany making changes. In a discussion of the ethics of educator as change agent, Ettling (2012) proposes a model for "walking an ethical path" (p. 544). A central component of this path, and what many other writers call for, is assessing and revealing one's own "ideological positioning and personal values" (p. 546). "Humility and comfort with personal disclosure seem essential to the transformative learning practitioner" and set "the stage for dialogue among learners and with us, as educators, creates the environment for change to occur, both in ourselves and in the learners" (p. 546).

Chapter Summary

Transformative learning theory has taken center stage in research and writing about adult learning. Whether it is as prominent in actual practice as it is in theory is debatable, although there is a burgeoning literature of accounts of educators trying to implement and assess this type of learning. What we have in this chapter is a snapshot in time, one that is likely to change even by the time this book is published. Nevertheless, we have tried to explain the different conceptualizations of this theory, reviewed where it takes place, the strategies used in fostering and evaluating this type of learning, and finally, examined some of the current issues inherent is this type of learning.

Linking Theory and Practice: Activities and Resources

1. Identify a major transformation in your thinking about some aspect of your life. What precipitated this transformation? What steps or stages did you go through in the process? What role, if any, did other people, including perhaps educators, play in your transformation? How have you acted on your new perspective?
2. Compare your transformational journey to the transformational models presented in this chapter. Did your journey resemble Mezirow's 10-step process? Was it more nonrational?

3. Read a biography or autobiography of someone who made a major change in his or her life. Nelson Mandela's autobiography, *The Long Walk to Freedom*, and Ed Husain's *The Islamist* are possibilities. Or you might read a fictional account, such as Kafka's *Metamorphosis* or Ibsen's *A Doll's House*, or view a movie about transformation such as *Educating Rita*, *The Doctor*, or *Norma Rae*. Analyze the process and outcome of the transformation.

4. Identify and interview someone who has experienced a change in their perspective on life as the result of a disorienting dilemma such as divorce, death of a loved one, surviving a major disaster and so on. "Map" this change according to transformative learning theory.

5. An excellent resource is the 2012 *The Handbook of Transformative Learning* edited by Edward W. Taylor and Patricia Cranton (Jossey-Bass publisher).

6. Create service learning experiences where learners engage in community issues through interviewing stakeholders, joining protests, meeting government officials, or taking field trips that will challenge learners' experiences or worldviews.

7. Engage in storytelling activities. One example is to have students write a very linear account of their problem or issue on an index card by writing one sentence completing this statement: "My issue/problem is _____." Next they complete this statement: "The prescribed solution is _____." Next they set the card aside and are assigned the task of writing a story about the problem that begins with "Once upon a time" and ends with "The End," embellishing as they see fit. Once they finish the story, they read it to a partner who then begins to identify and question assumptions they are hearing in the story. After back-and-forth dialogue, learners compare their linear problem/prescription index card with the story and insights gained from writing about it and sharing dialogue.

Chapter Highlights

- Transformative learning is about change in your perspective on yourself and your place in the larger social context.
- The transformative learning literature can be grouped into three categories. The cognitive rational perspective is primarily associated with Jack Mezirow and focuses on critical reflection. The beyond rational sees transformation as a psychic, emotional, or spiritual phenomenon.

Transformation as social change, the third perspective, is about systemic, sociopolitical change and is most associated with Paulo Freire.

- Sites of transformative learning can be the individual, the classroom, online, the workplace, and the community.
- Instructional strategies that involve critical reflection, dialogue, artistic modes of expression, and collaboration have been used to foster transformative learning. Also important is creating space in an instructional setting for it to occur.
- Evaluating transformative learning is most often done through self-report and interviews, though other means are being experimented with.
- Unresolved issues have to do with identifying what actually transforms in this type of learning, the nature of the process of transformative learning, the permanence of a perspective transformation or social transformation, and ethical considerations in engaging in this type of education.

CHAPTER SIX

EXPERIENCE AND LEARNING

"The more that you read, the more things you will know. The more that you learn, the more places you'll go," writes Theodor Seuss Geisel, widely known as Dr. Seuss, in his book *I Can Read With My Eyes Shut* (1978, p. 27). Indeed, our lives play out in a cyclical pattern, where learning often leads to new experiences and life experiences that are themselves sources of learning. This relationship between experience and learning is particularly prominent in adulthood when we are engaged in a continual flow of activities in the private, public, and professional spheres of our daily life. At the heart of adult learning is engaging in, reflecting upon, and making meaning of our experiences, whether these experiences are primarily physical, emotional, cognitive, social, or spiritual. In much of our understanding of adult learning including the foundational work in andragogy, self-directed learning, and transformative learning, an adult's life experiences generate learning as well as act as resources for learning. In this chapter we explore the relationship between experience and learning beginning with the foundational works of Dewey, Lindeman, and Kolb, followed by contemporary conceptualizations and models of experiential learning, reflective practice, and the learning theory of situated cognition.

On the Relationship Between Experience and Learning

Philosophers at least as far back as Aristotle have considered the role of experience in learning. For Aristotle, all knowledge or theory needs to be tested in the real world of our everyday experience: "Hence we ought to examine what has been said by applying it to what we do, and how we live; and if it harmonizes with what we do, we should accept it, but if it conflicts we should count it [mere] words. (Aristotle NE:1179a20)" (cited in Dyke, 2009, p. 303). But it was the philosopher and educator John Dewey and his book *Experience and Education,* first published in 1938, who has had the most influence on our understanding of the role of experience in learning. Dewey saw learning as a lifelong process involving applying and adapting previous experience to new situations: "What [one] has learned in the way of knowledge and skill in one situation becomes an instrument of understanding and dealing effectively with the situations which follow. The process goes on as long as life and learning continue" (1963, p. 44). Dewey called this the principle of continuity in which what one is learning in the present is connected to past experiences and has potential future applications. For example, perhaps you enjoy gardening and have moved from a northern to a southern climate. Learning what plants do well in the new climate involves new learning, but at the same time, you link this new learning to your gardening experiences in the previous setting; and of course this new learning evolves as it is creatively applied in the future.

Interestingly, Dewey recognized that not all experiences are "genuinely or equally educative" (1963, p. 25). Some experiences can be "miseducative." By this Dewey meant that some experiences have "the effect of arresting or distorting the growth of further experience" (p. 25). Dewey explains: "An experience may be such as to engender callousness; it may produce lack of sensitivity and of responsiveness. Then the possibilities of having richer experiences in the future are restricted (pp. 25–26) . . . Wholly independent of desire or intent, every experience lives on in further experiences. Hence the central problem of an education based upon experience is to select the kind of present experiences that live fruitfully and creatively in subsequent experiences" (pp. 27–28). A miseducative experience can occur in everyday life or in the classroom. For example, one might be fired from a job in such a way as to be bitter and angry, thus prohibiting learning from the experience. In the classroom, certain activities such as simulations, role playing, or critiques from fellow learners or a teacher might be so devastating as to inhibit future learning.

The role of experience in learning is also central to our understandings of *adult* learning. Lindeman, an early adult educator and a contemporary of Dewey, famously wrote that "the whole of life is learning" and "the resource of highest value in adult education is the learner's experience"

(1961, p. 6). He also wrote that "experience is the adult learner's living textbook" (p. 7). And certainly most adult learning occurs informally and incidentally as we go about our adult lives. But it was Knowles's formulation of andragogy that placed experience front and center in understanding adult learning. A protégé of Lindeman, Knowles highlighted experience as one of the major assumptions of andragogy in that an adult accumulates a growing reservoir of experience which is a rich resource for learning (Knowles, 1980). Clearly, as we age we have a variety of life experiences which can be drawn on in a learning situation, but which also stimulate the need for learning. Thus not only do we connect with our past experiences to foster new learning, our ongoing experiences often require new learning. Experience is thus a resource and a stimulus for learning. However, as Dewey noted, Knowles also acknowledges that an adult's prior experiences can act as a barrier to new learning: "But the fact of greater experience also has some potentially negative effects. As we accumulate experience we tend to develop mental habits, biases, and presuppositions that tend to cause us to close our minds to new ideas, fresh perceptions, and alternative ways of thinking" (Knowles, Holton, & Swanson, 2011, p. 65). There are also times when learning may first require us to "unlearn" previous learning, For example, those trained some years ago to administer CPR used a combination of mouth-to-mouth breathing and hand pressure on the victim's chest. After several studies found that hands-only CPR is as effective, if not more so, the American Heart Association in 2008 began recommending hands-only CPR. One would thus have to "unlearn" the earlier, traditional method. There's a similar notion of "unlearning" in Lewin's famous theory of organizational change (1951). His model consists of first "unfreezing" one's previous behavior or learning by introducing new information that reveals a discrepancy between present thinking and behavior and desired new behavior. The second phase is the change in knowledge and behaviors, followed by the third stage of "refreezing" the new knowledge and behaviors.

In an interesting wedding of andragogy and experiential learning, O'Bannon and McFadden (2008) propose a model of "experiential andragogy" for use with nontraditional adult experiential education programs (such as service-oriented programs, educational travel, or outdoor adventure-based programs). Their model has six stages of motivation, orientation, involvement, activity, reflection, and adaptation. A learner must be intrinsically motivated to participate and learn, become actively engaged in the experience, reflect individually or in a group, and "consider how they will apply what they have learned to future experiences" (p. 27). In their model "it is the process, the interaction between stages, which makes learning possible" (p. 25).

Experience is also important in two other conceptualizations of adult learning—self-directed learning and transformative learning. While self-directed learning is about taking control of your own learning (see Chapter 4), what you wish to learn, and how you go about it, involves life experience. For example, rising gas prices have led many people to figure out how to be more fuel-efficient. This learning might involve researching fuel-efficient cars, adopting driving strategies that cut down on fuel, carpooling, or learning to drive a motorcycle. Next steps might be implementing and assessing the results of some of these strategies.

Transformative learning (see Chapter 5) is a form of learning very much embedded in life experience. The process actually begins with an experience that causes us to question our assumptions about how the world works or how life is. There is something of a disjuncture between our experience and our understanding of it. Dewey noted that learning is stimulated when previous experience fails to explain a present situation. Dewey "regarded non-reflective experience based on habits as a dominant form of experience. The reflective experience, mediated by intelligence and knowledge grows out from the inadequacy and contradictions of the habitual experience and ways of action. For Dewey, the basis of, and reason for reflection was the necessity of solving problems faced in habitual ways of action" (Miettinen, 2000, p. 61). In transformative learning, because our previous beliefs, attitudes or habits fail to accommodate a present experience, we find new ways of thinking about and dealing with the problem. Transformative learning occurs when the way we make meaning of experience changes; that is, our meaning-making process has become transformed into one that is more accommodating of our real-world experience. In an interesting convergence of transformative learning and assessing prior learning, Stevens, Gerber, and Hendra (2010) report on a study with students in the University Without Walls at the University of Massachusetts, Amherst. Through the development of prior learning portfolios, adult students receive college credit for reflecting on learning from professional and personal experiences. The authors found that systematically reflecting on previous experience can lead to outcomes that are "transformative for the learner, facilitating the development of a new sense of confidence and ability to make new meanings of experience" (p. 377), in turn, "foster[ing] the capacity for transformative learning" (p. 401).

Models of Experiential Learning

A number of writers have mapped out the relationship between life experience and learning. We have selected several for discussion beginning with Kolb's experiential learning cycle which has influenced several subsequent models. Second, we will briefly present three models developed by adult educators including Jarvis' types of learning model, Tennant and Pogson's four levels of experiential learning, and Fenwick's five perspectives on experiential learning. It is important to note that these writers use the term "experiential learning" to represent various conceptualizations of the relationship between experience and learning. The term also refers to the use of certain instructional strategies and programs familiar to adult educators that are designed to make learning as authentic and like real-life as possible. Finally, "experiential learning" is also used to acknowledge an adult's previous life experiences that can be reflected upon and documented for academic credit (see, for example, the National Society for Experiential Education, www.nsee.org and the Council for Adult and Experiential Learning, www.cael.org). Our focus in this chapter is on understanding the reciprocal relationship between our learning and our life experiences as adults.

Kolb's Experiential Learning Cycle

A good place to begin a discussion of Kolb's experiential learning cycle is with his definition of learning itself. "Learning," Kolb writes, "is the process whereby knowledge is created through the transformation of experience" (1984, p. 38). Experience is at the heart of his understanding of learning. Kolb's learning model consists of four stages that learners go through in this learning process. As can be seen in Figure 6.1, the four stages are: concrete experience, reflective observation, abstract conceptualization, and active experimentation.

Effective learners are able to engage each aspect of the model: "Learners, if they are to be effective, need four different kinds of abilities—*concrete experience abilities* (CE), *reflective observation abilities* (RO), *abstract conceptualizing abilities* (AC) and *active experimentation abilities* (AE). That is they must be able to involve themselves fully, openly and without bias in new experiences (CE). They must be able to reflect on and observe their experiences from many perspectives (RO). They must be able to create concepts that integrate their observations into logically sound theories (AC) and they must be able to use these theories to make decisions and

FIGURE 6.1 THE EXPERIENTIAL LEARNING CYCLE AND BASIC LEARNING STYLES (KOLB, 1984)

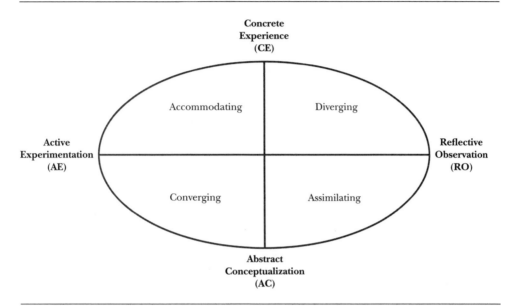

Source: Kolb, D.A., Boyatzis, R.E., & Mainemelis, C. (1999), Learning Theory: Previous Research and New Directions. Accessed at http://learningfromexperience.com/media/2010/08/experiential-learning-theory.pdf.

solve problems (AE)" (Kolb, 1984, p. 30). In recent publications Kolb has linked these four abilities with being mindful of one's experiential learning and proposed practices that maximize each ability (Kolb & Yeganeh, 2012; Yeganeh & Kolb, 2009). For example, for concrete experience we strive to turn off the autopilot of our mind by relaxing our body and focusing on our sense of touch, sound, sight and smell. For reflective observation we can "practice sitting with thoughts and feelings rather than acting on them" (Kolb & Yeganeh, p.10); abstract conceptualization can be enhanced by questioning assumptions, and seeing "shades of gray rather than dichotomous thinking"; finally for active experimentation, we can "practice novel questioning" and "experiment by responding to people and events in ways that you normally do not" (p. 10).

As can be seen in Figure 6.1, there are also four basic learning styles—diverging, assimilating, converging, and accommodating. Each learning style draws from its two adjacent learning abilities. For example, the diverging learning style relies on CE and RO in that these learners "are best at viewing concrete situations from many points of view. It is labeled 'diverging' because people with it perform better in situations that call for generation of ideas, such as a 'brainstorming' session" (Kolb, Boyatzis, & Mainemelis, 1999, p. 5). As another example, the accommodating learning style draws from AE and CE. These learners prefer hands-on activities and tend to "act on 'gut' feelings rather than logical analysis" (p. 6).

Green and Ballard (2010–2011) discuss a real-world application of Kolb's model in a teacher preparation program. Unlike most teacher preparation programs with a field experience as a student teacher, in the Professional Development School (PDS) program interns spend their senior year as both a student and as a full-time professional employee of the school system. "In contrast to the traditional student-teacher residency, the teaching intern (TI) is fully integrated into teaching practices for a full academic year, planning and making class decisions from the first day of in-service in August until the last work day in June" (p. 13). Green and Ballard explain how the intern is engaged in all four aspects of Kolb's model: "As they are immersed in the experience of teaching in an authentic classroom, they are learning curriculum—content and pedagogy required by the state for licensure—partially through the experience as it is embedded into their daily responsibilities and activities." At the same time, "they are engaged in pedagogy-based coursework where content is delivered in multiple modalities . . . they are synthesizing knowledge and engaging in reflective practice from the moment they step on the teaching and learning campus for in-service . . . Reflective opportunities occur as the University Liaison incorporates standards-based curriculum into discussions with the interns . . . and the teaching intern reflects and writes about the experience and learning gained" (p. 15).

The basic components of Kolb's experiential learning cycle have also been incorporated into training adult Girl Scout leaders (O'Bannon & McFadden, 2008). Their five-stage model includes experiencing (participating in a learning activity), publishing ("identifying and sharing reactions and observations" in a group), processing the experience, generalizing, which "occurs when theories and concepts are shared and inferences are made in regard to real world principles" (p. 25), and applying knowledge in future experiences.

To determine one's preferred learning style, Kolb has also developed an instrument, called the Learning Style Inventory (LSI). The LSI, now in its fifth version, is designed to assess a learner's preference for learning via Concrete Experience (CE), Reflective Observation (RO), Abstract Conceptualization (AC) and Active Experimentation (AE). It also assesses one's preference for abstractness over concreteness (AC-CE) and action over reflection (AE-RO). In all, the latest version of the LSI assesses nine learning styles. You can learn more about the LSI at www.learningfrom experience.com. (For a review of the LSI and its application with accounting students, see McCarthy, 2010).

Kolb's theory and Learning Style Inventory are not without their critics. The theory seems to be context-free; that is, experience and reflection on that experience seem to occur in a vacuum unimpeded by power dynamics present in any social context. One wonders, for example, how reflecting on experience and experimenting in a totalitarian regime might work out! Others suggest that the some learners may not move through the process as Kolb suggests. Rather, the model might "be viewed as a sparking chamber in which the learner makes contact with each point, but not in any specified mechanical order" (Dyke, 2006, p. 121). Still others note that novice facilitators are likely to teach from their own preferred style, rather than teaching to relate to all styles. Finally, "issues of reliability and validity persist with the LSI" (Bergsteiner, Avery, & Neumann, 2010, p. 31) and a number of researchers have gone on to construct learning style instruments that claim to have more validity and reliability (see, for example, Vermunt & Vermetten, 2004).

Three Models from Adult Educators

Perhaps because life experience is so central to understanding learning in adulthood, all those who write about adult learning consider the role of experience as Knowles did in proposing andragogy, or as can be found in the self-directed learning and transformative learning literature. Some adult educators have gone a step further and proposed models of experiential learning, three of which we briefly review in this section.

In 1987, British adult educator Peter Jarvis published his model of learning derived from participants in adult education workshops who were invited to compare their learning "cycle" with Kolb's four-stage learning cycle. Experience is central to his model as with his definition of learning as "the transformation of experience into knowledge, skills and attitudes" (1987, p. 32). The Jarvis model is considerably more complex than Kolb's and consists of nine routes, or types of learning. Three routes he labeled "nonlearning" in which the individual either presumes to already know (presumption), decides not to consider the opportunity to learn (nonconsideration), or outright rejects the opportunity to learn from the situation (rejection). The second three positions in his model constitute learning but nonreflective learning such as what goes on at a preconscious level, involves basic skills through practice, or involves memorization. The final three routes he termed "reflective learning." Here an individual can contemplate an experience and "either accept or change it" (contemplation), or "think about the situation and then act upon it, either confirming or innovating upon it" (reflective practice), or "think about the situation and agree or disagree with what they have experienced" (experimental learning) (Jarvis, 2006, p. 10).

In contrast to Jarvis' model, Kolb's experiential learning cycle seems rather simplistic and indeed has been criticized along these lines (see earlier discussion). While Jarvis used Kolb's model as a touchstone for deriving his nine-stage model, the Jarvis model has continued to evolve with Jarvis himself as its most ardent critic. He has identified a number of strengths such as "the centrality of experience in learning," and "an understanding of the interaction between the person and the social world as being significant for learning to occur" (2006, p. 11). Points of criticism have to do with the learning process, types of learning, and his definition of learning. For example, he now recognizes that "learning through the emotions is much more significant than I originally realized" (p. 12). Further, while the transformation of experience is still central to his definition of human learning, he has expanded the definition. Now it is the process in which the "whole person" engages in an experience that is processed "*cognitively, emotively or practically (or through any combination) and integrated into the person's individual biography resulting in a changed (or more experienced) person* (p. 13, italics in original).

Tennant and Pogson (1995) explain experiential learning not so much as a process as Jarvis does, but as the different ways experience can be acknowledged as resources for learning. They propose four "levels" or ways experience can be thought of in terms of incorporating experience into instruction—prior experience, current experience, new experience, and learning from experience. Our previous experiences can be called up, reflected upon, and linked to new learning. This strategy is reminiscent of Dewey's principle of continuity discussed above wherein new learning is connected to past experience and foreshadows future learning. Say, for example, that you are attending a workshop on "Brain Power: Improving Your Memory." You could be asked to recall a time when you learned and still remember detailed information, such as steps in a computer program, or the names of flowering plants, or a recipe for a popular dish. You would then examine *how* you remember this information so as to apply the strategy to future learning. Prior experience can even be applied to learning about yourself. In his recent book, Tennant (2012) speaks of the role of prior experience in learning about and knowing oneself: "Making sense of our past experiences to better understand our desires and interests is a route to self-knowledge" (p. 112).

A second category of experience is current experience. Here learning activities are connected to an adult's current experiences as family member, community member or worker. Following the example above, you might be running for a position on your local town council or the school board. You have a need to remember many people's names and positions. You can immediately employ one of the memory strategies learned in the workshop. By embedding instruction in the immediate circumstances of an adult's life, theory becomes very practical and learning highly relevant. New experience, the third category, is creating experiences through instructional techniques such as simulations, role playing, internships, or practicums that provide a base for new learning to occur. Continuing with the memory example, numerous techniques and strategies for aiding your memory would be demonstrated and applied. Their fourth category is learning from experience by which they mean the critical examination of prior experience: "Typically the meanings that learners attach to their experiences are subjected to critical scrutiny through the medium of the group. The adult educator may consciously set out to disrupt the learner's world view and stimulate uncertainty, ambiguity, and doubt about previously taken-for-granted interpretations of experience" (Tennant & Pogson, 1995, p. 151). Again, using the memory workshop as an example, you and the other participants would be led to explore previous experiences with memory in order to examine taken-for-granted assumptions about memory (such as it declines as we age). They sum up their model with the point that for learning to occur, "education must somehow stimulate learners to go beyond their experiences . . . Indeed, experience has to be mediated and reconstructed (or transformed) by the student for learning to occur" (p. 151).

While Jarvis (2006) maps the process of learning where experience is central and Tennant and Pogson (1995) consider experiential learning from an instructional perspective, Fenwick (2003) proposes a more philosophical lens for viewing experiential learning. For Fenwick, there are five possible ways to conceptualize experiential learning, each of which draws from a different theoretical paradigm. The first perspective is constructivist, that is, learning is the construction of meaning through engaging in and reflecting upon experience. This view underlies much of the experiential learning literature covered above. For example, an adult recently diagnosed with diabetes would reflect upon her experience with the disease, and learn what lifestyle and treatment options are best. A second perspective she calls "situative" (Fenwick, 2003, p. 25) wherein knowing or learning occurs in doing or in practice: "Learning is rooted in the *situation* in which the person participates, not in the head of that person as intellectual concepts produced by reflection" (p. 25, italics added). From this perspective the woman with diabetes would be attuned to her body, learning and knowing when blood sugar levels are high or low and adjusting accordingly. This situated approach to experiential learning will be covered in more detail in the next sections of this chapter.

Fenwick's third perspective is psychoanalytic and involves getting in touch with unconscious desires and fears. Our unconscious can interfere or conflict with our conscious desires and affect our learning. Following the example of being diagnosed with diabetes, unconsciously the person may deny she has the disease as it may conflict with her self-image as a healthy, active person. Such an unconscious fear might interfere with learning. A fourth lens is what Fenwick calls the critical cultural perspective in which "dominant norms of experience" are critically questioned and resisted (p. 38). From this perspective, the woman with diabetes may resist or challenge some of the assumptions about people with diabetes held by many (for example, that it is their "fault" for contracting the disease). The fifth perspective is lodged in complexity theory and is labeled "ecological." Here the focus is on "the *relationships* binding humans and non-humans (persons, material objects, mediating tools, environments, ideas) together in multiple fluctuations in complex systems" (Fenwick, 2004, p. 51). Learning from a complexity theory perspective is "the continuous improvisation of alternate actions and responses to new possibilities and changing circumstances that emerge, undertaken by the system's parts" (p. 53). The woman with diabetes may decide to form a support group for dealing with the disease. This group is itself a system with a shared objective, but each member brings experiences from their own lives, health care systems, and so on. Learning evolves as these systems interact.

Clearly, there are many ways to think about the connection between life experience and learning. In this section we have reviewed three models proposed by adult educators. Jarvis (2006) took Kolb's cycle as a starting point and came up with a model of learning from experience that has nine possible pathways. Tennant and Pogson (1995) viewed experiential learning from a pedagogical perspective and proposed four ways experience can be accessed in learning. Finally, Fenwick (2003) differentiates among five philosophical conceptions of experiential learning.

Reflective Practice and Situated Cognition

The connection between adult learning and life experience is so basic that it is difficult to think of any learning that occurs isolated from experience. Whether we are talking about one of the adult learning theories covered in previous chapters, holistic conceptions of learning involving body, emotions, and spirit, or even traditional learning theories such as behaviorism or cognitive psychology, all these understandings of learning involve the learner's experiences. Of course such experiences can be designed to bring about learning as in a classroom, or they can be everyday experiences that we attend to, think about, process, and construct meaning from. In addition to the models that we have already reviewed above, there are several others, three of which we feel resonate particularly well with *adult* learning—reflective practice, situated cognition, and communities of practice.

Reflective Practice

Reflective practice, or practice-based learning, as it is sometimes called, is learning that is acquired through reflection on or in practice (experience). The "practice" arena is most often thought of as whatever job or field we work in and thus there is much emphasis on reflecting on and improving our practice. Continuing professional education in particular has adopted reflective practice as an organizing concept. Reflective practice became very popular in education and other social science professions through Donald Schön's books, *The Reflective Practitioner* (1983) and *Educating the Reflective Practitioner* (1987). Indeed, many professional preparation programs strive to develop "reflective practitioners." Schön's basic premise is that the real world of practice is messy and that our "technical" preparation for this world is merely a starting point. It is in practice itself that really useful learning occurs.

Reflection-on-action and reflection-in-action are two key concepts in reflective practice. Reflection-on-action is what we commonly think of in experiential learning—we have an experience and consciously think about it after it has happened. For example, did you try a different way to handle a difficult colleague at work, or experiment with a new reporting procedure, or have an informal discussion with a friend about a health problem? If you reflected on any of these experiences, you would have engaged in reflection-on action. In evaluating these experiences, you may decide to do something similar or different in your future "practice."

Reflection-in-action is different from the above because the reflection takes place as you are engaged in the experience—it is simultaneous with practice. This kind of reflection "reshapes what we are doing while we are doing it" (Schön, 1987, p. 26). Reflection-in-action is what distinguishes the more expert practitioner from the novice. It characterizes the practitioners who "think on their feet," who experiment, change direction, and immediately respond to a changing context of practice. Reflection-in-action is also aligned with knowing-in-action or tacit knowing, that is, we know what to do without articulating it. For example, minutes before Laura was presenting her research at a conference, the allocated time slot was cut by 15 minutes. Instead of rushing through all of the slides and talking fast, she decided to delete the least important component of the presentation, which for this group of practitioners was the jargon related to the research methodology. Experienced practitioners, whether they are educators, health practitioners, administrators, support staff, or rank-and-file workers make adjustments to their practice as they reflect-in-action.

Reflective practice can also be approached by analyzing one's espoused theories versus one's theories-in-use (Argyris & Schön, 1974). Espoused theories are those ideas and beliefs we have about our practice while theories-in-use are what we actually *do* in practice. As defined by Argyris and Schön, "when someone is asked how he would behave under certain circumstances, the answer he usually gives is his espoused theory of action for that situation. This is the theory of action to which he gives allegiance, and which, upon request, he communicates to others. However the theory that actually governs his actions is his theory-in-use, which may or may not be compatible with his espoused theory; furthermore, the individual may or may not be aware of incompatibility of the two theories" (pp. 6–7). For example, we can believe that adults learn differently from children and that their life experiences are a resource for learning. This is our espoused theory. However, once in the classroom we may teach adults the same way we teach children, which is our theory-in-use. Another example is the administrator who espouses a participatory management style, but actually employs a top-down, authoritarian style. What we believe about our practice may not be the same as what we actually do in practice.

While Schön's work is considered central to theorizing about reflective practice, several other writers have elaborated on various aspects of reflective practice. Fenwick (2004) for example, acknowledges that practice-based learning "recognizes and celebrates knowledge generated outside institutions" (p. 43), challenges "expert" knowledge, and values personal experience. However, "experiences also can reproduce structural inequities and reinforce entrenched beliefs or traditions of practice that may be harmful or repressive" (p. 44). This may be particularly problematic for "educators who typically practice in isolation" dimming the potential for "systemic change" (p. 44). She proposes a model of reflective practice that is more complex, one that sees learning as embodied within complex systems.

Reflective practice/experiential learning has also been connected to the characterization of work-based learning (WBL). Being examined is how the theoretical frame of experiential learning can be applied to learning in the workplace—"What needs to be considered is how the learning processes take place in 'work'-related environments and how, by understanding the mechanisms of learning, the work-based environment can be formalized as an authentic learning environment and thus accepted as comparable but nevertheless different from the traditional on-campus one" (Chisholm, Harris, Northwood, & Johrendt, 2009, p. 319).

Others have assumed a more postmodern and critical stance on reflective practice (Brookfield, 1991; Dyke, 2009; Mezirow, 2000; Usher, Bryant, & Johnston, 1997). Key to this perspective is that learning from one's experience involves not just reflection, but *critical* reflection (see Chapter 11 for more information). For example, Brookfield proposes three phases of critical reflection:

1. The identification of "the assumptions that underlie our thoughts and actions;"
2. The scrutiny of "the accuracy and validity of these assumptions in terms of how they connect to, or are discrepant with, our experience of reality;"
3. The reconstituting of these assumptions "to make them more inclusive and integrative." (Brookfield, 1991, p. 177)

Popularized by Schön, the notion of reflective practice has taken hold in adult education, human resource development, other areas of education, and many applied fields. His ideas and subsequent thinking are popular because they resonate with what we adults know to be true about our learning. Our learning is rooted in practice/experience, even if the experience is one of formal education; and for learning to occur, we need to reflect on or in the experience.

Situated Cognition

Just as "reflective practice" signifies learning that occurs with reflection on or in practice, when we talk about "situated cognition" or as it is also referred to, "contextual learning," we are acknowledging the importance of *where* this learning occurs, that is, *the context itself shapes the learning.* Given situated cognition is solidly anchored in a constructivist learning perspective, we could have discussed this in the chapter on learning theories, but because situated cognition is first and foremost about learning in context or in an experience, we placed it in this chapter. Reflective practice is most often thought of as reflecting *on* experience or practice, whereas situated cognition is more akin to learning *in* practice in a context. The spotlight shifts from the individual to the context. Learning occurs as people interact with other people in a particular context with the tools at hand (tools can be objects, language, or symbols). For example, on a trip to Singapore Sharan set about learning the public transportation system. The context was Singapore's bus and train system, the tools consisted of a transit pass, maps, and the trains and buses themselves, and it was socially interactive as she and her husband "figured out" the system with the occasional help of a passenger or employee of the system. This example is reminiscent of several now famous examples from research by Jean Lave, who is considered the major architect of this theory. In one study, adults were asked to determine which of two products were a "best buy" and were given two ways to solve the problem, one using the "tools" and social interaction available to them in the grocery store—the size and shape of jars and containers, their location in the store such as a bargain aisle, people in the store—and then the more traditional mathematical paper and pencil test. In the context of the grocery store they got 98% correct; given the same problems in a paper and pencil test, they got 59% correct (Lave, 1988). In another example, Kim and Merriam (2010) studied how the context, tools, and social interaction shaped the learning of older Korean adults taking a computer class. The physical setting of the classroom, the "tools" of computer terminals and teacher's notes which were copied by the students, and Korean cultural values worked in concert to shape the learning that took place.

Viewing learning from a situated cognition perspective removes learning from that which only occurs within the person's mind and highlights the importance of context and social interaction as determinants of the learning that takes place. And context and social interactions are culturally and politically defined. For example, in the study cited above of Korean elderly learning computers, the nature of the interaction between teacher and students and among the students themselves was culturally defined; that is, respect for teachers in this culture precluded informal or spontaneous exchanges that one might see in a Western classroom.

Further, respect for age even among a group of all older adults meant that older students felt uncomfortable asking younger ones for assistance.

From a situated cognition or contextual learning perspective, the experiences from which one learns need to be as contextualized, that is as "authentic" as possible. In the classroom, role play, case studies, simulation games, and introducing problems or issues from outside the classroom are ways to make the learning more authentic. Cognitive apprenticeship, which can occur within or outside the classroom, is yet another strategy. Modeled after craft apprenticeships, in a cognitive apprenticeship, novices are taught to think about what they are doing as well as learning the skills associated with the activity (Fenwick, 2003). Like traditional apprenticeships in which the apprentice learns a trade such as auto repair or culinary arts by working under a master teacher, cognitive apprenticeships allow the master to model behaviors and the thinking that accompanies the task.

Brown, Collins, and Duguid (1989) were the first to articulate the steps involved. First, the master explains exactly what she is doing and thinking as she simultaneously models the skill. The learner/apprentice develops a conceptual model of the processes involved. The learner then attempts to imitate those behaviors with the master observing and providing support and coaching when needed. This is often called "scaffolding" the learning. Coaching is particularly critical at the skill level *just beyond* what the learner/apprentice could accomplish by him or herself. Vygotsky (1978) referred to this as the Zone of Proximal Development and believed that fostering development within this zone leads to the most rapid learning. The coaching process includes additional modeling if necessary, corrective feedback, and reminders, all intended to bring the apprentice's perform-ance closer to that of the master's. As the apprentice becomes more skilled through the repetition of this process, the feedback and instruction pro-vided by the master "fades" until the apprentice is, ideally, performing the skill at a close approximation of the master's level. Collins, Brown, and Holum (1991) characterize cognitive apprenticeship as "making thinking visible": "In traditional apprenticeship, the process of carrying out a task to be learned is usually easily observable. In cognitive apprenticeship, one needs to deliberately bring the thinking to the surface, to make it visible, whether it's in reading, writing, problem solving. The teacher's thinking must be made visible to the students and the student's thinking must be made visible to the teacher. That is the most important difference between traditional apprenticeship and cognitive apprenticeship" (p. 9). Clinton and Rieber (2010) describe how situated cognition and cognitive apprenticeship provided the foundation for a three-course graduate program in multimedia design called The Studio Experience. "Situated cognition posits that all thinking, learning, and knowledge arise from socially mediated activities embedded in authentic and meaningful contexts" (p. 766). Over the three courses students learn about the nature of design, develop skills in instructional design, and ultimately produce a multimedia project as a team. "The ultimate goal of the Studio is to help participants move toward full participation in this wider community [of multimedia design]" (p. 767). They also point out that the principle of scaffolding "is a particularly important component in the Studio's design. The overall 'scaffold' of support fades slowly over the three-course sequence" (p. 767).

Cognitive apprenticeship is an instructional strategy solidly grounded in the situated cognition framework. That is, it posits that learning is a function of the context in which it takes place, the tools in the context, and the social interaction between master (educator) and apprentice (learner). In many situations the social interaction includes other learners and educators, for example, as a more advanced apprentice explains a procedure to a less knowledgeable learner. Finally, a cognitive apprenticeship mode of instruction does not have to be only skill-based, such as learning to use a computer or learning to swim; it is equally applicable to learning which is primarily cognitive, as in solving a physics problem, or emotional, as in dealing with the grief, or even spiritual, as in learning to meditate.

Communities of Practice

Communities of practice, also often called learning communities, are yet another manifestation of a situated cognition perspective on how learning resides in the context, tools, and social interaction of learners. Wenger (1998, 2000; also, Wenger & Snyder, 2000) is most often associated with this concept. Communities of practice are everywhere as people informally come together around some common interest. We all belong to multiple communities of practice—our family is one, as is our workplace, our professional association, a civic organization we might belong to, and social websites such as Facebook. As Wenger points out,

> Communities of practice are an integral part of our daily lives . . . Although the term may be new, the experience is not. Most communities of practice do not have a name and do not issue membership cards. Yet, if we care to consider our own life from

that perspective for a moment, we can all construct a fairly good picture of the communities of practice we belong to now, those we belonged to in the past, and those we would like to belong to in the future . . . Furthermore, we can probably distinguish a few communities of practice in which we are core members from a larger number of communities in which we have a more peripheral kind of membership. (1998, p. 7)

Communities of practice are made up of learners who have different levels of knowledge and mastery of the knowledge, behaviors, attitudes, and norms of the group. There are those who know more than others; however, "mastery resides not in the master but in the organization of the community of practice of which the master is a part" (Lave & Wagner, 1991, p. 95). Newcomers, through engaging with others in the community, learn what they need to know to move from the periphery to the center of practice; over time newcomers become more engaged and more active. Think about your graduate studies program for which you might be reading this textbook. After enrolling in the program, you attended your first course; you were on the periphery of this community of practice. As you interacted with fellow students, instructors, and others associated with the program, and as you learned some of the practices, procedures, and jargon, you became more central to the community. After several semesters you become something of an "old timer" and can mentor new students into the community.

Learning is central to these communities because learning is what goes on in our daily lives as we move in and out, between and among various communities. These communities of practice have "*shared histories of learning*" (1998, p. 86). In the communities of practice and learning communities literature, a distinction is made between learning itself and designing for it to occur. "Learning cannot be designed" according to Wenger (p. 225). "Ultimately, it belongs to the realm of experience and practice. It follows the negotiation of meaning; it moves on its own terms. It slips through the cracks; it creates its own cracks. Learning happens, design or no design. And yet there are few more urgent tasks than to design social infrastructures that foster learning" (p. 225). In his theory, a community of practice becomes a learning community when learning is "not only a matter of course in the history of its practice, but at the very core of its enterprise" (pp. 214–215).

There is now a fairly large literature on communities of practice and learning communities, including a journal, *Learning Communities Journal.*

Though originally the idea of communities of practice was more about acquiring expertise through apprenticeship-type learning, and learning communities were more about learning in community with one another, over the years the distinctions between the two concepts has become less rigid. Communities of practice are most often studied and implemented in organizational settings and are sometimes linked to the concept of the learning organization (Senge, 1990). Fenwick (2008), for example, examines workplace learning from a community of practice perspective: "Learning is viewed as the ongoing refinement of practices and emerging knowledge embodied in the specific action of a particular community. Individuals learn *as* they participate in everyday activity within a community (with its history, assumptions and cultural values, rules, and patterns of relationship), with the tools at hand (including objects, technology, language)" (pp. 19–20, italics in original). Laura had an opportunity to consult with a division of Ford Motor Company that was implementing a learning organization model that sought to create learning communities among critical work groups such as management-labor councils and product launch teams. Employees were trained on learning organization principles such as developing a shared vision, engaging in generative dialogue, sharing and testing assumptions, building effective teams, and thinking systemically. Results were impressive with improved labor relations and product launches. Historically ineffective launches (late, lower quality, higher costs) shifted to launches as a result of the learning community initiative, launches that were on time, on budget, and of higher quality.

In education, online environments, and community-based organizations, communities of practice and learning communities seem to be used somewhat interchangeably. In one study, for example, 12 Latino Fellows participated in a year-long learning community of practice for development as community college leaders (Wiessner & Sullivan, 2007). Participants and researchers shared their experiences and insights enabling learning to occur on several levels—personal, by making their tacit knowledge explicit; professional, where roles and responsibilities as leaders became clarified; and disciplinary, which consisted of understanding concepts and theories of leadership. In a recent study of community activists in Australia, learning is analyzed from a social learning and community of practice perspective. Ollis (2010) writes: "The practices of activism are usually closely connected to communities, community development and social movements. Sites of community and social movements are the spaces and places where activists learn through socialisation with one another, by learning in 'communities of practice' (Lave & Wenger 1991,

p. 31). Learning in activism is a naturally social process; through time, and the opportunity to observe and interact with others, activists become more expert at what they do" (p. 246). The literature on learning communities in online environments has focused on how to establish a learning community online (Palloff & Pratt, 2009), and how professional development can be fostered through this medium (Cornelius & McDonald, 2008; Sherer, Shea, & Kristensen, 2003).

Reflective practice and situated cognition represent two other ways to think about the connection between experience and learning. Reflective practice, which has been widely adopted in adult education especially in continuing professional education, posits that reflecting on and in our experiences (our "practice"), is where learning occurs. The more we engage in reflective practice the more expert we become. Situated cognition is yet another way of looking at experience and learning. In this perspective, the context in which the learning occurs is critical to understanding and facilitating learning. Cognitive apprenticeships and communities of practice, direct outgrowths of this perspective, can be employed as instructional strategies to foster learning from and in experience.

Chapter Summary

In this chapter we have explored the interrelationship between life experience and learning. Whether we are in a formal class, at home, at work, or grocery shopping, we are engaged in experiences that hold the potential for learning. In turn that learning often leads us to new experiences and the cycle continues. In this chapter we have explored some of the ways scholars and the field of adult education and human resource development have conceptualized this relationship. First we reviewed Dewey's foundational work, followed by Lindeman, and then explained how an adult's life experience is recognized in andragogy, self-directed learning, and transformative learning theories. In the second section of the chapter we presented Kolb's model of experiential learning followed by three models developed by adult educators. Each of these three models focuses on a different aspect of experiential learning including the process (Jarvis), types of experiential learning and their instructional implications (Tennant & Pogson), and philosophical orientations (Fenwick). Finally, we reviewed the theories of reflective practice, situated cognition, and communities of practice for their contributions to understanding the connection between experience and learning.

Linking Theory and Practice: Activities and Resources

1. Trace a recent learning episode in your life from initiation of the learning, through to completion of the learning. To what extent does your learning cycle reflect Kolb's cycle? How would you "adjust" Kolb's cycle to better accommodate your learning?

2. Go to Kolb's website (www.learningfromexperience.com) and access the LSI to assess your learning style preference.

3. Pair off with another adult learner. Begin by teaching your partner something, then switch roles, with you being the learner and your partner teaching you something. What you teach and learn can be on *anything* that the teacher has some expertise in—how to play the guitar, cook an ethnic dish, learn a computer program, drive a motorcycle, appreciate opera, or employ APA citation style in an academic paper. Plan on two learning sessions so that you can reflect on the first session with the goal of improving instruction and learning in the second session. Set the learning event up as a cognitive apprenticeship wherein the teacher verbalizes the cognitive process while simultaneously demonstrating the learning. As the sessions proceed, the learner becomes more competent, thus reducing the need for "scaffolding" from the instructor. As an assignment in your class with adult learners, students can document through a reflective paper, oral presentation, or multimedia event, the experience and what they learned about themselves as learners, about teaching adults, and about cognitive apprenticeships.

4. Taking Tennant and Pogson's four levels of experience—prior, current, new, and learning from experience—select a topic and consider how instruction can be designed to address each of the levels of experience. (See the example of a workshop on memory in the Tennant and Pogson discussion in this chapter.)

5. Conduct a pilot study on espoused theory versus theories-in-use by first interviewing a practitioner about some aspect of their practice (what they believe and what they think they do); then observe the person in practice. Compare their espoused theory with their theory-in-use. This exercise can be done with a colleague in your field of practice (education, health, administration, nursing), or with a skill-based activity with which you are familiar, such as a sport or hobby.

6. Teaching Around the Circle: Reflect on a subject or course you teach and list the different activities you use. Now compare it to Figure 6.2 below and see if you are tending to the different quadrants of the Kolb Learning Cycle. Next, revise your course to incorporate at least one

FIGURE 6.2 TEACHING AROUND THE CIRCLE

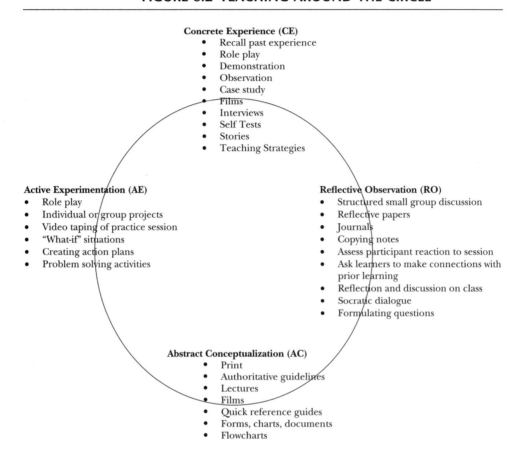

Concrete Experience (CE)
- Recall past experience
- Role play
- Demonstration
- Observation
- Case study
- Films
- Interviews
- Self Tests
- Stories
- Teaching Strategies

Active Experimentation (AE)
- Role play
- Individual or group projects
- Video taping of practice session
- "What-if" situations
- Creating action plans
- Problem solving activities

Reflective Observation (RO)
- Structured small group discussion
- Reflective papers
- Journals
- Copying notes
- Assess participant reaction to session
- Ask learners to make connections with prior learning
- Reflection and discussion on class
- Socratic dialogue
- Formulating questions

Abstract Conceptualization (AC)
- Print
- Authoritative guidelines
- Lectures
- Films
- Quick reference guides
- Forms, charts, documents
- Flowcharts

strategy from each quadrant around the circle. By ensuring a variety of active learning strategies that relate to a range of learning styles, you will create more powerful, effective learning experiences for adults.

Chapter Highlights

- The connection between experience and learning has been well documented through the years, from Greek philosophers to Dewey and Lindeman.

- Andragogy, self-directed learning, and transformative learning all have life experience as a central component to understanding learning.
- The most well-known model of experiential learning is Kolb's experiential learning cycle; adult educators Jarvis, Tennant, and Pogson and Fenwick have all advanced models of experiential learning focusing on adult learners.
- Reflective practice, or practice-based learning, as it is sometimes called, is learning that is acquired through reflection on or in practice (experience). Schön has written extensively about reflection on and in practice, and about espoused theories versus theories in use.
- The theory of situated cognition posits that learning is embedded in the context where it occurs, with the tools of that context, and through social interaction. Cognitive apprenticeships and communities of practice enable this form of experiential learning.

CHAPTER SEVEN

BODY AND SPIRIT IN LEARNING

"Why would anyone play a one-string guitar when there are five other strings?" asks Virginia Griffin (2001, p. 131). In most learning situations, she points out, the rational, cognitive mind is the one string we focus on at the expense of emotional, relational, physical, intuitive, and spiritual ways of knowing. In this chapter we bring two of these neglected "strings" to the forefront—learning in and through the body, and learning in conjunction with spirit. Not only are embodied learning and spirituality and learning two approaches receiving attention in adult learning theory, they are central pillars in the growing literature on holistic education.

The dominance of the rational mind in the West can be traced to the seventeenth-century French philosopher Descartes whose famous assertion, "I think, therefore I am" resulted in a mind/body split. (Some think that this famous dictum was based in doubt; that is, Descartes reasoned that if he doubted, then something or someone must be doing the doubting, therefore the very fact that he doubted proved his existence (Dupré, 2007)). He further declared that "I [that is, my mind, by which I am what I am] is entirely and truly distinct from my body" (Descartes, 1637/1960, p. 165, cited in Michelson, 1998, p. 218). For Descartes, "the mind, or consciousness, is thought of as having the properties of understanding and intelligence. In contrast, the body, and the physical and organic world more generally, are seen as having the property of spatial extension, and thereby as inert, or dumb" (Dall'Alba & Barnacle, 2005, p. 723). Eighteenth-century Enlightenment philosophers further elevated the mind as the source of reasoning and knowledge. Reason, rationality, and objectivity came to dominate all of education in the West as the most legitimate pathway to knowledge and learning. Indeed, even today, reasoning, critical thinking, evidence-based knowledge, and the "scientific" method are more highly valued than other forms of knowledge.

As with other areas of education, until recently a rational perspective on adult learning dictated both practice and research. Other than recognizing that adult learners were different from children, and that adults needed a psychologically comfortable environment to learn in, little was written about nonrational ways of knowing. Within the last twenty years, however, nonrational modes of learning have been attended to as legitimate pathways for learning. This chapter focuses on the two modes of learning that have recently received the most attention—the body and the spirit.

Embodied Learning

"The body," music educator Wayne Bowman (2010) points out, has had a "bad rap." The body is "other to the knowing mind; as a sense-dominated threat to intellectual clarity; as an emotional or feelingful contaminant to rigorous cognitive effort; . . . as a mere vessel housing (and following the directives of) the most distinctive and important human entity, the mind" (p. 2). Bowman goes on to say that "so pervasive and seductive are such assumptions—so much a part of the cultural 'air' we breathe—that even music educators, who should know better, invoke dubious claims like 'Music makes you smarter' to rationalize their existence" (p. 2).

But why have we ignored the body as a site of learning? The dominance of rationality as the source of knowledge is one explanation. Some writers have advanced other explanations. Speaking of her own bicycle accident and trauma to her body, Smears (2009) points out that "detachment from one's body [is] a means of distancing oneself from the associated feelings of distress or pain" (p. 106). Further, she reflects upon how the "embodied self becomes integral to the processes of power that permeate our institutions and their practices," such as the health care system (p. 105). Smears also finds that as a result of feeling she has lost agency and control, she can better relate to the vulnerability of her students: "I have been able to engage more with students' experience of fragility. I have been more willing to listen to students when they express concerns about how they feel anxious and out of control. I have been able to respond when they express how overwhelmed and excluded they feel in a Higher Education culture—a culture that speaks a 'foreign language,' which follows procedures that are unfamiliar and not understood" (p. 108). Others (Goldenberg, Pyszczynski, Greenberg, & Solomon, 2000) suggest we might distance ourselves from our bodies because our cognitive mind knows our body cannot escape the inevitability of death. In exploring dance as a way of knowing, Snowber (2012) writes that "body knowledge has become endangered within the human species, and we are often alienated in our own bodies" (p. 55). We need to move from worrying about how our outer body looks and return to the lived body: "The lived body is the felt body where we make connections to the multiple sensations around and within us. The feel of the wind on the skin, fingers typing at the computer, the pain in the lower back, the joy of one torso swimming, and the tears in the belly all connect us to the lived body" (p. 55). Attention to the body has come from feminist scholars who exposed ways in which the female body was linked to oppression and marginalization (Clark, 2001), and from neuroscientists who are exploring how the brain itself "learns" and changes (Taylor & Lamoreaux, 2008), However, for whatever reason, attention to the body as a site of *learning* has been sporadic.

What Is Embodied Learning?

In August 2011, a rare 5.8 strength earthquake occurred along the East Coast of the United States. For days afterwards, news shows reported the unusual behavior of animals and birds just prior to the earthquake— flamingos herded together in a protective stance in the Washington, D.C. zoo, dogs became agitated, and so on. But sensing danger is not limited to animals and birds. From the deadly December 2004 tsunami in Southeast Asia comes the remarkable story of the Moken village sea gypsies, a group of nomadic seafaring people living on islands off the coast of Thailand. Fearing the worst, a *60 Minutes* television show reporter visited the Moken after the tsunami and found that they and their animals had survived (www.cbsnews.com/video/watch/?id=681813n). They had noticed the signs, they "knew" and "felt" it was coming and they moved away from the sea to higher ground. Although their village was destroyed, "listening" to their bodies saved their lives.

We have all had times when our body reacts in a "knowing" way to something in our environment—perhaps we feel threatened or angry or elated or excited before we know the exact cause of these emotions. At the same time we often trace physical ailments back to stress in our lives and have been told that we need to "slow down," or "relax" before we get physically ill. The body and our mind and our emotions are indeed connected. The brain, where these connections occur, is a physical organ, a part of our body. Separating the two makes little sense; hence we can talk about "embodied" learning. Basically, unifying, rather than separating the mind and the body, is what embodied learning is all about. Rather than relegating physical knowing to the sidelines in our learning, we attend to it; we incorporate it into our understanding of the world in which we live. "Simply stated, embodied learning involves being attentive to the body and its experiences as a way of knowing" (Freiler, 2008, p. 40).

There are several terms used somewhat interchangeably in the growing literature in this area—embodied learning, embodiment, somatic learning, and embodied cognition. Somatic learning or knowing draws from the Greek word *soma*, which means body, and is most readily associated with learning that takes place in specific body-centered activities such as dance, yoga, or tai chi. Cheville's notion (2005) of embodied cognition "locates the human body at the intersection of culture and cognition" (p. 86). She illustrates this concept through her ethnographic study of a women's basketball team. She found that learning meant negotiating their physicality (associated with males) on the court with their femininity off the court, and that spatial and physical learning on the court was overlaid by differentials in power between coach and players and more and less experienced players. The nuanced differences among these terms are less important than the fact that all are referring to the body as a site of learning and knowing.

Many of us have had the experience of "knowing" that a certain applicant is not right for the job even though "on paper" he or she may look eminently qualified, or that you should circumnavigate around a particular person on the street, or that you know not to bring up a specific issue in the workplace at a particular meeting. These are examples of tacit or intuitive knowledge that we all have acquired but rarely articulate. Such knowledge is "embodied" within us and can be seen as expressions of embodied knowing. It is knowing without reasoning and transcends the cognitive. It is knowing that we experience rather than think about. Lawrence (2012a) in fact defines embodied knowing as an intuitive process: "Intuition is spontaneous, heart-centered, free, adventurous, imaginative, playful, nonsequential, and nonlinear (Lawrence, 2009). We access intuitive knowledge through dreams, symbols, artwork, dance, yoga, meditation, contemplation, and immersion in nature. Most of these processes call upon embodied knowing" (Lawrence, 2012a, pp. 5–6). She also reminds us that "the most primal way of accessing knowledge is through the body as our earliest forms of knowing are preverbal" (p. 7). Küpers also (2005) points out that tacit knowledge is "a personal skill or capability, something individuals can rely on in everyday life without being aware of it, let alone understanding it . . . Tacit knowledge is a bodily competence [which] Polanyi calls 'embodied knowledge' (Polanyi, 1966,1969). But not only do we 'know more than we can tell' (Polanyi, 1966, p. 4) . . . we are immersed in an embodied world of experience in which the lived is always greater than the known" (p. 117). Schuyler (2010) proposes that leadership training which "tends to be primarily cognitive and conceptual" would be more effective if the body were brought into the experience "creat[ing] change at the level of *tacit knowledge*—familiarity with a subject that lets a person act effectively without being able to fully describe how. It is from this part of the human "knowing" that change in values and long-standing habits is believed to be possible" (p. 24, italics in original). And as Gallagher (2005) suggests in his book titled *How the Body Shapes the Mind*, some scientists believe that the mind itself is shaped by the body in fundamental ways through perception, social cognition, and language; the body has created knowledge which is "behind the scene" (p. 141)

Though Griffin (2001) lists intuition and emotion as separate strings on the guitar, we see both as entwined with embodied learning. Speaking of the role of emotions in adult learning, Dirkx (2001) writes, "personally significant and meaningful learning is fundamentally grounded in and is derived from the adult's emotional, imaginative connection with the self and with the broader social world" (p. 64). We feel these emotions in our body, that is, they are embodied, "providing us with a means for developing self-knowledge. They are an integral part of how we interpret and make sense of the day-to-day events in our lives" (p. 65). Emotions, experienced through the body, are part of how we know and how we learn. In an edited volume titled *Adult Learning and the Emotional Self* (Dirkx, 2008), the emotional, embodied dimensions of adult learning are explored in various settings including literacy programs, higher education, online contexts, the workplace, and nonformal educational settings. Emotions felt through our bodies are also central to what has been called "emotional labor" (Malcolm, 2012), "emotion work," or "emotion learning" in human resource development. Here the concern is the emotional well-being of workers and their relationship to the organization. Bierema (2008) comments on this connection: "The emotional well-being of workers is a complex process that intersects with the organization culture, history, structure, policies, and politics. Emotion has a significant impact on well-being, identity development, and power relations. It is important to value and develop the emotional wellbeing of workers, but it should be done in conjunction with a broader commitment to promoting organizational well-being" (p. 62).

Griffin (2001) agrees that our bodies reflect our emotions and we can learn about ourselves by attending to our body. We can also listen to our body to direct our learning: She cites Castenaga who writes "any path is only a path . . . Look at every path closely and deliberately . . . Then ask yourself, and yourself alone, one question . . . Does this path have a heart? If it does, the path is good, if it doesn't it is of no use" (Castaneda, 1968, cited in Griffin, p. 108). Mulvihill (2003) discusses the link between the rational mind and the emotional body:

> There is no such thing as a behavior or thought, which is not impacted in some way by emotions. There are no neurotransmitters for "objectivity"; rather even the simplest responses to information signals are linked with possibly several "emotional neurotransmitters" (Haberlandt, 1998). Because the neurotransmitters, which carry messages of emotion, are integrally linked with the information, during both the initial processing and the linking with information from the different senses, it becomes clear that there is no thought, memory, or knowledge which is "objective," or "detached" from the personal experience of knowing. (p. 322)

Embodied learning, then, is seeing our body as an instrument for learning. Some of this learning is unconscious as in tacit knowing, and some of the learning has an emotional component. We now turn to some examples of embodied learning and offer suggestions as to how it might be fostered in an educational setting.

Embodied Learning in Practice

The study of embodied learning in adult education is still fairly new, so while we have examples from several areas of practice, we will also briefly consider how embodied learning is embedded in experiential learning, andragogy, and transformative learning.

It is not surprising that studies of embodied learning can be found in activities where movement of the body is featured, such as dance (Barbour, 2011; Snowber, 2012) or basketball (Cheville, 2005). Amann (2003) calls this form of embodied learning kinesthetic learning, wherein "movement and action . . . often yields lessons about discipline, diligence, dealing with stress, or solving problems" (p. 28). Amann's notion of kinesthetic learning is reminiscent of one of Gardner's (1993) multiple intelligences, that of "bodily-kinesthetic" intelligence. (See Chapter 9.)

The body also figures prominently in health care, especially in nursing, where patient care is about care of the human body. Wright and Brajtman (2011) explore how nursing ethics is firmly embedded in relational knowing (encounters with others) and embodied knowing. As they point out, "We experience the world through our bodies, and our sense of our own body is inexorably linked to our sense of self. Therefore, any assault to the integrity of the body will inevitably threaten integrity of the self. Recognition of every person as an embodied being-in-the-world is fundamental to ethical nursing practice" (p. 25).

A group of nursing students were the participants in Freiler's study (2008) incorporating "experiences of embodiment" and "attention to body awareness" to promote embodied learning. While participants "initially found embodiment difficult to verbally express as a concept," they were eventually able to give "expression to a developed sense of embodied being-in-the-world. Visceral, emotive, and physiological connections of intensified embodied awareness were described by participants as 'being in tune' to or with their bodies, 'listening to' the body as it talks to them and tells them something, and 'being more aware' of attending to body experiences and one's surroundings" (p. 42). In another medical area, psychotherapy, Panhofer, Payne, Meekums, and Parke (2011) state that "knowing can happen in the body, in an unconscious, preconscious, and or non-languaged, way" (p. 10). They explore how embodied practices such as dance and writing, can be effective tools in psychotherapy supervision; in particular, they propose a model of self-supervision which promotes accessing "the knowledge of the body when reflecting on practice day to day" (abstract). Finally, King (2012) explored her eight-year struggle with debilitating illness and came to realize that her journey involved more than dealing with the healthcare system. It involved the realization (in itself a transformative learning experience) that "health included more than the absence of illness, and instead involves connecting and communicating among the mind, body, and spirit" (p. 49).

The workplace is another site for fostering embodied learning. An interesting study of coal miners' use of embodied knowing to promote workplace safety is reported by Somerville (2004). The author herself was required by her interviewees to go down into the mine—"to experience (my) body at the site of (their) work" (p. 59). Survival "depends on sensing minute changes in sounds, smell, feel of air" (p. 60). "Pit sense," as the miners call it, is dependent on the miners' "keen sensory awareness of one's surroundings in relationship with the mines but also on reliance on other miners inhabiting the same place in the mines" (p. 60). As one miner told Somerville, "All the blokes have got pit sense. They know that the roof's bad, they know by hearing it, they know by smell, they know by the sense of just being there and being uncomfortable, the heaviness of the air, that you're in a place where you shouldn't be, lack of oxygen or gas" (p. 60).

Embodied learning and the workplace has further been explored in management, organizational and leadership development education. In her feminist analysis of human resource development, Metcalf (2008) writes,

> As Sinclair suggests, management education should not be "shamelessly reproducing a false mind–body dichotomy, or ignoring bodies in the mistaken belief that their effects will be inert" (2005;, 98). In other words, "doing HRD" through the body, and the relationships between HRD and learners, is as much about the gender (and race, age, ethnicity) of the HRD professional, as well as the training content, or client task itself. That is, HRD is not an action, nor a transaction, but becoming/evolving. It is an interactive and embodied process that requires an intellectual and emotional connection between HRD and learners (see Lee 2004; Perriton, 1999). Bodies can be an important source of knowledge, both interior and exterior. (p. 456)

Likewise, Schuyler (2010) makes a strong case for leadership development being more than a cognitive activity. She has found combining mindfulness and somatic experiences can lead to "leaders who can remain calm and aware, who can notice and immediately uproot negative emotions, who can be inclusive of people regardless of their status in an organization, and who can truly appreciate all the people they lead" (p. 35). But incorporating embodied learning into the workplace requires, Meyer (2012) writes, "a mind-set shift from workplace to playspace" (p.

25). Meyer presents several examples of companies that have successfully incorporated embodied learning in the workplace. She concludes from these case examples that "creating playspace for and fostering practices that allow people at all levels of the organization to engage their whole selves and their whole bodies can set the stage for people to play new roles and discover new capacities . . . Those who risk stepping out of their comfort zone and into their bodies not only enjoy their own personal rewards; they might also give permission to others to explore new frontiers in their own learning and development with previously unimagined organizational value" (p. 32). And in an interesting discussion of the value of embodied implicit and narrative knowing in organizations, Küpers (2005) points out that such knowledge management techniques have some limitations: "Organizational control of embodied emotional knowing can cause various negative effects, like dissonance, demotivation and alienation" (p. 123). Further, these "forms of knowing are not always fulfilling needs for specific relevant knowledge efficiently. They are much less predictable media, in their content and process, than other organizational knowledge sources" (p. 123).

Finally, given that so much of our learning today takes place in online environments, some have wondered what role the body can and does play in a medium that is characterized by anonymity. In their article "Embodied Knowing in Online Environments," Dall'Alba and Barnacle (2005) encourage educators to think of embodied knowing as the interface between mind/body and human/machine. They write, "The way that bodily perceptions, particularly sight and hearing, are facilitated through modern technologies is such that the instruments and machines that we use cannot be treated simply as "tools", or as objects for consciousness. Since perception is aided, enhanced or even obstructed by technologies, ICATAs are not merely objects of inquiry. Instead, they become the means of inquiry: technologies become an extension of us. Perceptions are embodied through instruments, artifacts and the like, from the pen and the keyboard through to complex imaging and audio devices" (p. 740). Teachers and learners, they argue, need to become acquainted "with their own embodiment and technology relations and, thereby, promoting recognition that knowing, acting and being are integrated" (p. 741).

Although work explicitly about embodied learning in adult education is fairly recent (Clark, 2012; Lawrence, 2012a), links can be drawn between embodied learning and experiential learning (Chapter 6), andragogy (Chapter 3), and transformative learning (Chapter 5). Beginning with experiential learning, for example, not only do people learn from reflecting *on* an experience, they learn *in* an experience. Fenwick (2003) writes that "Learning is rooted in the situation in which the person participates, not in the head of that person as intellectual concepts produced by reflection" (p. 25). Indeed, experience is "the adult learner's living textbook" (Lindeman, 1961, p. 7). Experience, which involves one's body, emotions and spirit, and not just the mind, is also a key assumption in Knowles's andragogy. He proposed that not only do adults bring more and varied life experiences to a learning situation, which differentiates them from children, these experiences are a resource for learning; that is, adults can connect new learning to their life experiences as well as share their experiences to assist others in their learning (Knowles, 1980).

The key to recognizing life experiences as sites of embodied learning is to recognize that it is not just the mind that is having the experience, but the body—and attending to what we are learning through the body is embodied learning. Finally, much of the recent work on transformative learning suggests that it involves more than rational discourse and critical reflection as Mezirow (2000) first proposed. A more holistic approach to transformative learning appears to be taking hold. This approach "recognizes the role of feelings, other ways of knowing (intuition, somatic), and the role of relationships with others in the process of transformative learning. Dirkx (2006) suggests it is 'about inviting 'the whole person' into the classroom environment, we mean the person in fullness of being: as an affective, intuitive, thinking, physical, spiritual self' (p. 46)" (Taylor, 2008, p. 11).

The Spirit in Learning

The dominance of the rational mind in learning has made it difficult to think of learning in other ways, or as Griffin (2001) proposed, using other than one string to play the guitar. We have just explored the place of one's body in learning, which is perhaps easier to grasp due to its physical sensations than spirit in learning. But interestingly, the concept of spirituality and learning has actually received *more* attention in the media, popular books, and scholarly writing than has embodied learning. In the arena of health, for example, there are investigations into the role of meditation and prayer in fostering health and wellness; in corporate settings, "workplace spirituality" has been studied since the mid-1990s; and further, *Teachers College Record* (Miller, 2009) devoted an entire issue to spirituality and education as did *Adult Learning* (English, 2001). In this chapter we will first define what is meant by spirituality and its role in learning, then review its connections to the field of adult education, and finally, suggest how it might be fostered in practice.

Spirituality and Learning

Linked to the Latin *spiritus*, meaning breath, spirituality is often equated with soul, grace, flow, and life force; it is somehow more than, or beyond the corporal body. It is simply "an awareness of something greater than ourselves" (English, 2005, p. 1171). Physicist and philosopher David Bohm defines spirit as "an invisible force—a life-giving essence that moves us deeply, or as a source that moves everything from within" (cited in Lemkow, 2005, p. 24). Mackeracher (2004) adds the notion of connection to her definition of spirituality as "the experience of feeling expanded beyond the normal limits of my body and mind, of feeling connected to aspects of the external world that are of value to me—to others, to the earth, and to a greater cosmic being" (p. 172). Connection, whether it be to the self, to others, to the world, or to a higher being, is often a central component of definitions of spirituality.

Spirituality is not, most writers point out, the same as religion. Religion has to do with an organized system of beliefs, and human institutions where participants express their faith. Although for some people religion and spirituality overlap, significant spiritual experiences need not be related to religion or take place in a religious setting. The birth of a child, viewing a spectacular sunset, or being moved by a musical performance can all be spiritual experiences. As Tisdell (2007) notes, "the most important spiritual experiences themselves actually occur in a wider context of people living out their lives" (p. 539). In addition to separating spirituality from religion, Tisdell writes that spirituality is about connection, meaning-making, identity development, constructing knowledge through "unconscious and symbolic processes," and that it is always present in the learning environment, and often happens by surprise (p. 535).

It seems to us that it is the connection to *meaning-making* or knowledge construction that affords spirituality a legitimate place in our understanding of its place in adult learning. As Tisdell (2001) explains, "Spirituality is one of the ways people construct knowledge and meaning. It works in consort with the affective, the rational or cognitive, and the unconscious and symbolic domains. To ignore it, particularly in how it relates to teaching for personal and social transformation, is to ignore an important aspect of human experience and avenue of learning and meaning-making. This is why spirituality is important to the work of adult learning" (p. 3).

Much of the current literature on spirituality addresses its role in education, from primary school through higher and adult education. Schoonmaker's years of experience as a classroom teacher and her study (2009) of children's responses to literature with spiritual themes has led her to believe that the classroom is a spiritual space. Experiences of mystery and wonder "are a natural form of human awareness, transcending religious and cultural boundaries" (p. 2714). This kind of learning can be nurtured and acknowledged by carving out "spaces for children's wholeness within the classroom" and learning to really listen to what children say (p. 2729). Spirituality is a popular topic in higher education also, with writers exploring what it is exactly, and how to foster it in this setting (see for example, Astin, 2004; Chickering, Dalton, & Stamm, 2006; Jablonski, 2001). The authors of a recent review of the research on the impact of meditative practices in higher education found support for this spiritual practice in three areas—"the enhancement of cognitive and academic performance, the management of academic-related stress, and the development of the 'whole person'" (Shapiro, Brown, & Astin, 2011, p. 496).

Spirituality in Adult Education

Given the nature of spirituality, there is of course overlap in defining it and uncovering how it manifests itself in different areas of education. Whether primary or higher education, spirituality appears to enable meaning-making or knowledge construction in a learning situation. So too in adult education. The presence of spirituality has been particularly observed in three areas—adult development, social movements, and the workplace.

It used to be thought that like a butterfly emerging from its cocoon, once someone reached adulthood they were fully formed and changed little as they aged. However, decades of research into how adults grow and change as they age has revealed otherwise. As we age we often change the way we see the world and ourselves in it. Numerous models of adult development have mapped out psychosocial stages of development. One of the best known of these is Erikson's (1963) theory of eight stages of ego development. While all issues are present at all stages of development, each stage is characterized by a particular issue or crisis that needs to be addressed. In older adulthood, adults must deal with what he calls ego integrity versus despair. In this final stage of development, adults need to feel a sense of self-worth, of integrity about their lives, work and accomplishments, or despair will set in. Erikson's model and others suggest that as adults move into midlife and beyond, there is a turning in to the self in contemplation of the meaning of life and one's existence. Some research suggests adults become more spiritual as they age. For example, Wink and Dillon's 2002 longitudinal study of adult spiritual development found that "all participants, irrespective of gender and cohort, increased significantly in spirituality between late middle (mid 50s/early 60s) and older adulthood" (2002, p. 79).

Tisdell (2008) also makes the case that attending to spirituality in adult learning is important in "the ongoing development of identity" (p. 33). And this identity development is about developing authenticity. An authentic identity, Tisdell writes, is "operating from an identity defined more by one's self rather than by others' expectations" (2007, p. 551). Our authentic identity is our core self, and moments of spirituality in the learning environment can enable us to not only get in touch with, but develop our authenticity. This is especially likely to happen in adult learning contexts where we examine how we are all shaped by our culture, race, class, and gender.

In addition to the arena of authenticity in identity development, spirituality has played a major role in adult education's historic mission of social justice and social action. In fact, in an interesting study of women in the Catholic Worker Movement of the 1930s and 1940s, Parrish and Taylor (2007) found that women in this movement sought both independence and authenticity. They felt that caring for the poor allowed them "to live an authentic life as a Christian" (p. 233). The authors write that the women in the Catholic Worker Movement "were seeking out a more authentic expression of the Catholic faith than they found in some church and school settings . . . This disconnection with institutional structures propelled them toward social movement involvement that resulted in a new framework or worldview and had a dramatic impact on the rest of their lives" (p. 244).

Two other book-length studies of social activists in adult education have uncovered the link to spirituality. Daloz, Keen, Keen, and Parks (1996) interviewed 120 men and women active in social change and found that 82% claimed a strong sense of spirituality (though not necessarily religion) as a reason for their commitment to the common good. Tisdell's study (2003) of 31 culturally diverse educators involved in social action found that spirituality intersected with their practice in several ways, each of which involved learning: through being involved in or witnessing significant human experiences such as giving birth; "sacred moments" of synchronicity that "offered new learning about hope, healing, or direction in times of difficulty" (Tisdell, 2008, p. 31); special moments in nature and meditation on the everyday context of their lives; and in the claiming of their own unique identity, wherein gender and culture were acknowledged.

English (2005) makes the case that social change and spirituality are central to the mission and practice of adult education. Spirituality, an awareness of a force greater than ourselves, can be both private and individual in nature, but also public and secular as in social movements. Through references to movements and individuals, English builds a strong case for how spirituality and social change have permeated adult education in the United States, Canada, and elsewhere. While she addresses some of the challenges with bringing these two intertwined purposes together in today's world, she is hopeful that:

> In a world struggling to understand the aftermath of the war in
> Iraq, the threat of further violence, and the vain struggles of world
> leaders to negotiate the complex politics of religion and its
> relationship (if any) to the violence, the time is ripe for adult
> educators to contribute to a wide variety of purposes and causes, yet
> to establish some core concerns and commitments . . . Adult
> educators can move beyond the polarized views of education and
> training, spirituality and religion; we have much to teach the world
> about how it balances, negotiates, and embraces difference and
> how it moves beyond binaries to effect spiritual growth and social
> change. (p. 1188)

A third major site for discussions and research about spirituality is the workplace. Much of our adult life is spent in the workplace, and the notion that we bring our whole self to work, not just our body and brain, has generated much interest in the literature in adult education and human resource development, organizational development, management, and leadership. There have been literally dozens of popular books and articles and upwards of two hundred studies on this topic in the last twenty years. There is an online resource center, The Association for Spirit at Work (www.spiritatwork.com), and a journal published by Routledge, *Journal of Management, Spirituality and Religion.* Karakas (2010) speculates that this burgeoning interest may be due to a paradigm shift from seeing the workplace as a controlled environment with a solely economic focus "to a balance of profits, quality of life, spirituality, and social responsibility" (p. 89). As with all the literature on spirituality, workplace spirituality has

various definitions but most have to do with "the recognition that employees have an inner life that nourishes and is nourished by meaningful work
that takes place in the context of community" (Ashmos & Duchon, 2000,
p. 137). Pawar (2009) suggests that there are three levels from which
workplace spirituality might be approached: the individual level, which is
about meaning in work; a group level involving a sense of community at
work; and an organizational level wherein the focus is on one's spirituality
and its alignment with organizational and corporate values.

In another conceptualization of workplace spirituality, Karakas (2010)
reviewed 140 articles on workplace spirituality and how it supports organizational performance. In his review of the research, he found that spirituality is connected to organizational performance and productivity in three
ways. The first construct, employee well-being, referring to incorporating
spiritual practices at work, was found to "increase employees' morale,
commitment, and productivity; while decreasing their stress and burnout
at work" (p. 94). Second, attention to fostering a sense of meaning and
purpose (such as asking, "What is the meaning of the work I am doing?"
or "What do I want for my life? Why?") increases productivity and commitment of employees. The third construct is about a sense of community
and connectedness. "This perspective contends that incorporating spirituality at work provides organizational members a sense of community and
connectedness, and thus increases their attachment, loyalty, and belonging to the organization" (p. 96). Though it would seem from this review
of the research that promoting spirituality at the workplace is a win-win
situation, Karakas also presents some drawbacks such as the danger of
proselytizing, incompatibility with corporate culture, spirituality as a fad
or management tool to manipulate employees, and the "ambiguity and
confusion about the concept, definition, meaning, and measurement of
spirituality" (p. 100).

Leadership, which cuts across organizations and areas of adult education practice, has also been studied with regard to spirituality. An early
acknowledgment of the importance of spirituality was expressed by learning organization guru Peter Senge (1990): Leaders "must give up the old
dogma of planning, organizing and controlling and realize the almost
sacredness of their responsibility for the lives of so many people. A manager's fundamental task . . . is providing the enabling conditions for
people to lead the most enriching lives they can" (p. 140). And in a study
of the role of spirituality in the practice of adult education leaders, Fleming
and Courtenay (2006) found four ways in which spirituality had an impact
on their practice. First, participants claimed spirituality served as a resource

in times of challenge; second, spirituality shaped the leader's perception of power in that instead of using it to control others, power was something to be shared or even given away; third, their spiritually influenced ethical framework affected their decision making; and fourth, it affected communication with coworkers. Of this last factor they write, "The model of communication which appears to be used by a spiritually influenced leader is more of a triangle with a connection to a Higher Being located between the two [sender and receiver]. We visualize this as spirituality performing the role of an uplink satellite through which communication is channeled" (p. 128).

If spirituality in the learning environment is thought of as in integral part of meaning-making for many adults, then our task as educators is to promote the conditions where it can happen. First, we need to make space in the learning situation for it to "happen." But what does it mean to "make space"? Vella (2000) writes such a space is safe, supportive, and open, a "sacred" space where dialogue can take place and learners can share their experiences related to the topic at hand without being judged by other learners or the facilitator. Others suggest that we should not be overly programmed and that should one of these moments arise, we need to be flexible enough to abandon our plans and go with the flow. Lauzon (2007) bemoans the prevalence of the "banking approach" to education where information is poured into the heads of students "and in doing so squashes the human spirit" (p. 44). What we need to do, he says, is "create spaces in which learner experience can be used in meaningful ways, not merely as an adjunct to the 'main' learning, and there is sufficient fluidity to allow for undetermined learning outcomes. This is the learning of spirit, arising from learners creating meaning, constructing knowledge" (p. 45).

In summary, the keen interest and vast number of publications on spirituality as it manifests itself in adult education practice and in the workplace suggests that for many adults, the spiritual dimension of their lives is as important, if not more important than, other aspects of knowing and learning.

Chapter Summary

In bringing this chapter on the body and spirit in learning to a close, we would like to return to Griffin's image (2001) of the guitar that we opened with. Indeed, engaging the body and the spirit are two other strings or pathways for learning that we can access in promoting adult learning. As she says, "Wouldn't it be worth a little effort and openness to what could be? Wouldn't you rather play all the strings of your guitar and teach others to play more beautiful music on their guitars?" (p. 131).

Linking Theory and Practice: Activities and Resources

1. Most who have written about embodied learning in educational practice suggest that you first must attend to how *you* "learn" through your own body. Unless you already meditate or engage in one of the mind/body practices such as yoga, you need to experiment with listening to your body, acknowledging the gut-level intuitive and emotional responses you have to everyday experiences. Keep a diary for a day, jotting down any physical feelings or responses that accompany your thinking as you go through your day. This can be as basic as feeling too cold in an air-conditioned meeting room, avoiding someone in the hallway, laughing at a funny story, and so on. Most people are surprised at how much their body is "talking" to them, once they start listening to it!

2. Try to implement activities in your instruction to draw attention to the relationship of rational knowing with embodied learning. This of course is easier to do in areas like athletics, dance, art, and the health professions where the body is central to the discipline. However, even in subjects that are more cognitive in nature, the body can be accessed as a learning site. Experiment with space in your classroom, for example, different seating arrangements, the position of the instructor, or change the location of the class altogether, meeting in a coffee shop, outdoors, in an auditorium, and so on, to see how changing the position of the body affects learning. Rational knowing can also be enhanced through embodied learning experiences. Crowdes (2000), for example, dealt with issues of power and social inequity in her critical social analysis courses. She implemented an activity called "bowing" in which partners in dyads were assigned roles, with one being superior and all-powerful to whom the other must bow. The roles were reversed in the second step and students were asked how they "felt" in each role. The third step consisted of each partner bowing to the other in a mutually loving and respectful way.

3. The use of symbol (such as asking participants to share an object or symbol that represents something meaningful in their lives), storytelling,

dreams, art, music, poetry, literature, movies, and other noncognitive expressions of subject matter can also stimulate both embodied and spiritual learning. Freiler (2008) points out that incorporating such techniques into your instruction "needs to be carefully weighed about when, where, and how to integrate experiences of embodiment to enhance learning" as there may be some "resistance and discomfort" on the part of learners who prefer "a more traditional, rational approach to learning. Thus timing, relevance, and establishment of a comfortable space that affords support and choices for exploration in direct experience need to be sensitively navigated in learning spaces" (p. 45). Tisdell (2007) speaks of the "cultural imagination" in which "image, symbol, music, ritual, art, poetry, often touch off memory in conscious and unconscious ways, which sometimes connects to spirituality." Such techniques can be combined with "the intellectual and critical analysis aspects of higher education to facilitate greater student learning and greater equity in society" (p. 532).

4. Promoting spiritual learning also involves making space for it to occur. Then it is important to incorporate dialogue and discussion around topics and readings that allow for "the interpersonal connections and interchanges among people that encourage and promote their spiritual development" (English, 2000, p. 34). It might be recalled that connection with self, with others, with the earth or with a higher force is central to most definitions of spirituality. Whether face-to-face or online, classroom dialogue and discussion is but one way to build connections. Connections can also be fostered through personal contact and through listservs, e-mail, or text messaging. Also related to fostering connections is establishing a learning community, or community of practice, within the classroom. Finally, from working with Native peoples, Orr (2000) advocates "talking circles" where everyone is invited, in turn, to speak on the topic while others listen respectfully.

5. Mentoring and coaching are other instructional techniques through which spiritual learning might be fostered. Mentoring has been found to facilitate an adult's developmental journey and spiritual development may be part of that journey (Daloz, 2012). English, Fenwick, and Parsons (2003) point out that even in the corporate setting, mentoring "is not about increasing the bottom line. It is about relationship, support, and increasing the human spirit" (p. 93) and that "the spirituality of the relationship" (p. 95) is key to learning in this way.

6. Below is a list of activities for facilitating embodied and spiritual learning:

   a. Use Play-Doh, clay, or Legos to build a model to represent a concept, theory, or idea.

   b. Use silence perhaps combined with visualization exercises to help learners focus, relax, or connect with the material.

   c. Have learners draw a symbol or picture or write a song to represent something about themselves or the lesson.

   d. Take a field trip and then write, draw, and talk about what was learned.

   e. Use simulation games to illustrate complex principles, for example *The Beer Game* (http://www.beergame.lim.ethz.ch/), or cultural dynamics, *Ba Fa Ba Fa* (http://www.stsintl.com/business/bafa.html); computer-assisted simulations or games could also be used.

   f. Have small groups create embodied/active learning exercises for the whole class to illustrate a concept or model.

   g. Begin your class session with a contemplative quote, a reading, or music followed by an opportunity for silence and reflection, and class dialogue about reactions and insights.

Chapter Highlights

- Learning is a holistic process involving our body and our spirit as well as our rational mind.
- Embodied knowing is about attending to our body as a site of knowing and learning.
- Learning in and from our everyday life experiences involves our physical body and our emotional responses to these experiences.
- Spirituality in learning is about connections to others, to the world around us, to a force beyond ourselves. For some, spirituality is an avenue of meaning-making in learning.
- Spirituality in adult education has been studied in three areas—adult development, social action and social justice movements, and the workplace.
- Embodied and spiritual learning can be fostered through the use of ritual, art, poetry, cultural symbols, storytelling, music and other creative instructional techniques.

CHAPTER EIGHT

MOTIVATION AND LEARNING

You are in the midst of reading this book. Why are you doing it? What impels you to continue? This chapter is about motivation—why we do what we do. Are you reading because you just want to know more about the topic? Or are you reading in order to achieve a promotion at work or receive a good grade in a course? Take a moment and consider what motivates or demotivates you to continue reading. You may find yourself with a list of many items, for motivation is a complex, fluid phenomenon. Asking what motivates learning is an important question to contemplate both as learners and educators. Several factors affect learners' stamina to continue. How can we ensure that we are enhancing, rather than eroding, learners' enthusiasm?

While the adult learning theories discussed in Chapters 3, 4, and 5 implicitly involve motivation, this chapter is a much more thorough review of what we know about motivation and how it affects learning. This chapter will examine definitions and introduce theoretical bases of motivation showing how they apply to adult education and learning. We will explore the complexities of adult access to and participation in education. Barriers to adult participation in education will be considered and we will also review contemporary issues in motivation across diverse contexts. Finally, we will share strategies for fostering your own motivation for learning, as well as how to take motivation into consideration when planning learning activities with adults.

Motivation Defined

The word, "motivation" comes from the Latin *motivus*, meaning "a moving cause" (Ahl, 2006, p. 387). Motivation is the drive and energy we put into accomplishing something we want to do. We cannot see or touch it, but it is ever present in our thought and action. Wlodkowski (2008) suggests that motivation is basic to survival and that it means being purposeful. He describes its signs—"effort, perseverance, completion—and we listen for words: 'I want to . . . ,' 'I will . . . ,' 'You watch . . . ,' 'I'll give it my best!'" (p. 2). Motivation can also be described as educational engagement or "the time and energy students devote to educationally sound activities inside and outside the classroom, and the policies and practices that institutions use to induce students to take part in these activities" (Kuh, 2003, pp. 24–25).

Motivation can be either extrinsic or intrinsic. Extrinsic motivation usually provides a means to an end and is derived from factors outside the person, such as seeking approval or attaining credentials. External motivators might be receiving recognition from your teachers or classmates, getting a promotion, earning a certificate or diploma, and so on. Intrinsic motivation is usually an end in itself, internal to the person. Intrinsic motivation tends to be grounded in challenge, curiosity, and mastery (Pintrich, Smith, Garcia, & McKeachie, 1991). Intrinsic motivators might be learning for the love of the intellectual challenge, or desiring to achieve mastery of a topic or practice for the satisfaction it brings you.

In his bestselling book on motivation, *Drive*, Daniel Pink (2009) argues that much of what we know about motivation is wrong—making erroneous assumptions about human potential and individual performance, such as believing that short-term incentive plans or pay-for-performance schemes work. Pink argues that we are not only "extrinsically motivated profit maximizers"—essentially motivated by things like raises and approval of others, but also "intrinsically motivated purpose maximizers"—"Because for growing numbers of people, work is often creative, interesting, and self-directed rather than being unrelentingly routine, boring, and other-directed" (p. 31). Pink offers a "Twitter Summary" of his premise: "Carrots & sticks are so last century. *Drive* says for the 21st Century work, we need to upgrade autonomy, mastery & purpose" (p. 218). *Autonomy* is the yearning to direct our own lives, or in other words to control task, time, team, and technique (what we do, when we do it, whom we do it with, and how we do it). Autonomy is synonymous with self-directedness. *Mastery* is the compulsion to progress and improve around things that matter. According to Pink, "Mastery is a mindset: It requires the capacity to see your abilities not as finite, but as infinitely improvable. Mastery is a pain: It demands effort, grit and deliberate practice. And, mastery is an asymptote: It's impossible to fully realize, which makes it simultaneously frustrating and alluring" (p. 223). The third aspect of Pink's model, *purpose*, is to work for something larger than ourselves. He faults businesses with not taking the quest for purpose seriously and instead favoring profit maximization over purpose maximization. Pink argues they go hand-in-hand in what he calls a "purpose motive" that connects goals, words, and policies in ways that promote both purpose and profit maximization. The principles from *Drive* are highly aligned with adults' propensity toward self-direction, especially when it comes to learning things that are both relevant and important to the learner. Adults are also driven by generativity—the legacy they will leave for others, so this model is very appropriate to consider for adults. Although Pink's book is written for the context of work, his ideas can be transferred to education and learning situations where we can make deliberate linkages between learners' purpose and achieving learning goals.

Much of the motivation research is conducted on traditional age undergraduate students (18–22 years old) engaged in formal education, although nontraditional students are increasing with those over age 25 becoming the fastest growing group of undergraduates in North America (Bye, Pushkar, & Conway, 2007). Bye, Pushkar, and Conway surveyed 300 traditional and nontraditional undergraduates aged 18 to 60 on measures of intrinsic and extrinsic motivation to learn. Not surprisingly, nontraditional students reported higher intrinsic learning motivation. Given adults' interest in learning what is relevant and timely to their lives, it seems fitting that there would be a stronger internal drive to learn. Bye, Pushkar, and Conway advocate balancing intrinsic and extrinsic learning motivators when teaching. They also suggest validating nontraditional students as active partners in a shared learning experience to increase intrinsic motivation and positive affect. They suggest that unnecessary criticisms or directives should be avoided as they have counterproductive effects on motivation. They also advocate for humor, respect, and social support to nurture learning.

Motivation Theory

You have probably studied motivation theory in a psychology course. These same theories apply to learning. Ahl (2006) provides a thorough overview of classical motivation theories as depicted in Table 8.1.

TABLE 8.1 CLASSICAL MOTIVATION THEORIES

Humans as	Are motivated by
Economic/rational	Rewards and punishments
Social	Social norms, groups
Responsive to stimuli (behaviorism)	Stimuli and/or rewards
Need-driven	Inner needs
Cognitive	Cognitive maps

Source: Adapted from Ahl, 2006, p. 387.

Economic or rational motivation theory is traceable to Adam Smith's *The Wealth of Nations* (1776/2000). Economic motivation theory views humans as rational actors who seek to maximize self-interest and outcomes yielding the highest economic returns. Economic motivation theory is best known through Frederic Taylor's *The Principles of Scientific Management* (1911). Scientific management became popular during the Industrial Revolution and is visible in work and reward systems that are designed to maximize productivity through specialization and piecemeal work. Educationally, economic motivation might mean you select a college major that promises a good income (business) rather than something you are more interested and passionate about (art). You might enroll in a training seminar that gives you better chances of a promotion at work, or you might be motivated to get good grades to avoid the consequences of not doing so. Economic or rational motivation is also extrinsically oriented.

Social or human motivation theory emerged as a reaction to scientific management through the work of Elton Mayo (1933) and the Hawthorne Studies. Mayo and his collaborators concluded that factors other than pay and physical working conditions, such as social and emotional aspects of working in well-functioning groups, affected work motivation. Their work challenged the economic model that assumed workers rationally sought profit maximization and instead argued that workers were social beings motivated by relationships. The Human Relations School emerged out of these discoveries and served as a precursor to the rise of Human Resource and Organization Development. The influence of social motivation theory in education is evident in the humanist philosophy that underlies several adult learning models and theories such as andragogy, self-directed learning, and social learning.

Behavioristic motivation theory, popularized by Pavlov, Thorndike, and Skinner, assumed that behavior and learning were based on providing a stimulus to provoke a desired response. The learner would then be conditioned through punishments and rewards. Learning occurs when appropriate stimuli are presented and the learner is subsequently rewarded for exhibiting the desired behavior. These views were dominant through the 1960s (Ahl, 2006), and still influence many education and training programs.

Need-driven motivational theories grew out of Abraham Maslow's hierarchy of needs (1954). Maslow contended that although humans are partially motivated by external factors, innate, intrinsic human needs are the main drivers of human behavior. He created the hierarchy of needs with the lowest needs being physiological ones such as safety and sustenance. Higher order needs include belonging, recognition, cognitive, and aesthetic, with the highest order needs having to do with self-actualization. Humanistic educational philosophy and practice falls under this theory that assumes learners would not be motivated by things that already satisfy basic needs and requirements, but rather by the higher order needs. In other words, you probably would have little interest or motivation in a course on financing your first home if you have already done so (safety needs), but would be more enthusiastic about a course on how to improve your landscaping (aesthetic). Humanism has had a major influence in adult education through models and practices such as andragogy, self-directed learning, and learner-centered teaching.

Cognitive motivation theory is concerned with our thoughts and how they influence our actions. These models assume that there is not one unequivocal reality that affects our thought and action, but perceptions of reality that vary between individuals. Kurt Lewin (1935) and Victor Vroom (1964/1995) were early theorists in this area. These theories dominate motivation research today. According to this theory, a reward for learning will have different meanings and importance from person to person. History is also a key factor in that how you conceive of reality today depends on how you thought of it yesterday and how you will interpret it tomorrow. We might also liken this perspective to critical and postmodern understandings of learning that regard knowledge as fluid, changing, and dependent on the learner.

Classical motivation theory provides insight into adult motivation to learn, and how it affects adults' access to and participation in learning activities. It also serves as a historical glimpse into how the field of adult education has evolved from more rational models that assumed external motivation was the impetus to learn, to social models that explain how group dynamics and relationships influence motivation and learning. Next came behavioristic explanations of motivation that are interested in providing the best stimuli to provoke a learning response, to the more humanistic or need-driven models that undergird much of adult education practice today, to more cognitive understandings of motivation and that how adults create and interpret knowledge differs. Behaviorism, Humanism, and Cognitivism have been particularly influential in the development of adult learning theory and practice and are discussed in more detail in Chapter 2. Now that we have a foundation in motivation, we will turn our attention to how it plays out with adults in educational endeavors.

Motivation in Adult Education

The literature discussing adult motivation to learn is diverse, drawing on psychology, educational psychology, anthropology, and sociology (Schlesinger, 2005). Exploration of motivation in adult learning was initiated by Houle's 1961 publication of *The Inquiring Mind*, around the same time need-driven and cognitive motivation theories were gaining popularity. Houle's book reported an in-depth study of 22 adults engaged in continuous learning. He interviewed adults about their learning experiences and self-perceptions of themselves as learners. He identified three types of learning orientations in his analysis. *Goal-oriented learners* engage in learning as a means to attaining another goal. Goal-oriented learning tends to be extrinsic and economically motivated. For instance a person might attend a training program to become competitive for a promotion or learn woodworking to start a cabinet-making business. *Activity-oriented learners* participate for the opportunity to socialize with other learners and for the sake of the activity. A person might attend a photography class to meet new people and engage in conversation, or join a book club to meet new friends with similar interests. Activity-oriented learning might be extrinsically or intrinsically motivated and driven by social and need-driven motivation. Finally, *learning-oriented learners* are focused on developing new knowledge for the sake of learning. For example, a person might devour everything available on the U.S. Civil War based on a love of the subject. Learning-oriented learners are likely intrinsically and cognitively motivated. Motivation is fluid and our motivations toward learning activities can include multiple goals or change. Suppose you take a watercolor painting class for the joy of learning it, then discover you are good at it and start a business selling your paintings. A primary "learning" motivation becomes also "goal-oriented."

Boshier (1991), building on the work of Houle, developed the most extensive instrument to measure adult motivation to learn with his Education Participation Scale (EPS). It measures factors related to adult engagement in learning. These factors can be accounted for by several general motivation theories as noted in the listing in Table 8.2. Boshier and Collins (1985) also tested Houle's original typology (goal, social, and learning orientations) by analyzing responses from 13,442 learners from Africa, Asia, New Zealand, Canada, and the United States. They reported results similar to Houle's.

Dia, Smith, Cohen-Callow, and Bliss (2005) evaluated the Boshier and Collins measurement model and theory underlying the Educational Participation Scale-Modified (EPS-M). They surveyed 225 licensed social workers in Maryland and found the EPS-M to be a valid and reliable measure for identifying motivational orientations of social workers that pursue continuing professional education. Participants most often cited professional knowledge as their primary motivator that is consistent with interest and participation in work-related learning among other occupational groups.

Motivation theory helps us understand what drives people to pursue activities such as learning. What it does not account for are the many vari-

TABLE 8.2 COMPARISON OF BOSHIER'S ADULT LEARNING MOTIVATIONAL FACTORS WITH CLASSICAL MOTIVATION THEORY

Boshier's Factor	Example	Links with Classical Motivation Theory
1. Communication improvement of verbal and written skills	ESL course Writing workshop Toastmasters	Economic/rational Behaviorism Cognitive
2. Social contact	Meeting people Making friends Continuing education	Social Need-driven
3. Educational preparation and remediation of past educational deficiencies	GED education GRE test preparation	Economic/rational Behaviorism Need-driven Cognitive
4. Professional advancement	Promotion New career opportunities	Economic/rational Need-driven
5. Family togetherness	Relationships across generations	Social Need-driven
6. Social stimulation	Escaping boredom	Social Need-driven
7. Cognitive interest	Learning for the sake of learning	Cognitive

ables that affect access to and participation in education. For instance, you might be economically motivated to attend learning that improves your job prospects but cannot attend due to financial or family constraints. Motivation is not always enough if other variables prevent us from pursuing education. McClusky's Theory of Margin, a lesser-known theory of adult learning, illustrates the complex dynamics adults face when attempting to learn.

McClusky's Theory of Margin

McClusky (1963) believed that humans had unlimited potential during their lifetime and viewed adulthood as a dynamic process of continuous development, change, and challenge requiring energy and resources for addressing daily life. His major contribution to adult education was the 1963 Theory of Margin, also known as the power-load-margin (PLM) formula. The formula, which is a conceptual model, addresses motivation as a measure of how many resources (power) the learner has to offset the demands (load) that potentially diminish motivation for learning. He defined the theory as "Margin is a function of the relationship of load to power. By load we mean the self and social demands required by a person to maintain a minimal level of autonomy. By power we mean the resources, i.e., abilities, possessions, position, allies, etc., which a person can command in coping with load" (McClusky, 1970, p. 27). McClusky posited that adults need enough margin to handle life's load of challenges, changes, and crises. Low margin might indicate that the adult is under undue stress or illness. Excess margin might indicate a life that has too little load where the adult is not fulfilling her potential (Stevenson, 1982). Although McClusky never developed an instrument to study his formula, Stevenson constructed an instrument for her research in nursing and identified six key areas for measuring margin including self, family, religiosity/spirituality, body, extrafamilial relationships, and environment.

Load and power are affected by the interacting internal and external variables such as those depicted in Table 8.3 (Baum, 1978; Main, 1979). *Load* might be family commitments, occupational responsibilities, or goals. *Power* is the ability to deal with the load, such as economic wealth, physical health, social contacts, or coping skills. *Margin* is the dynamic relationship between load and power. Margin "is surplus power or power available to a person over and beyond that required to handle . . . load . . . Margin is essential to the mental hygiene of the adult . . . *A margin allows a person to invest in life expansion projects and experiences including learning experiences*"

TABLE 8.3 LOAD AND POWER

Load—Self and Societal Demands on Learner	Power—Learner's Resources to Cope with Load
External motivators • Family commitments • Occupational responsibilities • Social obligations • Civic duties	External resources and capacity • Physical health • Economic wealth • Social abilities • Social contacts
Internal, personal motivators • Expectations of self • Ideals • Goals • Values • Attitudes	Internal skills and experiences • Resiliency • Coping skills • Personality

(Main, 1979, p. 23, italics in original). An adult will be more motivated to learn by maintaining a power surplus and less motivated with a load surplus (Infed, n. d.)

Main (1979) offered illustrations of the PLO Formula in an *Adult Education Quarterly* article to clarify the principles of the model. Here are some examples based on his work:

$$\frac{2(\text{Power})}{4(\text{Load})} = 0.5(\text{Margin}) \quad \frac{\text{Deficit of Power to Handle Load}}{\text{Crisis of Excess Load Pressures}}$$

$$\frac{7(\text{Load})}{7(\text{Power})} = 1.0(\text{Margin}) \quad \frac{\text{Breaking Even}}{\text{Barely Holding On}}$$

$$\frac{4(\text{Power})}{2(\text{Load})} = 2.0(\text{Margin}) \quad \frac{\text{Surplus of Power to Handle Load}}{\text{Space to Maneuver}}$$

Adults can carry a high load, presuming they have comparable power resources to handle it. For example, many adults continue their higher education while holding down full-time jobs, managing households, juggling children's needs and activities, and participating in their communities. To successfully manage this level of load requires power such as a supportive spouse, internal drive, physical health and stamina, economic stability, and a supportive work environment. The load would be very different for a single parent who is working two jobs with little familial or workplace support to continue her education. In this scenario, the load would likely exceed power making perseverance and success at higher education more difficult. McClusky (1971) also identified barriers to learning related to adult life stages including: the unexpected loss of margin (job loss, relocation, illness, loss of spouse), time allocation (finding scarce time to engage in learning), resistance to learning (time pressures, personality, unwillingness to admit need for change, fear of risk, inability to reorder life commitments), viewing the self as a "non-learner," and declining sense of discovery.

McClusky's Theory of Margin is also relevant in teaching. Hiemstra and Sisco (1990) point out that instructors can unknowingly create surplus "load" for learners by assuming a traditional, authoritarian stance and not respecting learners' opinions or experience. Other instructor behaviors that contribute to learner load might be disorganization, distracting mannerisms, inappropriate assignments, or unclear evaluation guidelines. They suggest that it is imperative for instructors to carefully craft the learning environment to avoid creating additional load for learners. Clearly, following good adult education practice that honors and respects the learner is important for giving learners more power to engage in educational activities.

The relationship between an individual's margin in life (MIL) and their readiness for change (RFC) across four organizations was studied by Masden, John, Miller, and Warren (2004). Using a scale to assess MIL, their survey of 464 employees found "that employees who have higher MIL levels (meaning they feel more energy, strength, joy, and power from their work and nonwork lives and environments) may be more open and ready for changes the organization may require of them. Furthermore, employees who feel good and are not burdened down by various work (job in general, job demands, relationship with boss, workplace social support, job knowledge and skills, and commitment to the organization) and possibly nonwork (family, balancing work and family, physical and mental health) appear to be ready to make the changes that may be needed by the organization" (p. 765). They suggested certain interventions that might help employees in dealing with both MIL and RFC such as supporting employees' life balance needs with flextime, child-care assistance, and job sharing. They also recommend offering wellness programs, improving management-employee communications, providing development to augment job knowledge and skills, and programming to enhance employee commitment.

Now that we have considered how margin affects learning, take a moment to figure out your margin by creating your own formula. Write down the elements making up your "load" on a scale of 1–5 and then the elements of your "power," also on a scale of 1–5, to counter it. What is your margin? What does it say about your motivation toward reading this book? Learning? We will now consider how motivation affects adult learning environments.

Wlodkowski's Integrated Levels of Adult Motivation

Wlodkowski (2008) offers two critical assumptions of learning and motivation: "If something can be learned, it can be learned in a motivating manner . . . every instructional plan also needs to be a motivational plan" (pp. 46–47, italics in original). In his view, instructors who motivate learners exhibit expertise, enthusiasm, clarity, and cultural responsiveness. Wlodkowski (2008) presents the most comprehensive exploration of motivation in his book *Enhancing Adult Motivation to Learn.* He suggests that the value of his framework is that it provides both a model of motivation and an aid for instructional design. He cites four intersecting motivational conditions that are essential to attend to when teaching adults and being culturally responsive including: establishing inclusion, developing attitude, enhancing meaning, and engendering confidence.

The first condition, establishing inclusion, involves creating an atmosphere that promotes a learning community so that everyone feels respected and connected. Wlodkowski (2008) suggests that this is best accomplished at the beginning of the lesson. Fostering connection and respect "invites adults to access their experience, to reflect, to engage in dialogue, and to allow their histories to give meaning to particular academic or professional knowledge—all of which enhance motivation to learn" (Wlodkowski, 2008, p. 103). One strategy for establishing inclusion is introducing yourself and the learners. This important activity builds rapport, trust, and care, not to mention lowers anxiety at the beginning of a lesson. Making introductions and building connections is time well spent as it facilitates learning for the duration of the class or semester. Another inclusion strategy is building in opportunities for multidimensional sharing such as introductory exercises, personal anecdotes, potlucks, or other activities both inside and outside the classroom. Wlodkowoski advocates any activity that gets the learners laughing and learning each other's names. The next strategy is for you, as the instructor, to announce your "cooperative intention to help" (p. 138) the learners learn. Wlodkowski advocates taking the fear out of learning for learners by being available through office hours, during breaks, or at other times to partner with learners in ways that make it okay for them to ask for help.

Another strategy is to share something of value with your adult learners such as self-deprecating humor or credible intense experiences such as teaching failures, mistakes, or difficult learning experiences related to the teaching topic. Other important ways of sharing are giving learners individualized attention and being willing to share something personal about ourselves such as favorite television programs, sporting events, travel, or other life anecdotes. Wlodkowski offers several pedagogical strategies that help promote learner inclusion, including: using collaborative and cooperative learning; clearly communicating learning goals and objectives, and connecting what is being learned to the learners' personal lives and experience; conducting a needs analysis to ensure course relevance for learners; establishing course ground rules; providing solid rationale when giving mandatory assignments; and acknowledging different ways of knowing and being in the classroom.

The second condition of the motivation framework, also recommended for attention at the start of the lesson, is developing an attitude of favorability toward the learning by helping learners see its relevance to their experience. A key element of promoting favorable learning attitudes involves eradicating learner anxieties toward failure, public humiliation, disrespectful interpersonal dynamics, or inadequate feedback (Wlodkowski, 2008). Promoting positive learner attitudes is facilitated by providing physically and psychologically positive conditions in the classroom, presenting lessons at a reasonable pace, providing ample notice on assignments and tests (in other words, no pop quizzes), and creating a safe learning environment that is free from humiliation or shame when students do not know the answer or are unfamiliar with the subject. Wlodkowski advocates that instructors positively confront any erroneous beliefs, expectations, or assumptions feeding negative learner attitudes. He also offers a pedagogy supportive of positive attitudes which includes diversifying instruction to promote learning, providing very clear expectations and evaluation criteria, scaffolding complex learning tasks, giving learners control over their learning, using learning contracts, and helping them own accountability for their learning successes.

The third motivational condition is enhancing meaning through creating challenging and engaging experiences that value the learners' viewpoints and values. Wlodkowski (2008) asks, "What do we need to do to gain learner attention?" (p. 227). Meaning may involve making connections cognitively between previous and new knowledge, or it may connect experiences with our values and purposes. "Though adults may feel included and have a positive attitude, their involvement will diminish if they cannot find learning meaningful. By making the learners' goals, interests, and cultural perspectives the context of challenging and engaging learning experiences, instructors can secure their continuing participation" (p. 109). Wlodkowski recommends addressing this condition throughout the lesson with strategies such as providing frequent opportunities for learners to respond to the content through Q&A, sharing opinions, reflecting on practice, solving problems, demonstrating concepts, reviewing research, role playing, simulating the learning issue, engaging in service learning, studying cases, and reacting to feedback. Keeping learning active and inventive is a key focus of Wlodkowski's recommendations in this area. It is also a good idea to vary your presentation style, type of instruction, and the learning materials when engaging learner attention. Learners must also see how the learning relates to their own individual interests and values.

The fourth motivational condition is engendering confidence by helping learners see that they have been successful at their learning, whether according to their own standards or social standards. This condition is best addressed throughout the lesson and at the end. Key ways of promoting learner self-efficacy in this condition are through providing timely feedback that avoids cultural bias, and making assessment tasks and criteria explicit to learners prior to completing assignments. Assignments and activities should also be carefully selected to ensure they are authentic—that is as close to real life context as possible. Authentic assessment, according to Wlodkowski (2008) is realistic, requires judgment and innovation, asks the learner to "do" the subject rather than regurgitate it, replicates or simulates real context, and assesses the learners' ability to integrate and synthesize knowledge. It is also important to include opportunities for learners to self-assess their progress and to provide a positive closure experience at the end of the learning episode.

Wlodkowski (2008) not only lays out a comprehensive framework for motivating adult learners, but also includes multiple strategies for doing so. He recommends that instructors conduct a self-assessment for applying the motivational framework by reflecting on the following issues: "(1) your perception of your role as instructor; (2) your assumptions about the motivation of the adults you teach or train; and (3) your perceptions of your instructional situation" (pp. 379–380). His strategies are summarized in Table 8.4.

TABLE 8.4 INSTRUCTIONAL ACTIVITIES: WLODKOWSKI'S SUMMARY OF MOTIVATIONAL STRATEGIES

Major Motivational Condition	Motivational Purpose	Motivational Strategy
Inclusion (beginning learning activities)	To engender an awareness and feeling of connection among adults	1. Allow for introductions. 2. Provide an opportunity for multidimensional sharing. 3. Concretely indicate your cooperative intentions to help adults learn. 4. Share something of value with your adult learners. 5. Use collaborative and cooperative learning.
	To create a climate of respect among adults	6. Clearly identify the learning objectives and goals for instruction. 7. Emphasize the human purpose of what is being learned and its relationship to the learners' personal lives and current situations. 8. Assess learners' current expectations, needs, goals, and previous experience as it relates to your course or training. 9. Explicitly introduce important norms and participation guidelines. 10. When issuing mandatory assignments or training requirements, give your rationale for them. 11. Acknowledge different ways of knowing, different languages, and different levels of knowledge or skill among learners.
Attitude (beginning learning activities)	To build a positive attitude toward the subject	12. Eliminate or minimize any negative conditions that surround the subject. 13. Positively confront the erroneous beliefs, expectations, and assumptions that may underlie a negative learner attitude.
	To develop self-efficacy for learning	14. Use differentiated instruction to enhance successful learning of new content. 15. Use assisted learning to scaffold complex learning. 16. Promote learners' personal control of learning. 17. Help learners effectively attribute their success to their capability, effort, and knowledge. 18. Help learners understand that reasonable effort and knowledge can help them avoid failure at learning tasks that suit their capability.
	To establish challenging and attainable learning goals	19. Use relevant models to demonstrate expected learning. 20. Encourage the learners. 21. Make the criteria of assessment as fair and clear as possible. 22. Help learners understand and plan for the amount of time needed for successful learning. 23. Use goal-setting methods. 24. Use learning contracts.
	To create relevant learning experiences	25. Use the entry points suggested by multiple intelligences theory as ways of learning about a topic or concept. 26. Make the learning activity an irresistible invitation to learn. 27. Use the K-W-L strategy to introduce new topics and concepts (Learners Identify what they KNOW, what they WANT TO KNOW, and what they have LEARNED).

(Continued)

TABLE 8.4 (Continued)

Major Motivational Condition	Motivational Purpose	Motivational Strategy
Meaning (during learning activities)	To maintain learners' attention	28. Provide frequent response opportunities to all learners on an equitable basis.
		29. Help learners realize their accountability for what they are learning.
	To evoke and sustain learners' interest	30. Provide variety in personal presentation style, modes of instruction, and learning materials.
		31. Introduce, connect, and end learning activities attractively and clearly.
		32. Selectively use breaks, settling time, and physical exercises.
	To deepen learners engagement and challenge	33. Relate learning to individual interests, concerns, and values.
		34. When possible, clearly state or demonstrate the benefits that will result from the learning activity.
		35. While instructing, use humor liberally and frequently.
		36. Selectively induce parapathic emotions.
	To enhance learners' engagement, challenge, and adaptive decision making	37. Selectively use examples, analogies, metaphors and stories.
		38. Use uncertainty, anticipation, and prediction to the degree that learners enjoy them with a sense of security.
		39. Use concept maps to develop and link interesting ideas and information.
		40. Use critical questions to stimulate engaging and challenging reflection and discussion.
		41. Use relevant problems, research, and inquiry to facilitate learning.
		42. Use intriguing problems and questions to make initially irrelevant material more meaningful.
		43. Use case study methods to enhance meaning.
		44. Use role playing to embody meaning and new learning within a more realistic and dynamic context.
		45. Use simulations and games to embody the learning of multiple concepts and skills that require a real-life context and practice to be learned.
		46. Use visits, internships, and service learning to raise awareness, provide practice, and embody the learning of concepts and skills in authentic settings.
		47. Use invention, artistry, imagination, and enactment to render deeper meaning and emotion in learning.

Competence (ending activities)	To engender competence with assessment	48. Provide effective feedback.
		49. Avoid cultural bias and promote equity in assessment procedures.
		50. Make assessment tasks and criteria clearly known to learners prior to their use.
		51. Use authentic performance tasks to deepen new learning and help learners proficiently apply this learning to their real lives.
		52. Provide opportunities for adults to demonstrate their learning in ways that reflect their strengths and multiple sources of learning.
		53. When using rubrics, make sure they assess the essential features of performance and are fair, valid, and sufficiently clear so that learners can accurately self-assess.
		54. Use self-assessment methods to improve learning and to provide learners with the opportunity to construct relevant insights and connections.
	To engender competence with transfer	55. Foster the intention and capacity to transfer learning.
		56. When necessary, use constructive criticism.
	To engender competence with communications and rewards	57. Effectively praise and reward learning.
		58. Use incentives to develop and maintain adult motivation in learning activities that are initially unappealing but personally valued.
		59. When learning has natural consequences, help learners to be aware of them and their impact.
		60. Provide positive closure at the end of significant units of learning.

Source: Adapted from Wlodklowski, R. J. (2008). *Enhancing adult motivation to learn: A comprehensive guide for teaching all adults* (3rd ed.). San Francisco: Jossey-Bass, pp. 382–385.

Ahl (2006) challenges the assumption that motivation is a phenomenon existing only within the individual learner because it suggests a deficit. Ahl takes issue with the notion that adult learners must be recruited and kept, thus assuming that they are neither easily recruited nor retained. She contends that adult learners do not have motivational problems, but rather that the problem lies in the relationship between the learner and those providing learning opportunities who have their own motives. Through the motivation discourse, Ahl argues that we have created "the unwilling adult learners [who] are both the reasons for and the solutions to societal problems, while those who formulate the problems, and the basis for the formulation of the problem remain invisible. They are made invisible because they represent normality, the ideology in power, and knowledge that is always taken for granted" (p. 401). Her critical assessment of adult learning motivation literature shows how motivation theory stigmatizes people we regard as "unmotivated" because motivation problems are only attributed to the individual. Ahl argues that motivation should be reconceptualized as a relational phenomenon that is not just situated within the individual. She urges that "instead of asking what motivates adults to study, research should focus on *who states that this is a problem, and why, and the reasons for this conclusion*" (italics in original, p. 385). She suggests that her approach would reveal power relations and show how the discourse of lifelong learning constructs adults as inadequate. She also notes that the majority of motivational recommendations in the adult education literature are pedagogical, putting much confidence in educators to counteract the many variables that can affect motivation to learn that have little to do with teaching. Ahl offers us an important counternarrative to the dominant discourse about unmotivated learners. Presumably, she would not agree with Wlodkowski's approach (2008) given its reliance on pedagogy and teacher behaviors as the keys to unlocking learner motivation.

Chapter Summary

Adult motivation to learn is affected by many variables and contexts. It is important to take a holistic view that considers the learner and her personal context; the social context that incorporates other learners, instructors, and the macro dynamics in society; and how these variables intersect to influence the context of learning. The next section focuses on how to apply the ideas presented in this chapter.

Linking Theory and Practice: Activities and Resources

1. *Use Wlodkowski's Summary of Motivational Strategies to Design Instruction.* Take a course you regularly teach and evaluate it for motivational elements against Table 8.4. Revise your course to include strategies for each of the four major motivational conditions listed in the summary.

2. *Apply Strategies from the Motivation Book Drive.* Pink (2009) offers several suggestions for both individuals and organizations to sustain motivation in his book *Drive.* Here are some particularly relevant to learning and mastering new knowledge and skill:

   a. *Give Yourself a "Flow" Test.* Based on the creativity work of Csikszentmihalyi (1990), set an alarm or reminder on your computer or smart phone to go off randomly 40 times during the week. Each time the alarm rings, write down what you are doing, how you are feeling, and whether you are in "flow," a state of consciousness where you experience deep enjoyment, creativity, and a complete engagement with what you are doing. Record your observations and see if you can decipher patterns. At the end of the week, consider the following questions:

      i. Which moments produced a feeling of "flow"? Where were you? What were you doing? Who were you with?

      ii. Do you have certain times of day that are more "flow-friendly" that others? How might you restructure your time based on your findings?

      iii. How might you increase the number of opportunities to be in "flow"?

      iv. What insights has this exercise given you about your work, studies, or other activities?

      v. What does this exercise tell you about your true source of motivation? (adapted from Pink, 2009, pp. 153–154).

   b. *Just Say No—With a List.* We all have to-do lists. Pink recommends following management guru Tom Peter's advice and create a "to-don't" list—an inventory of behaviors and activities that drain your energy and distract your focus. In essence you should create an agenda of avoidance to keep you away from the things that are draining your motivational energy. "To-don'ts" might be ending unimportant or unnecessary obligations or eliminating time wasting distractions such as meetings or email. Pink cites Peters, noting,

"What you decide *not* to do is probably more important than what you decide to do" (p. 158).

   c. *Get Unstuck by Going Oblique.* Pink offers this as a fun way to curb a creativity drought or writer's block. You can create your own index cards with a question or statement to jolt you out of your mental rut such as "What would your closest friend do? Your mistake was a hidden intention. What is the simplest solution? Repetition is a form of change. Don't avoid what is easy" (p. 157). You can purchase a deck of these cards at http://www.enoshop.co.uk/product/oblique-strategies or follow a Twitter accounts that touts the strategies at http://twitter.com/oblique_chirps.

3. Reflect on some of Pink's (2009) "Questions About Motivation":

   a. As you think about your best work, what is most important to you? Autonomy over what you do (task), when you do it (time), how you do it (technique), or with whom you do it (team)? Why? How much autonomy do you have in your learning or teaching right now? Is that enough?

   b. Does education today put too much emphasis on extrinsic rewards? What is the best way to build more intrinsic motivation into the accountability equation?

   c. What really motivates you? Make a list. Now, jot down how you spent your time last week. How many of those 168 hours were devoted to those things? How might you do better?

4. *ARCS Model of Motivational Design.* Keller's ARCS model (1983) of motivational design of instruction notes four components of motivation: Attention, Relevance, Confidence, and Satisfaction. This model posits that instruction will be more motivating if it captures student *attention* (task engagement), includes content and activities that learners perceive as *relevant*, increases learner self-*confidence* and sense of self-efficacy, and results in *satisfaction* in what was learned. Reflect on or discuss how you can incorporate these four components into adult learning and instruction. See http://www.arcsmodel.com/Mot%20 dsgn.htm for more information.

5. *Self-Directed Project Reflection and Dialogue.* Ask learners to consider their own self-directed learning projects. What sustained them in these learning endeavors? What understandings of their own motivation can they conclude from these projects? How would they describe their motivational ups and downs? What type of barriers did they encounter to sustaining learning?

6. *Learning Memos.* Laura uses a weekly "learning memo" that is sent electronically to students to help keep them motivated and on track with their readings and assignments. The major headings are: updates, what to read, what to do online, what to turn in, and just for fun—a section profiling interesting websites, articles and links. Develop some type of regular communication to share with your learners. This becomes even more important for motivating online learners.

7. *Class Evaluation.* Analyze a class or learning module to determine what was (and was not) motivating about it. Discuss.

8. *Dialogue Topics.* Facilitate a dialogue around this topic: "How do you create a motivational atmosphere in your classes? Online environments?" or "What makes you feel least/most motivated as a learner?

9. *Calculating Margin.* Have learners use McClusky's Power-Load-Margin formula to assess how their personal circumstances are affecting their motivation as described in the chapter.

10. *Reflective Practice.* You can use this exercise to either reflect on your teaching or learning. What steps can you take to understand and enhance your own motivation to learn? First, determine what motivates you:
    - What are key extrinsic motivators?
    - What are key intrinsic motivators?
    - What type of learning orientation or combinations of orientations would you have according to the Houle Typology (Goal, Social, or Learning Orientation)?
    - Take Boshier's Education Participation Scale to see which of the seven factors and their corresponding motivation theory pertain to your learning.

    Next, reflect on your own learning in courses and workshops. Recall your teachers. Which ones made you feel passionate and excited about learning? What did they do? What can you infer about your own learning motivation based on this experience? How do you emulate past motivating teachers in your own practice?

11. *Resources and Web Links:*
    a. "Dan Pink on the Amazing Science of Motivation." This TED Talk discusses motivation by a well-known popular press author. http://www.ted.com/talks/lang/en/dan_pink_on_motivation.html
    b. "Tony Robbins Asks Why We Do What We Do?" A TED talk on what motivates our actions. http://www.ted.com/talks/tony_robbins_asks_why_we_do_what_we_do.html

   c. MindTools: Self-Motivation Quiz—an inventory to assess your motivation. http://www.mindtools.com/pages/article/newLDR_57.htm

   d. For a comprehensive literature review of McClusky's Theory of Margin and copy of Stevenson's Margin-in-Life Scale, see: Walker, B. H. (1997). *Margin-in-Life Scale: A predictor of persistence for nontraditional students in higher education.* An unpublished dissertation. University of Georgia.

   e. Free Motivation Newsletter: *Motivation Times* http://www.true-motivation.com/motivational-times.html

   f. *Professional Learning to Promote Motivation and Academic Performance Among Diverse Adults* (Ginsberg & Wlodkowski, 2010) http://raymondwlodkowski.com/Materials/ProfessionalLearning.pdf

   g. National Center for Educational Statistics (NCES). You can find a wealth of reports and statistics on learning in the United States. Search under "adult" for reports relevant to our field. http://nces.ed.gov/

   h. NCES Adult Participation Data. Specific data on adult participation and links to multiple reports. http://nces.ed.gov/programs/coe/indicator_aed.asp

   i. National Household Education Surveys, 2001: Participation in Adult Education and Lifelong Learning. http://nces.ed.gov/pubs2004/2004050.pdf

Chapter Highlights

- Motivation is the drive and energy we put into accomplishing something we want to do. We cannot see or touch it, but it is ever present in our thought and action.
- Motivation can be either extrinsic or intrinsic.
- Houle identified three types of learning orientations in his analysis. *Goal-oriented learners* engage in learning as a means to attaining another goal. *Activity-oriented learners* participate for the opportunity to socialize with other learners and for the sake of the activity. *Learning-oriented learners* are focused on developing new knowledge for the sake of learning.
- McClusky's Theory of Margin posits that motivation to learn is a function of how adults are able to balance the load of life by offsetting it with power or resources, a ratio known as Margin in Life.

- Wlodkowski (2008) offers two critical assumptions of learning and motivation: *"if something can be learned, it can be learned in a motivating manner . . . every instructional plan also needs to be a motivational plan"* (pp. 46–47, italics in original).
- At least three key contexts affect adult motivation to participate in education: personal, societal, and learning.

CHAPTER NINE

THE BRAIN AND COGNITIVE FUNCTIONING

At the age of 37, brain scientist Jill Taylor had a massive stroke that left her unable to walk, talk, read, or write. In her book, *My Stroke of Insight* (2009), Taylor writes of the morning of her stroke, "*Wow, how many scientists have the opportunity to study their own brain function and mental deterioration from the inside out?*" (p. 44, italics in original). It took her eight years but she retaught her brain and today she is living a normal life and once again conducting research on the human brain. Her book is a testimony to "the beauty and resiliency of our human brain because of its innate ability to constantly adapt to change and recover function" (p. xv). Indeed, our brain is an amazing organ in our body, one that changes as we learn. In this chapter we begin with a short overview of how the brain works, then we go on to discuss several dimensions of cognitive functioning including memory, intelligence, cognitive development, and wisdom—all with an eye to how our learning maximizes each of these functions.

Brain Basics

The brain, which is attached to the spinal cord, can be thought of as the control center of the human organism. This control center is constantly monitoring all functions within our bodies such as heart rate and breathing, in addition to what is going on immediately around the body. This outside data comes into the body through our senses—seeing, hearing, touching, tasting, and smelling. The brain continually processes all this data, making adjustments as necessary to keep the human organism out of danger and responding appropriately to incoming data. Over the years scientists have mapped the brain, identifying which part does what. We will now look at two of these maps—the three-part triune brain, and the two-part hemispheric brain.

Figure 9.1 shows a cross section of the triune brain with the three areas, each having a different function in the processing of information. At the base of the skull closest to the spinal cord is what most people know as the "reptilian brain," labeled as such because it is the oldest, most primitive part of the brain and is found in reptiles, birds and mammals. This innermost part of the brain reacts instinctively—the so-called "fight or flight" response to perceived danger. It also is engaged in insuring survival through urging humans to feed and mate.

The second part of the triune brain, the limbic system that wraps around the reptilian brain, developed while mammals evolved from reptiles. The limbic system takes in sensory data and converts these data into units that are then processed in the neocortex. Interestingly, it is in the limbic system that "the emotional content of experience is processed *before* meaning is processed . . . The limbic system controls the individual's basic value system, enhances or suppresses the short-term memory . . . [and] determines how the brain will respond to all information received" (Mackeracher, 2004,

FIGURE 9.1 THE TRIUNE BRAIN

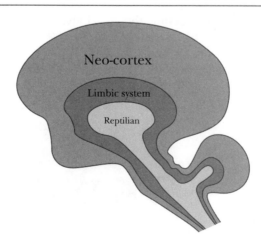

p. 96; italics added). For example, "if the experience that originally created the memory was associated with positive feelings (happiness or pleasure), then the response to the new experience will also be positive"(p. 96). Although "we may think of ourselves as *thinking creatures that feel,* biologically we are *feeling creatures that think*" explains a lot of what we know about adult learning (Taylor, 2009, p. 17, italics in original). When presented with a learning experience that rouses a previously threatening or painful memory, this new experience will be avoided or, at best, seen as negative. Likewise, a learning event that connects with a memory of a positive learning experience will be embraced and seen as positive.

The neocortex is the third part of the brain and is distinct to primates and humans. It extends over the top of our brain and covers the limbic system. If we had to locate the "mind," the neocortex would be the closest candidate! All learning occurs in the neocortex: "It reasons, plans, worries, writes poems, makes lists, invents engines, paints pictures, and programs computers. Its products are foresight, hindsight, and insight . . . It co-ordinates our relationships with the outside world through its centres for vision, hearing, taste, smell, bodily sensations, and motor responses" (Mackeracher, 2004, p. 97). While the neocortex is essentially the "control tower" of human thinking and activity, "it is dependent on the lower levels of the brain to pass on information, yield control over various activities, and keep the entire system activated" (p. 97).

The hemispheric brain with its left and right hemispheres, offers another map to help us understand how the brain works. Try putting your thumbs next to each other, side by side, fingernails pointing up; then fold your hands into fists. What you have formed is the dual hemisphere model of the brain with the corpus callosum, a nerve fiber (that is, where your thumbs are), connecting the two halves (see Figure 9.2). Research in

FIGURE 9.2 THE HEMISPHERIC BRAIN

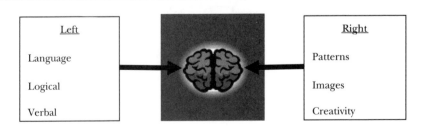

which this bridge between the two hemispheres has been disconnected has revealed that each half has distinctively different mental functions. The left hemisphere controls the right side of the body and is verbal, linguistic, analytical, and sequential. People like Jill Taylor whose stroke occurs in the left hemisphere, have their language and analytical abilities impaired. She writes: "When I lost my left hemisphere and its language centers, I also lost the clock that would break my moments into consecutive brief instances . . . I shifted from the doing-consciousness of my left brain to the being-consciousness of my right brain . . . I stopped thinking in language and shifted to taking new pictures of what was going on in the present moment" (2009, pp. 70–71). The right hemisphere's strength is nonverbal, more holistic, pictorial, and spatial. Damage to this side of the brain may result in not being able to interpret the nonverbal, emotional content of a message.

While our educational system tends to favor the verbal and analytical strengths of the left brain, it is important to note that learning is maximized when the strengths of *both* sides of the brain are activated. Learning activities that draw upon our creative, emotive, and physical sides along with verbal and analytical assignments generates brain activity in both hemispheres. For example, one can learn economic theory by reading about it and perhaps working through some mathematical formulas. But say this learning is supported by setting up a simulation game in which the classroom becomes an "economy" where people and businesses buy and sell, save and spend. This experiential dimension activates the right brain, reinforcing the left brain learning.

The triune brain and the hemispheric brain are but two glimpses into what might be the most amazing organ in our body. Enabled by new techniques that allow neuroscientists to study the brains of living persons, it is becoming quite clear that the brain learns and changes as it learns. This process, called neuroplasticity or just plasticity, refers to the brain's ability to rewire or expand its neural networks (Cozolino, 2002). Again, Taylor (2009) speaks to this amazing ability of the brain to learn: "On the morning of the stroke, this massive hemorrhage rendered me so completely disabled that I describe myself as an infant in a woman's body . . . Following surgery, it took eight years for me to completely recover all physical and mental functions. I believe I have recovered completely because I had an advantage. As a trained neuroanatomist, I believed in the plasticity of my brain—its ability to repair, replace, and retrain its neural circuitry" (p. 35). New information enters the brain in the form of electrical impulses; these impulses form neural networks, connecting with other networks and the stronger and more numerous the networks the greater the learning. The brain learns when challenged: "When a mental process is easy, it is either trivial or needs only previously well-stabilized synapses. Such processes certainly qualify as brain use, but not as learning. Brain use then, is quite a bit different from brain change, and it is the latter we are trying to elicit" in learning (Leamnson, 1999, cited in Gravett, 2001, p. 32). Zull (2006) points to a study "demonstrating change in the human neocortex when learning. In particular, an increase in the density of a small sensory region of the neocortex, the region that senses movement, was demonstrated when people learned to juggle. The density of this region decreased when people forgot some of their juggling skills (Draganski and others, 2004) . . . This and many other experiments have shown that increased signaling by cortical neurons generates the growth of more branches" (p. 4).

Further, years of research with placing rats in standard, enriched, and impoverished environments has revealed that an enriched environment leads to an increase in the weight of a rat's brain; in addition, rats equivalent in age to humans in their sixties and seventies were found to increase their brain weight "by 10 percent when they lived with younger rats in an enriched environment" (Gross, 1999, p. 25). This is really exciting research from the perspective of learning and aging. Obviously, you *can* teach an old dog new tricks! And we do not need to be "taking a class" for our brains to learn. We need only challenge ourselves with ideas and opportunities in an enriched environment to maintain and enhance brain functioning. Even popular culture has picked up on the ability of the brain to learn. There are now brain institutes and brain "trainers" offering programs to boost brain power, Internet sites where one can learn exercises for the brain, and popular magazine articles such as AARP's recent article titled "Age-Proof Your Brain: 10 easy ways to stay sharp forever " (Howard, 2012). Among the suggestions are engaging in physical exercise, learning new skills, and reducing stress.

Memory

As with the other cognitive functions presented in this chapter, memory is one of the brain's activities. Information coming into the brain is processed and put into memory in the neocortex. However, what we process and remember may well depend on our feelings at the time, a characteristic of the limbic system. As discussed above, we first react with our senses and emotions to stimuli before these data are processed in meaningful ways. Further, because no two persons have had the exact same prior experiences, each person attends to, processes, and remembers information differently from the next person. This helps explain why several people can witness the same car accident or purse snatching, for example, but when asked to recall the event, remember it slightly differently.

Historically, memory has been compared to a computer in which information is first entered (input), stored (throughput) and at some later point, retrieved (output). More commonly, memory is divided into sensory memory, working memory, and long-term memory, all processes that take place in the brain. We will first describe these three components of memory, and review what we know about memory and aging, and memory and learning.

In order for us to remember something, that "something" has to enter through our senses, that is, we have to attend to something that we see, hear, taste, smell, or touch. Since we are constantly bombarded by stimuli to our senses, especially sight and hearing, we have to consciously select what we want to remember. Say you are at a social event and are introduced to someone. If you do not hear their name clearly, there is no chance you will remember it later. You have to hear the name and attend to it in order for it to move from sensory, to working, to long-term memory. As people age they often think they are losing their memory. In fact, research suggests that the problem may lie with loss of hearing or vision because once something is clearly seen or heard, there is actually minimal decline in sensory memory (Foos & Clark, 2008).

Working memory, located in the neocortex, is where the information you attended to is processed. "As the name implies, this part of memory does the real work of paying attention to information in the sensory memories (or ignoring that information), encoding, abstracting, selecting, retrieving, and other mental processing" (Foos & Clark, 2008, p. 131). Working memory can move between sensory memory for more information, and long-term memory where information can be retrieved to help form a new memory. Encoding information into working memory does seem to exhibit some decline with age, although it is not clear why. Researchers have speculated that processing information takes longer as we age, and perhaps older adults do not have the mental energy they once had; further, older adults have no patience for dealing with "irrelevant and confusing information" (Bjorklund, 2011, p. 111).

Information that is processed in working memory enters long-term memory where it is stored for future use. We can think about the difference between working memory and long-term memory as the difference between the top of your desk and the file cabinet next to your desk. Decisions are made about items that come across your desk—do you discard the item, set it aside to deal with later, or attend to it, that is, process it so that you can file it in your file cabinet? The desktop is your working memory. Once we move to the file cabinet (long-term memory), there are three types of stored memories—procedural/habituated, episodic, and semantic (Tulving, 1985). Procedural/habituated memories have to do with cognitive and motor skills we have learned like how to read, play cards, mow the lawn, or drive a car. Once we've learned these skills we rarely think about what we are doing when engaging in them. Episodic memories are memories of past events or experiences and they are recalled with the sights, sounds and feelings of the original experience. For example, you might recall some early school experience when you felt embarrassed or humiliated, an experience that comes to mind when you are in an educational situation as an adult. It is these episodic memories of earlier school experiences that sometimes impede adults from pursuing learning later in life. Semantic memories, the third type of memory, have to do with knowledge, facts, understanding, and meaning that we have acquired as a result of life experiences and learning. We know who George Washington was, where China is located, what it means to love someone.

Getting memories into long-term memory involves encoding, or the strategies we use to place information into long-term memory. "Rehearsing information or trying to form a mental image or associating information with prior information are considered forms of encoding processes. The more distinctive these encoding operations are, the better the *copy* in permanent memory . . . The better the copy, the easier it will be to find at another time" (Foos & Clark, 2008, p. 134). Finding the memory, or retrieval, is the other major process in memory activity. Taylor (2009) talks about trying to regain her memory after her stroke: "Opening old files in my mind was a delicate process. I wondered what it would take to recall all those filing cabinets lining my brain, which contained the details of my previous life. I knew that I knew all of this stuff; I just had to figure out how to access the information again" (p. 101). In some research older adults show some decline in ability to recall or retrieve past memories, but it must also be kept in mind that as we age we accumulate thousands of memories. A 70-year-old trying to recall a particular birthday celebration or trip to the beach has many more memories to sort through than a 20-year-old asked to do the same thing. There is also a difference in whether adults are asked to recall information (as in an essay exam, for example), or recognize information (as in a multiple-choice exercise where one answer is correct). In recognition activities there is little difference between younger and older adults, although it may take older adults longer to recognize an answer.

All that we have come to understand about memory and the brain has major applications to adult learning. We know, for example, that if we consciously attend to what we are trying to learn, the information will enter our working memory to be processed for long-term memory. Further, there are dozens of techniques we can use to improve our memory and many self-help websites (Luminosity, PositScience, and Brain Metrix, to name just a few), and popular books we can access (see for example, Joshua Foer's *Moonwalking with Einstein: The Art and Science of Remembering Everything* (2011), which combines research about memory and memory techniques, Norman Doidge's *The Brain That Changes Itself* (2007), or Komblatt and Vega's *A Better Brain At Any Age* (2009)). Many of us have figured out some of these strategies on our own such as coming up with a word where each letter represents an item we want to buy at the grocery store. If we need eggs, cheese, tomatoes, apples, and hamburger, our word might be "teach." A common strategy for remembering sections of a talk is to peg each section of the talk to a room as you mentally "walk" through your home. For example, if this chapter were to become a speech, the introduction would be tagged to the front door/hallway, the living room would be where information about the brain would be placed, and in the kitchen we would place the section on memory, and so on. In sum, with regard to memory and the brain, physical exercise and mental exercise in the form of continuing learning, experiencing, and challenging ourselves, have been shown to enhance brain functioning in many ways including storing and retrieving memories.

Intelligence

If you were asked "What makes a person intelligent?" what would you say? Many might say an intelligent person is one who is "smart," or who "knows a lot." In a school setting, an intelligent person might be defined as one who learns easily and seems to remember what they learned more readily than others. Some think of intelligence as the score they received from taking an intelligence test. There is evidence of all of these understandings in the traditional perspective on intelligence, one that is dominated by isolating and measuring aspects of intelligence. We will review this perspective first, then look at some of the more recent models or "theories" of intelligence, all with an eye to how the brain, learning, and aging intersect with these understandings.

Early research on intelligence can be traced back to the first few decades of the twentieth century when several researchers such as Wechsler, Spearman, and Binet sought to define and measure intelligence, first with children then with adults (Foos & Clark, 2008). Spearman in particular proposed what he called a "general factor" of intelligence commonly called the "g" factor. This "g" factor stands for one's general intellectual capacity, measured by scores on an intelligence test. The "g" factor is the same as what has come to be known as one's intelligence quotient or "IQ." The notion of a "g" factor or "IQ" is still in use in research today (Bjorklund, 2011; Jensen, 2002).

Fluid and Crystallized Intelligence

Thinking of intelligence as a single construct such as the g factor has proved problematic to those who see intelligence as a set of multiple abilities or dimensions. Thurstone (1938) was one of the first to take this position and developed the Primary Mental Abilities measure for understanding adult intelligence. This instrument had seven distinct measures: spatial relations, reasoning, word fluency, verbal meaning, numbers, perceptual speed, and memory. However, it was Cattell (1963) and then Horn and Cattell (1966) in the mid-1960s and their theory of fluid and crystallized intelligence that has had the most influence in thinking about intelligence, especially as it relates to aging. They reasoned that fluid intelligence is "hard-wired," dependent on the central nervous system, and involves abstract reasoning, pattern recognition, and response speed. Crystallized intelligence is dependent on life experience and education. "It consists of the set of skills and bits of knowledge that we each learn as part of growing up in any given culture, such as the ability to evaluate experience, the ability to reason about real-life problems, and technical skills learned for a job and other aspects of life (balancing a checkbook, counting change, finding the salad dressing in the grocery store)" (Bjorklund, 2011, p. 106). An example of a test item for fluid intelligence might be to determine what comes next in a series of shapes. One would have to recognize the logic of the pattern of the given shapes (that is, number of sides, amount of shading) to select the next logical shape. A test item for crystallized intelligence might be to select a word that means the opposite from the given word.

Research suggests that as adults age, fluid intelligence decreases, perhaps due to the slowing down of response rate with age, while crystallized intelligence increases giving a fairly stable measure of intelligence over time. This can be seen in Figure 9.3. Combining the two measures of intelligence at a point in young adulthood, for example, will yield an average similar to combining a high crystallized score with a low fluid measure in older adulthood. Recent research on crystallized and fluid intelligence suggests, however, that culture might affect each of these components and it's possible that the above pattern will not hold for future generations (Zelinski & Kennison, 2007). For example, generational increases in fluid intelligence might be partially attributed to "changes in processing from more characteristically verbal to more iconic representations due to the rise of visually oriented modalities in film, television, computer games, and other media" (p. 547). Thus, it is hypothesized that "larger cohort increases will be observed for the fluid-like cognitive skills that have been more emphasized in recent decades than previously, whereas crystallized skills that have been consistently emphasized over the past century would show less cohort change" (p. 547).

The notion that culture and context play a role in shaping what is considered "intelligent" behavior and that intelligence might be more than verbal and analytical reasoning underlies several other models of intelligence proposed within the last thirty years or so. There has also been the recognition that the West has so privileged the notion that intelligence is an individual, innate ability measurable by tests that other dimensions of what might be considered "intelligent" behavior in a real-world,

FIGURE 9.3 FLUID AND CRYSTALLIZED INTELLIGENCE

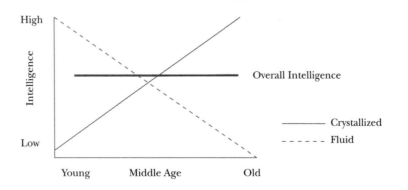

multicultural context have been overlooked. Here we review three such contributions to understanding intelligence as more than what IQ tests measure—Gardner's theory of multiple intelligences, Sternberg's triarchic model, and Goldman's proposal of an emotional intelligence.

Gardner's Multiple Intelligences (MI)

From early in his career, Howard Gardner of Harvard University questioned the dominance of intelligence as a single, inborn capacity assessed by IQ tests. Rather, he raised the question, "how did the brain/mind evolve over many thousands of years, in order to allow individuals (and the species) to survive across a range of environments?" (Gardner, 2000, p. 28). From cross-cultural studies of intelligence, research on universal skills and studies of people who are gifted, autistic, and idiot savants, he defined intelligence as "a biopsychological potential to process information that can be activated in a cultural setting to solve problems or create products that are of value in a culture" (Gardner & Moran, 2006, p. 227). He initially identified seven forms of intelligence, added an eighth in the mid-1990s (naturalist, one who can recognize and classify patterns in the natural world), and is considering a ninth, that of existential intelligence "that captures at least part of what individuals mean when they speak of spiritual concerns" (Gardner, 2000, p. 28). Here he speaks of the seven original intelligences: "In addition to the linguistic and logical-mathematical forms of intelligence that are at a premium in the schools, I proposed five additional intelligences . . .: musical (composer, performer); spatial (sailor, architect); bodily-kinesthetic (athlete, dancer, surgeon); interpersonal (therapist, salesperson); and intrapersonal (individual with keen introspective skills)" (p. 28). These types of intelligences are present in all cultures, and individuals have individual patterns of these intelligences; that is, every individual is talented in some of these intelligences and may have little capacity in others.

Gardner's theory of multiple intelligences has been widely accepted by educators who have long observed that students can be "intelligent" or talented or highly skilled in areas not necessarily captured in standard IQ tests. It has been somewhat less embraced in higher education and adult education. Historically of course, higher education has emphasized and rewarded verbal and analytical reasoning, first through test scores for admission, then through academic courses and even into testing for graduate school or professional training. In a discussion of implications of

Gardner's theory for higher education, Kezar (2001) points out that institutions focusing on a liberal arts education where language, math, art, dance and music are part of the curriculum already draw on his theory. Kezar suggests that the theory also has implications for today's trends in higher education regarding access, diversity in learning needs, and accountability and assessment. With regard to access, for example, admission criteria could be expanded beyond the verbal and math tests that assess only two of Gardner's intelligences. With regard to teaching and learning methods efforts could be made to incorporate "collaborative learning, working in groups to develop knowledge collectively, [which] has the potential to develop interpersonal and intrapersonal intelligences" (p. 148). With regard to accountability, Kezar suggests that many higher education institutions' mission statements already endorse goals around intrapersonal (such as developing oneself) and interpersonal (developing leaders) intelligences as part of the higher education experience. He recommends that processes be developed to both bring about these outcomes and be able to appropriately assess them (Kezar, 2001).

A major application of Gardner's theory to adult education has been in adult literacy. Under the auspices of the National Center for the Study of Adult Learning and Literacy (NCSALL), teachers in adult literacy programs in five states developed and implemented learning activities that maximized learners' multiple intelligences. For example, in an exercise to learn about geometric angles, learners were offered seven ways to express their learning such as: "Using your arm and elbow make five angles," "Using play dough and/or paper, show the angles 180, 135, 90, and 45," or "Write a poem, song, chant, or rap using some of the words about angles: figure formed by two lines, intersection, elbow, notch . . . acute, point of view, perspective," or "Find or make five triangles. Measure each angle and find the total number of degrees in each triangle by adding up the sums of the three angles" (Kallenbach & Viens, 2004, p. 61). The authors note that "MI-based learning choices made adult learners more confident about taking greater control of their own learning . . . [and] prompted adult learners to see themselves as learners in a more positive light after identifying and reflecting on their own abilities" (abstract, p. 58). One outcome of this project was the development of a sourcebook reviewing the MI theory and containing resources for developing learning activities responsive to learners' strengths (Viens & Kallenbach, 2004). Other reports and materials are available at the NCSALL website (http://ncsall.net).

Sternberg's Triarchic Theory of Intelligence

Another challenge to the traditional view of intelligence as a verbal and analytical school-based measure comes from Sternberg and his associates (2000) who assert that "the problems faced in everyday life often have little relationship to the knowledge and skills acquired through formal education or the abilities used in classroom activities" (p. 32). Sternberg's triarchic theory of intelligence consists of three components of intelligence—analytical, creative, and practical. Analytical intelligence is comparable to "general intelligence" and what is typically measured by IQ tests. Creative intelligence is the ability to think "out of the box," or creatively, and practical intelligence has to do with how we deal with everyday experience in real-world contexts. Practical intelligence involves acquiring and using tacit knowledge—that knowledge which we come to know through experience and which we rarely articulate. Reflecting Sternberg's ideas, in his recent book *Thinking, Fast and Slow*, neuroscientist Daniel Kahneman (2011) explains that there are two systems at work in our thinking. System 1 is the intuitive, tacit knowing that "operates automatically and quickly, with little or no effort and no sense of voluntary control" (p. 20). System 2 is "the conscious, reasoning self that has beliefs, makes choices, and decides what to think about and what to do" (p. 21). He gives numerous examples of how system 1 (thinking fast) and system 2 (thinking slow) work. One puzzle he presents is "A bat and ball cost $1.10. The bat costs one dollar more than the ball. How much does the ball cost?" He explains: "A number came to your mind. The number, of course, is 10 cents. The distinctive mark of this easy puzzle is that it evokes an answer that is intuitive, appealing, and wrong. Do the math, and you will see. If the ball costs 10 cents, then the total cost will be $1.20 (10 cents for the ball and $1.10 for the bat), not $1.10. The correct answer is 5 cents" (p. 44).

Sternberg sees practical, creative, and analytical forms of thinking (or intelligence) as working together as we go about living and managing our lives. Being able to select how and when to use which type of intelligence is what Sternberg (2003) calls "successful intelligence." And an important component of "mental management of one's life in a constructive, purposeful way" (Sternberg, 1988, p. 11) is the ability to select an environment for both working and living that best suits our personality, skills, and abilities. Successful intelligence is the ability to adapt to an environment, shape or modify an environment, or select a new environment.

From an adult learning perspective, Sternberg's major contribution has been the promotion of the valuing of experiential learning and the "practical intelligence" that accompanies that learning. "For educators of adults [his theory] provides rich evidence that adult intelligence is much more than academic abilities and measures on the more traditional IQ tests, but also encompasses what many of us have believed it to include all along: everyday or practical intelligence" (Merriam, Caffarella, & Baumgartner, 2007, p. 380).

Goleman's Emotional Intelligence

In 1995, Goleman published *Emotional Intelligence* in which he argued that success in life is equally, if not more dependent, on how well one understands and employs emotions than the more academic aspects of IQ. Underlying Goleman's theory is the fact, discussed above, that the our brain first responds on a sensory and emotional level: "Because it takes the rational mind a moment or two longer to register and respond than it does the emotional mind, the "first impulse" in an emotional situation is the heart's, not the head's . . . This rapid-fire emotional reaction takes over in situations that have the urgency of primal survival" (p. 293). There is also a "slow path" to emotion, one that "simmers and brews first in our thoughts before it leads to feeling. This second pathway to triggering emotions is more deliberate, and we are typically quite aware of the thoughts that lead to it" (p. 293). Goleman's emotional intelligence (1995) is comparable to Sternberg's interpersonal and intrapersonal intelligences and consists of five domains. He credits Salovey and Mayer (1990) with these five domains: (1) knowing one's emotions—"self-awareness—recognizing a feeling as it happens—is the keystone of emotional intelligence" (p. 43); (2) managing emotions—handling feelings so the emotional response is appropriate; (3) motivating oneself—this is the ability to marshal "emotions in the service of a goal" (p. 43); (4) recognizing emotions in others. "Empathy," he writes "is the fundamental 'people skill'" (p. 43); and (5) handling relationships. This is "skill in managing emotions in others" and this ability undergird[s] popularity, leadership, and interpersonal effectiveness" (p. 43).

Although solid evidence still needs to be presented in support of emotional intelligence as a separate type of intelligence, this notion of emotional intelligence has resonated with adult educators and human resource development practitioners (see, for example, Thory, 2013) and others who have known that there is more to success in life than just IQ. It may also help explain why some people are highly skilled at interpersonal relationships or how some become leaders. Several tests have been constructed to measure EQ with one, the Mayer-Salovey-Caruso Emotional Intelligence Test, or MSCEIT, seemingly high in reliability (see McEnrue and Groves [2006] for a review of current EQ tests). There are also popular versions of EQ tests available on the Internet (see resources at the end of this chapter).

In summary, intelligence is a very complicated construct. Its relationship to the brain is clear in that general intelligence involves the intake and processing of information. We have reviewed some of the more common understandings of intelligence beginning with general intelligence, or what standard IQ tests measure. This general intelligence has been parsed into fluid and crystallized forms of IQ, a concept which helps explain changes in functioning as we age. However, general IQ (whether seen as "g" or a combination of crystallized and fluid), has proven inadequate in capturing the many types of abilities and skills people exhibit in their everyday lives. Gardner's multiple intelligences, Sternberg's triarchic theory, and especially his notion of practical or successful intelligence, and Goleman's emotional intelligence all seem to resonate better with what we know about adult learning and adult functioning in an ever-changing world.

Cognitive Development and Wisdom

We can look closely at members of our own family for some hints as to how thinking patterns change as we age. Babies who seem to put everything in their mouths are using their bodies and in particular their senses to learn about their world; teenagers often have very strong opinions as to what is right or wrong; the grandparent seen as "wise" is one who has learned from life experience, and takes many factors into consideration when coming up with an insightful suggestion for dealing with a problem. Cognitive development is about how thinking patterns change as we age.

There are numerous theories and models about cognitive development and many begin with the foundational work of Jean Piaget (1966). Piaget proposed four age-related stages of cognitive development beginning with the sensory motor stage of infants, to the pre-operational stage (2 to 7 years old) wherein symbols and words are used to represent objects, to concrete operational where children, 7 to 11 years old can understand concepts and relationships, to formal operational that involves reasoning hypothetically and thinking abstractly. He first thought this fourth stage was obtained between 11 and 13, but revised this saying the development of formal operational thought may occur up to the age of 20 (Piaget, 1972). If these four stages are thought of as playing with a pack of cards, infants would take hold of some cards and likely put them into their mouth. A 4-year-old could probably sort the kings, queens, and jacks into piles; a 10-year-old could play a simple card game using all the cards, and a young adult could play a sophisticated card game like poker or bridge.

Though critiqued on a number of issues (for example, the invariant structure or the lack of attention to context), Piaget's theory did provide a foundation for future work in cognitive development. Neo-Piagetians (those who came after Piaget) have suggested there is development past formal operations, perhaps a fifth stage of cognitive development called problem-finding (Arlin, 1975, 1984), post-formal thinking (Sinnott, 2010), or dialectical thought (Basseches, 1984). These formulations of adult cognitive development take into account conditions of adult life that are complex, involving real-world issues and situations. Mackeracher (2004) has identified several such conditions:

- Adults must be able to "transfer knowledge from one context to another" a skill not accounted for by Piaget's formal operations (p. 120).
- Adults develop specialized knowledge and skills, which become part of their personality which in turn "may affect cognition" (p. 120).
- Sometimes a problem is best addressed by reformulating it, that is, the problem finding or problem posing cognitive skill proposed by Arlin (1975).
- Adults live in contexts and deal with situations that might require "the development of projective images of future possibilities," and they may need to monitor the implementation of these images (p. 120).
- Formal operations, the highest stage of cognitive development in Piaget's model cannot resolve "*uncertainties, doubts, and ambiguities*" so characteristic of adult life (p. 120, italics in original).
- Living in situations of life and work where there are "complex systems of roles and relationships" requires systems thinking (p. 121).
- "The cognitive strategies required for learning how to learn and for reflective practice involve the development of executive cognitive strategies to guide and control other cognitive strategies. Executive cognitive strategies are not accounted for in formal operational thought" (p. 121).

- Critical thinking in which adults identify and examine assumptions underlying their ideas, values and behaviors calls for "cognitive processes allowing one to think about or operate on formal thoughts" (p. 121).
- Finally, "adults need to be able to deal with *paradoxical situations*. Doubt, ambiguity, uncertainty, systems thinking and self-reflective thought tend to give rise to paradoxes." Further, "a paradox can only be resolved by moving outside the frame of reference (or personal model of reality) that contains it, and beyond the cognitive strategies that are creating it" (p. 121, italics in original).

These "conditions" characteristic of adult life support the idea that adult cognitive thought needs to be creative and critical in negotiating these aspects of adult life—thus the need for cognitive development models that go beyond that of Piaget's model.

There have been other models of development which have been heavily influenced by Piaget such as Perry's stages of moral and ethical development (1999), Kohlberg's stages of moral development (1981), reflective thinking (King & Kitchener, 2004), ego development (Loevinger, 1976), faith development (Fowler, 1981), and self-development (Kegan, 1982, 1994). Another model influenced by Piaget, Perry, and Kohlberg is from the study titled *Women's Ways of Knowing* (Belenky, Clinchy, Goldberger, & Tarule, 1986). In the authors' study of 135 women of different ages, classes, and ethnic backgrounds, they delineated five categories of knowing consisting of silence, received knowing, subjective knowing, procedural knowing, and constructed knowing. They maintained that these positions were not hierarchical, although they have sometimes been interpreted as such. Briefly, silence is where women have no voice; received knowing is that state where what one knows comes from external authorities such as fathers, husbands, or religious leaders. Subjective knowing is what women know intuitively; knowledge is personal and comes from the self. In both procedural and constructed knowing, women are more active learners. Procedural knowing involves active learning and applying objective procedures in gaining knowledge; constructed knowing is when women see themselves as creators of knowledge and view knowledge as contextually bound, rather than neutral as in procedural knowing. Their model has generated quite a bit of research and follow-up reflections by the original authors (Clinchy, 2002; Goldberger, Tarule, Clinchy, & Belenky, 1996).

Wisdom is sometimes thought of as the end point of cognitive development; that is, it is the way people *think* about real-life problems and issues. In fact, Baltes and colleagues who have studied wisdom have defined wisdom as "expert-level knowledge in the fundamental pragmatics of life" (Baltes & Smith, 1990, p. 95), or "good judgment and advice in important but uncertain matters of life" (Baltes & Staudinger, 1993, p. 75). Sternberg (2003), whose triarchic theory of intelligence was reviewed earlier, believes wisdom draws upon "practical" or "successful" intelligence and creativity, and that wisdom is about "balancing various self-interests (intrapersonal) with the interests of others (interpersonal) and of other aspects of the context in which one lives (extrapersonal)" (p. 152).

There are others who tie wisdom to post-formal or dialectic thinking. Those who see wisdom from this cognitive development perspective "conceptualize wisdom as the integration, usually, of three dimensions (cognitive, affective, and behavioral). The integration occurs through the use of dialectical thinking which can also be seen as the logic of paradox and the recognition that uncertainty and the limits of knowledge frame human existence and force resolution of seemingly irresolvable dilemmas" (Bassett, 2006, p. 299). Bassett also proposes that wisdom, including her model of wisdom (available at www.wisdominst.org), could be the result of "exceptional self-development" tied to the notion of ego- or self-transcendence (p. 292).

This developmental perspective is certainly reminiscent of Erikson's well-known theory of eight stages of human development. Negotiating each of the eight stages includes gaining a strength for each stage. For example, the infant stage of "basic trust versus mistrust," if successfully negotiated, results in having "hope." The "intimacy versus isolation" of young adulthood results in "love." Erikson's eighth and last stage of older adulthood of "ego integrity versus despair," if successfully resolved, results in "wisdom" as the moral "strength" (Erikson, 1963). In this stage, which occurs in late life, adults must achieve a favorable balance between a sense of integrity about their lives versus feeling despair. In so doing, they achieve the strength of wisdom. For those who study wisdom from this perspective, the key is that wise persons are highly developed and their perspective includes "self-transcendence, depth of understanding of the meaning of life, philosophical commitments or spiritual development reaching a sense of the basic unity of self with universe, and recognition of the limits of human knowledge" (Bassett, 2006, p. 293).

One of the key questions about wisdom is its relationship to age. The preceding models would certainly suggest that it is as we age that we develop mature cognitive functioning central to thinking and acting wisely. But we also know some younger adults we might call "wise" and sometimes we even say children are "wise beyond their years." In 2005, Sternberg published a review of the literature on this very question. He concluded that perhaps due to the variation in how wisdom is defined and measured, there is yet no definitive answer to the question of whether wisdom increases with age. However, he does conclude that wisdom appears to be related to the situation, rather than the person, and that "cognitive variables, personality variables, and life experiences" are more important than age in the development of wisdom (p. 21). Sternberg humorously points out that "there is a joke about how many psychologists it takes to change a light bulb. The answer is it doesn't matter, so long as the light bulb wants to change. Similarly, people must want to develop their wisdom-related skills in order for them actually to develop, and then must adopt the attitudes toward life—openness to experience, reflectivity upon experience, and willingness to profit from experience—that will enable this development to occur" (p. 21).

The many facets of wisdom—the nature of wisdom, what it means to be wise, and how adult education can foster the development of wisdom—are receiving growing attention from adult educators. For example, Tisdell and Swartz (2011) have compiled an edited volume on *Adult Education and the Pursuit of Wisdom* which contains chapters ranging from the neuroscience behind wisdom, to teaching strategies to foster practical wisdom, to cross-cultural perspectives on wisdom and adult education. Again, the complex nature of wisdom is captured in Tisdell's (2011) description: "Wisdom involves both head knowledge and soul knowledge; it is what helps us weave together connections within our own being, and in human relations with others as individuals and across gender, culture, race, and religious differences and academic disciplines to facilitate wise action. It is about embracing paradox and dialectics that potentially pulls us open to something new—and to our very creativity . . . it is borne of an integration of these multiple ways of knowing, which allows us to both critique and create as we engage (hopefully) in wise action in the world" (p. 12). Most recently Swartz and Tisdell (2012) are working toward building a theory of wisdom and adult education. They maintain that such a theory should consist of the three dimensions of how adults *access* wisdom, how adults *act* with wisdom, and how we can *educate* to foster wisdom. For example, accessing wisdom might include use of emotion and intuition; acting with wisdom means wise action "grounded in complex connections within and across all systems levels" (p. 325); and educating to foster wisdom must include diverse experiences such as embodied learning and storytelling.

Chapter Summary

This chapter began with discussing the brain and how it functions, and then moved to related cognitive dimensions of learning and knowing including memory, intelligence, cognitive development, and wisdom. While none of these functions could happen without the brain learning, processing, and changing, it is interesting to note that the body and especially our senses play a key role in what enters our brain for processing. Memory and intelligence are not purely cognitive processes, nor are cognitive development and wisdom. Life experiences and learning play major roles in all of these processes.

Linking Theory and Practice: Activities and Resources

The following are suggested activities for linking theory and practice on the topic of the brain and cognitive processes:

1. A discussion centering on intelligence might begin by asking learners to write down their definition of "intelligence." Compiling these definitions into a list, then deriving what some of the commonalities are across the definitions usually results in uncovering several of the main components of intelligence.
2. A similar activity is fun to do with regard to wisdom. First ask learners to think of someone they know, or a public figure whom they would call "wise." Then ask for some reasons why they identified this person— what makes someone "wise." This can be followed up by compiling the ages of these nominated wise people to explore the notion of the relationship between wisdom and age.
3. Access an instrument on the Internet to determine your "emotional IQ" score.
4. Have students design a learning activity on one of the topics in this chapter such as the brain or memory or cognitive development wherein they plan learning activities employing several of Gardner's multiple intelligences. For example, they might make a clay model of the triune brain, or write a song about sensory, working, and long-term memory, or act out Piaget's four stages of cognitive development.

5. Some might be interested in learning about those with extraordinary intellectual capacities or memory such as geniuses or savants. These are interesting case studies of how the brain, memory, and intelligence intersect.

6. Resources and Web Links

   a. Taylor, J. (2009). *My Stroke of Insight.* New York: Plume/Penguin. This popular book describes her experience having a stroke, then what she did to "teach" her brain to recover all of her functions. There is also a list of suggestions for interacting with people who have had a stroke.

   b. "The Mystery of Consciousness: Neuroscience Offers New Insights." This video is an illustrated talk by Antonio Damasio, a neuroscientist who explains how the brain, emotions and consciousness are interrelated. www.ted.com/talks/lang/en/antonio_damasio_the _quest_to_understand_consciousness.html

   c. The Consortium for Research on EI (emotional intelligence) in Organizations. This website compiles all kinds of information about emotional intelligence such as the latest research, books on EI, tests of EI, and conferences on the topic of EI. www.eiconsortium.org

   d. Simply Google "brain hemisphere dominance" and dozens of websites will appear. You can take a test to assess whether you are right- or left-brain dominant (see especially the "dancer" test), link brain dominance to learning style, and engage in "mind games" to enhance your use of both sides of the brain.

   e. See the following websites for information and activities related to the brain and memory: Brain Metrix http://www.brainmetrix.com/; Luminosity http://www.lumosity.com/; PositScience http://www .positscience.com/

   f. Visit the blog of neuroscientist Bradley Voytek for his collection of the "top 10" neuroscience TED talks. TED (technology, entertainment, design) is a nonprofit organization devoted to sharing ideas on a variety of topics. One of the TED talks at this site is given by Jill Taylor, author of *My Stroke of Insight,* from which we quoted in this chapter (http://blog.ketyov.com/2011/01/top-10-neuroscience -ted-talks.html?m=).

Chapter Highlights

- Our brain is the control tower of our body, continually monitoring inside and outside stimuli. Interestingly, the brain continually expands its neural networks, in effect "learning" as it is challenged by new information.

- There are three parts to our memory—sensory memory, working memory, and long-term memory. Many techniques can be employed to enhance our memory.
- Intelligence is a complex phenomenon generating numerous models and theories such as the "g" factor, fluid and crystallized intelligence, Gardner's multiple intelligences, Sternberg's triarchic theory, and Goleman's emotional intelligence.
- Overall measures of intelligence appear to remain stable as we age.
- Models by Piaget and others suggest that the way we think changes as we age with many suggesting post-formal, dialectical reasoning and wisdom being characteristic of adulthood.

CHAPTER TEN

ADULT LEARNING IN THE DIGITAL AGE

Think of the last news story you scanned, purchase you made, book you read, bank transaction you performed, information you looked up, or friend you contacted. Chances are some or all of these activities were computer-mediated, that is, enabled by a computer rather than human-to-human contact. As we discussed in Chapter 1, technology is a major variable affecting adult learning. Just as the topics we've addressed elsewhere in this book, including learner characteristics, motivation, experience, self-directedness, and brain function affect learning, so too does the social, political, and technological contexts. Increasingly, learners are turning to the World Wide Web, whether it is to immediately access information or take a course. We live in the Digital Age (also known as the Information Age or Computer Age), where we freely exchange and have instant access to information. The ability to search the Internet has changed our access to and relationship with information. Information is now at our fingertips 24/7, information that previously would have required a trip to the library or consultation with an expert. Say you want to install tile in your bathroom. Just a few years ago you might have gone to your public library, local bookstore, or home improvement center to find out how. Or, you might have sought an expert tile installer for advice. Today, you can Google "tile installation" and have immediate access to blogs, instructional videos, product information, patterns, photos, and step-by-step instructions.

Our ability to access information has facilitated learning in a way that is particularly meaningful to adults: it is just-in-time, relevant, and self-directed. It can also be overwhelming, inaccurate, and misguided. The Digital Age is a shift away from the Industrial Age; information and its manipulation have replaced manual labor and manufacturing. With the emergence of the Digital Age comes new challenges: training and recruiting knowledge workers, bridging cultural and economic divides created by increased mobility, and addressing cultural conflict and misunderstanding (Bennett & Bell, 2010). Our first image of the digital learning context may be to picture a formal online course. Yet, the vast amount of adult engagement online is informal (King, 2010). Although digital learning, or eLearning, is an undeniable trend for both informal and formal learning, it is not something that educators have been traditionally rewarded for adopting, nor do they often have the resources, time, or support to effectively integrate technology into their teaching (Kenney, Banerjee, & Newcombe, 2010). The purpose of this chapter is to consider how the Digital Age affects adult learning and education. The chapter begins with an examination of technology and how it is shaping our lives across multiple contexts such as work, family, and community. Next we explore adult learners in the digital context to understand their characteristics and engagement with technology, and how they negotiate the challenges of a wired world. Finally, we assess the teaching context and examine how we can help learners become critical consumers of information, and how technology is challenging and changing our role as educators.

The Technology Context

"These days, being connected depends not on our distance from each other but from available communications technology" (Turkle, 2011, p. 155). We live in a world where it is difficult to "unplug," that is, we are constantly tethered to devices such as smartphones, e-mail and Twitter accounts, social networking pages, blogs, and so forth that link us to information and others. This "plugged in" life has created an environment that permeates all others: "Technology is not just a device that is utilized as a tool. Rather, technology has infused every aspect of society to essentially change the thought process in learning" (Parker, 2013, p. 55). How does this context affect learning and how we manage and process information?

What impact does it have on teaching? This section highlights the demography of our digitized lives, reviews the demand for eLearning, and troublesome issues of access created by the Digital Divide.

The Connected Adult Learner

Just how are we linking with others, whether across the hall or across the globe? Computer-mediated communication (CMC) refers to the many technologies and options for connecting virtually. "CMC illustrates communication taking place through a technology-enhanced medium that has the ability to span time and space; two or more people are sending and receiving messages" (Joosten, 2012, p. 11). CMC is viewed as potentially creating a more egalitarian and democratic learning experience for diverse learners on a global basis, particularly because it is open, free, and accessible to most individuals (Joosten, 2012).

A 2012 *Time* magazine report illustrates how wireless phones are changing our lives worldwide. Although 29% of respondents fear society places too much emphasis on technology, 68% sleep with their mobile device next to their bed and 44% indicate their wireless device is the first and last thing they look at every day. Sixty-six percent of Brazilians feel wireless technology helps them maintain closer contact with friends, while 79% of the Chinese said they are better informed about news, and 62% of United Kingdom participants said their devices made it easier to be away from family. Forty-eight percent of South Koreans reported that they spend too much time looking at their mobile device and not enough time observing the world. Seventy-three percent of Indians maintain closer contact with family via mobile devices.

According to the U.S. Bureau of the Census (2012), 71% of U.S. households had an Internet connection at home and 80% of households accessed the Internet either at home or via a mobile device. The U.S. Census report shows household Internet usage by race at almost 88% in Asian households, 82% in White households, and 73% in both Black and American Indian/Alaskan Native households. In 2010, 55% of all adults had made online purchases and 80% had sought health or medical information. A Pew Research Center report indicates that one in three adults uses the Internet to confirm medical diagnoses for themselves or others with medical professionals more likely than not to confirm the diagnosis (Fox, 2013) (http://e-patients.net/archives/2013/01/health-online-2013-survey-data-as-vital-sign.html). Increasingly technology is our link to family, friends, community, and the world.

Demand for eLearning

Beginning with correspondence courses tracing at least to the 1840s in England and extension education in the United States in the late 1800s, educators have been creating ways to reach learners who are unable to come to the educational institution itself. Instructional radio and television have been widely used for decades. With the Internet, a wide range of educational opportunities exists from synchronous, instruction that is in real time with learners meeting online to engage in discussion, lecture, or activities, to asynchronous, instruction that is not bound by time and can be accessed at learners' leisure, 24/7. With Internet learning also comes variation in delivery, such as blended or hybrid courses that are a mixture of face-to-face and web-based instruction, to fully 100% online instruction.

With the explosion of information and increasing access to the Internet comes a demand for eLearning, particularly in higher education. *Going the Distance: Online Education in the United States, 2011* (Allen & Seaman, 2011) is the ninth annual report on online learning in higher education based on over 2,500 colleges and universities. According to the report, online learning enrollments continue to grow steadily with over 6.1 million students taking at least one online course in 2010, an increase of 560,000 students from 2009. The online enrollment growth rate during the nine-year period from 2002 to 2011 is 18.3% as compared to just over a 2% growth of the overall higher education student population. The emergence of online universities such as Capella, Strayer, Walden, and the University of Phoenix has made higher education more readily accessible to a wide, international audience and created new forms of competition for traditional universities. According to their 2010 Academic Annual Report, the University of Phoenix had 470,800 students, a faculty of more than 32,000 and almost 600,000 alumni (http://www.phoenix .edu/about_us/publications/academic-annual-report/2010.html), although enrollments in these institutions are decreasing with University of Phoenix dropping to 328,000 in 2012 (http://www.huffingtonpost .com/2012/10/19/enrollment-falling-at-for_n_1989856.html).

Although demand for online education is high, its effectiveness may be low as innovation in technology is far ahead of corresponding changes in pedagogy (Sonwalker, 2008). "The computer as a learning platform is proving to be an ineffective and boring medium" charges Sonwalker (p. 45) noting barriers to effective university online teaching such as poor course management systems that support information exchange but lack pedagogy for online learning, the expectation that faculty be available 24/7 to answer e-mail and questions, the lack of a pedagogical framework for effective online teaching, the delays in feedback from faculty to students and vice versa, and the difficulty in knowing how students are doing in the course.

The Digital Divide

The Digital Divide refers to the differences between those who have access to the Internet and those who do not. According to an INTEL (2012) report, there are an estimated 2.4 billion Internet users globally, although access is lagging in developing countries with Africa having the lowest use at 16% of the population. Twenty-eight percent of Asia's population has access, with 40% in the Middle East, 43% in Latin America and the Caribbean, 64% in Europe, 68% in Oceania/Australia, and 79% in North America. There is also a gender gap, particularly in the developing world. "On average across the developing world, nearly 25 percent fewer women than men have access to the Internet, and the gender gap soars to nearly 45 percent in regions like sub-Saharan Africa. Even in rapidly growing economies the gap is enormous. Nearly 35 percent fewer women than men in South Asia, the Middle East and North Africa have Internet access, and nearly 30 percent in parts of Europe and across Central Asia. In most higher-income countries, women's Internet access only minimally lags that of men's, and in countries such as France and the United States, in fact exceeds it" (INTEL, p, 10).

The Pew Internet Project (Zickuhr & Smith, 2012) surveyed 2,260 adults age 18 and older in both English and Spanish during 2011 to measure differences in Internet use in the United States. They found that one in five U.S. adults does not use the Internet, particularly senior citizens preferring to be interviewed in Spanish, those with less than a high school education, and those living in households earning less than $30,000 per year. As we know from learning about andragogy in Chapter 3 and motivation in Chapter 8, adults seek learning that is timely and relevant to their lives. It is not surprising then, that of the nonusers of the Internet, nearly half remain offline because they do not view the Internet as relevant to them. The 27% of U.S. adults living with a disability are also at a distinct disadvantage with only 54% going online versus 81% of the population. Although adoption rates have leveled in recent years, adults engaged online are doing more activities, such as making purchases, social networking, and banking. Significant access differences remain and are attributed to age, income, and education. The report notes that the wide adoption of mobile phones is "changing the story . . . Groups that have traditionally been on the other side of the digital divide in basic Internet access are using wireless connections to go online. Among smartphone users, young adults, minorities, those with no college experience, and those with lower household income levels are more likely than other groups to say that their phone is their main source of Internet access" (p. 2). The Digital Divide today is not based significantly on race or gender. "Instead, age (being 65 or older), a lack of high school education, and having a low household income (less than $20,000 per year) are the strongest negative predictors for internet use" (p. 6). Bridging the digital divide remains an ongoing global concern.

The Knight Foundation undertook a project to bridge the Digital Divide in Detroit, Michigan, focusing on high-poverty neighborhoods to provide a broadband network and digital literacy training. This project yielded five recommendations for increasing access: (1) focus on digital literacy through adult education courses held in public places such as libraries to encourage adoption; (2) provide computers; (3) remove other financial barriers required by Internet providers such as security deposits or credit checks that make it more difficult for low-income users to get service (nonprofits exist to help defray these expenses); (4) establish low Internet rates; and (5) partner with local community organizations, private companies, libraries, and government for success (Martinez & Patel, 2012). Clearly adult education can play an important role in bridging the digital divide, particularly through a focus on digital literacy. For more information on the Digital Divide, view Aleph Molinari's TED Talk listed in the "Linking Theory and Practice" section at the end of this chapter.

Adult Learners in the Digital Age

As we have already shown, online learning is an undeniable trend that we must become adept at navigating both as learners and educators. Online learning is happening across adult learning settings such as ABE/GED, the workplace, continuing education, and communities. It is also exploding in higher education. This section explores online adult learners in various settings, examines the effectiveness of learning online, and considers the negative aspects and challenges of learning in the context of technology.

Adult Learners Online

The European Commission conducted a study to understand how life-long learning was affected by computer-mediated communication (CMC) technologies (Ala-Mutka, 2010). This study was based on assumptions that lifelong learning is important for being effective in changing jobs and environments, and that CMCs have promise in supporting lifelong learning in new ways. According to the study, online networks and communities are creating innovative lifelong learning patterns such as supporting new ways of both intentional and nonintentional learning. Online platforms, networks, and communities facilitate lifelong learning, including new skill development and personal growth. For online lifelong learning to be most effective, learners should have technical skill and open attitudes toward online learning; be prepared for and interested in learning; and belong to online communities that encourage participation within a positive, sociable community. Being prepared for lifelong online learning may be frustrating to many adult learners as the technology continues to advance, creating challenges for both learners and educators to keep pace.

Online learners are engaged in everything from informal surfing on topics of interest to formal higher education courses. Most adults in the United States log onto the Internet dozens of times daily to learn new information and its growth has been explosive. Only 0.4% of the world population used the Internet in 1995. Today, over 32% have access with the highest being in North America as we saw in the previous section that discussed the digital divide. With over 2 billion people using the Internet worldwide, online learners can sign up for continuing education, or free courses through such organizations such as the Khan Academy or Coursera. Mobile apps are available for tracking medical conditions, studying for the GED, learning English, or any other self-directed learning topic you can imagine. Online learning is being used in the workplace as well to provide cost-effective education that is not bound by geography or time zone. This section discusses three particular contexts of adult learning online: higher education, social networking, and communities of practice.

Higher Education. Stavredes (2011) notes that in the United States, online learning's main audience has been nontraditional adult learners. According to the 2011 Noel-Levitz *National Online Learners Priorities Report,* based on 99,000 students at 108 institutions in the United States, the majority of learners are Caucasian adult females in courses that are delivered primarily online, taking a full class load at the undergraduate level. Specifically: 67% of online learners are female, with 85% of the sample age 25 and older. Eighty-seven percent take courses primarily online versus blended or face-to-face. Online students report higher levels of overall satisfaction with their experience than those who reside on campus but take online courses. Thirty percent of the students are pursuing graduate studies, 62% are in undergraduate education, with 4% pursuing "other" studies. Challenges that face online learners include: finding clearly defined assignments in the syllabus, experiencing quality of instruction, receiving faculty responses to their needs, feeling their tuition is worth the investment, and getting timely feedback about their progress.

The Noel-Levitz (2011) report ranks factors that influence learners to enroll in online courses. These factors, in descending level of importance, include: convenience, flexible pacing, work schedule, program requirements, institution reputation, cost, availability of financial assistance, ability to transfer credits, future employment opportunities, distance from campus, and employer recommendation. Although this survey looked at learners in higher education, most of these variables hold for adults regardless of their educational goals. Adult online learners want convenience and flexibility in meeting their educational goals (Stavredes, 2011).

Social Networking. Ready access to technology has bred an information explosion with which no one can keep pace. Participation in social media is widespread and growing. According to Pring (2012), 66% of adults who use the Internet are connected to one or more social media platforms such as Facebook or Twitter, and 53% of American cellphone users now have a smartphone such as an iPhone or Android. In one day on the Internet, for example, enough information is consumed to fill 168 million DVDs, 294 billion e-mails are sent, 2 million blog posts are written (enough posts to fill *TIME* magazine for 770 million years), 172 million people visit Facebook, 40 million visit Twitter, 22 million visit LinkedIn, 20 million visit Google+, 17 million visit Pinterest, 4.7 billion minutes are spent on Facebook, 532 million statuses are updated, 250 million photos are uploaded, 22 million hours of TV and movies are watched on Netflix, 864,000 hours of video are uploaded to YouTube, more than 35 million apps are downloaded, and more iPhones are sold than people are born (Pring, 2012). And of course by the time this book is published, these numbers will have likely more than doubled. By 2015, for example, brands will be generating 50% of their web sales through social media and mobile platforms with a projection of $30 billion (Pring, 2012).

Social networks offer informal opportunities for learners to explore topics of interest, network with other learners, and share information. Such networks represent unique opportunities to tap skill development, for instance career and leadership development (Bierema & Rand, 2008) and for educators to support learners through the creation of social networking pages (such as Facebook, LinkedIn, or Twitter) that enhance courses.

Online Learning Opportunities. The technological age offers new prospects for learners such as opportunities to form online communities of practice (see Chapter 6) with others sharing common interests related to work and leisure, or as a means to connect with others who share similar values such as political views. Online communities of practice (OCoP) differ from social networking because they require members to share expertise around a particular skill or topic, such as adult learning, and they use the virtual space to engage in collaborative learning and activities around the shared interest. OCoPs are actively engaged in creating shared meaning, instruction, and dialogue around the topic of interest and are sustained over time. OCoPs also enable access to new career and employment opportunities through job posting and networking sites such as Monster.com or LinkedIn.com; linkages with fundraising and grant writing opportunities through web-based searches, access to medical databases, and the means for new forms of lifelong learning through eBooks, online courses, and readily available information (Bryan, 2013). OCoPs represent readily available, geographically boundless opportunities for learners to connect with other learners who share the same interests. For example, the University of Georgia, Adult Education, Learning, and Organization Development program's LinkedIn page connects a global community of people interested in adult learning (http://www.linkedin.com/groups/UGA -Adult-Education-Learning-Organization-3836262?gid=3836262&trk=hb _side_g>).

Effectiveness of Online Learning

Online learning is also proving effective. The U.S. Department of Education (2010) compared online learning conditions with face-to-face instruction among older learners and found that "Students in online conditions performed modestly better, on average, than those learning the same material through traditional face-to-face instruction" (p. xiv). Key findings include that blended instruction (a combination of face-to-face and online) was more beneficial than either totally face-to-face or online. Learners also had better outcomes in courses where the online instruction was collaborative or instructor-driven than when learners were left to be self-directed on their own. The study concluded that online learning is effective across a range of content and types of learners, making it a good option for adult learners. According to the findings, giving learners control over their interactions with media led to reflection, activity, and self-monitoring, again underscoring the importance of good adult education practice. The study also found that providing group-level guidance is less effective than one-on-one feedback and coaching with individual learners.

Retaining online learners is a challenge and drop-out rates are higher among this population than traditional, on campus learners (Allen & Seaman, 2011). Given the demographics of online learners, gender and age may be confounding variables for persistence. Persevering at online learning is also affected by computer and information literacy, time management, reading, writing, and online communication skills. Learners also have non-school-related external constraints that impact their ability to remain enrolled such as finances, employment, family obligations, support systems, and unanticipated crises such as illness, divorce, or job loss. Internal variables such as self-esteem, feelings of belongingness in the online program, and the ability to develop interpersonal relationships with peers, faculty, and staff also affect online learner retention (Stavredes, 2011). As with adults in traditional classrooms, online learners face similar challenges to their participation.

Navigating the Negative Aspects and Challenges of the Technology Context

Accessing and using information are fundamental to functioning well in today's world, yet we are constantly challenged by the pace of rapid change and information overload. Bryan (2013) points out, for example, that as of 2012, information is doubling every 72 hours. This torrent of information includes daily text messages sent and received exceeding the planet's population, and with U.S. citizens having "access to over 1,000,000,000,000 web pages, 65,000 iPhone apps, 10,500 radio stations, 5500 magazines, and 200+ cable TV stations" (Bryan, 2013, p. 2), the sheer volume is not only overwhelming, but incomprehensible. Bryan (2013) cautions that the exponential information overload may be difficult for some learners to process, especially when it conflicts with prior learning or other sources. An important learning task will be for learners to critically assess the value and relevance of new information. Other concerns that come with the information explosion are the loss of privacy through surveillance and the permanency of anything that is put on the Web. Language is also changing as idioms, emoticons, and Tweets become standard ways of communicating. Adult learners also need to be wary of technology and Internet crimes such as identity theft, stalking, cyberbullying, cyber pornography, sexting, and other issues.

Information overload is a consequence of being connected 24/7 and Rock (2013) suggests it has negative implications for brain function noting, "We won't let people work 20-hour factory shifts anymore, but we're okay to let them *respond to emails 24/7.* We organize workplaces to minimize physical injuries, yet we expect people to process huge volumes of data for hours on end. We mandate that people have vacations, yet more people are connected on vacation than ever. We are not respecting the needs of the brain largely because they are not obvious, maybe it is time we made them more so" (emphasis in original, Rock, 2013). Work at the NeuroLeadership Institute outlines seven types of mental activities that the brain needs to optimize healthy function and recover from being continually plugged-in, including: focus time (tending to tasks in a goal-oriented way, deeply challenging and making connections in the brain), play time (spontaneous, creative, or novel experiences that also make new connections in the brain), connecting time (engaging with other people to activate the brain's relational circuitry), physical time (movement, especially aerobic, to strengthen the brain in myriad ways), time in (reflection time to better integrate the brain), down time (nonfocused, non-goal-oriented time to let the mind wander and relax to help the brain recharge), and sleep time (rest time to allow the brain to consolidate learning and recover from experiences of the day) (Rock, 2009; Rock & Siegel, 2011; Siegel, 2012).

Carr's (2008) article "Is Google Making Us Stupid?" laments how ready access to hyperlinks, books, statistics, blogs, news, and facts on the Internet is diminishing his ability to concentrate and is changing how he thinks. He also assumes that he is not alone in this phenomenon. Noting that media are not neutral or passive information channels, "They supply the stuff of thought, but they also shape the process of thought . . . My mind now expects to take in information the way the Net distributes it: in a swiftly moving stream of particles. Once I was a scuba diver in a sea of words, now I zip along the surface like a guy on a Jet Ski" (p. 90). Although we may be reading more today than we did in the 1970s or 1980s, Carr observes that "it's a different kind of reading, and behind it lies a different kind of thinking—perhaps even a new sense of self" (p. 91). As the Internet privileges the immediacy and efficiency of information, our capacity for deep reading and reflection without distraction is replaced by the act of decoding information without making key linkages and associations. Our attention is scattered when we are reading an article on the Web and receive notification we have an e-mail. The same thing happens now on televised news with text crawls, and magazines with pop up ads and short summaries of articles, for those who don't have the time or capacity to read full articles. Although the Net's presence in our lives is dominant and all-encompassing, we've paid little attention "of how, exactly, it's reprogramming us" (p. 93). We are at risk of losing quiet spaces that promote deep thinking and deep reading.

The Teaching-Learning Context of the Digital Age

So far we have considered how the technological context is affecting our lives and adult learning. Now we turn to an assessment of the teaching and learning context and examine how we can help learners become critical consumers of information, and how technology is challenging and changing our role as educators.

Helping Learners Become Savvy Consumers of Online Learning

Adults are accessing the Internet in unprecedented numbers to find information on everything from recipes to directions to health. Bryan (2013) suggests that educators need to help learners evaluate new information for credibility, relevance, and accuracy; assess information for its currency, objectivity, and purpose; confirm that qualified experts have provided information; and participate in the dissemination, examination, and adoption of information to expand the knowledge base. Yet, not all web sources are equally reputable, nor are all learners adequately web literate. By web or information literacy we mean how well the learner can assess the accuracy, reliability, and validity of various web sources. There is a lot of information to help consumers review web sources with a critical eye. For instance, Penn Libraries has a tutorial on web literacy (http://gethelp .library.upenn.edu/guides/tutorials/webliteracy/). The U.S. Food and Drug Administration has an extensive site on evaluating food and dietary supplements (see http://www.fda.gov/food/dietarysupplements/consumer information/ucm110567.htm). The University of Maryland Libraries has a checklist for evaluating websites that is also quite useful: http:// www.lib.umd.edu/guides/webcheck.html.

Wright and Grabowsky (2011) provide a valuable discussion of how to help adults assess and select quality health information that is applicable to information on the Web in general. They note that evaluating the quality and accuracy of web-based information is often challenging for adults, particularly those with low reading comprehension and limited access to technology. They urge adult educators to help learners critique information sources on the web and provide specific examples of quality websites. Wright and Grabowsky also recommend that adult educators actively evaluate websites with learners and provide opportunities for learners to self-evaluate and discuss websites.

Key skills learners need to develop for savvy web consumption include developing effective search strategies, critically evaluating information, and finding reputable information (Wright & Grabowsky, 2011). For example, if a learner wants to know about managing depression, a first step is to write down key words that will help in the search for information such as depression, symptoms, stress, and treatment. An effective search string might be "depression AND symptoms" or "depression AND treatment." There are two key ways of being a more savvy web consumer: applying criteria for evaluating sites and finding reputable information. Next we will take a look at these strategies.

Applying Evaluative Criteria to Websites. These days, anyone can create a website, whether or not they have any expertise, credentials, or authority on the topic. The problem with information on the Web is that it can be wrong or biased. Wilkas (2002) reports that a 2001 Rand study of 18 top-rated health sites yielded complete and correct information only 63% of the time. As with any published work, just because it is on the web does not mean it is valid or of quality. Gorski (2000) observes that the criteria for evaluating traditional media such as textbooks or films is applicable to the Web but also that websites need to be evaluated for accuracy, potential bias, authorship, appropriateness, accessibility, timeliness, relevance, validity, and aesthetics. This type of critique is particularly important, given that websites are neither reviewed by peers nor publishing companies before they go public.

Wright and Grabowsky (2011) advise us to behave like investigative reporters when assessing websites by finding out the "who, what, where, when, and how" (p. 81). By this they mean, *who* is responsible for creating the website? Are the author's qualifications and credentials prominently listed? Are the affiliations clear? Gorski (2000) emphasizes asking what motivated the creator of the website and who funded it. He also advocates examining what voices have been privileged versus excluded, and for what purpose. Consider the depression example. A treatment site that is sponsored by a drug company will likely promote its product as the best cure. This would be biased information that only a savvy consumer might detect. The person seeking treatment information on depression would be much better served by a nonprofit organization or medical group not affiliated with pharmaceuticals. The health field is especially resourceful when it comes to critiquing websites, probably due to the severe consequences of misinformation related to health. Wilkas (2002) highlights websites devoted to preventing fraud or quackery such as The National Fraud Information Center (http://www.fraud.org/), or the U.S. Food & Drug Administration (http://www.fda.gov/). Another popular website devoted to validating or debunking urban legends, folklore, myths, rumors, and misinformation is Snopes (http://www.snopes.com/).

It is also important to determine *why* a website exists. "Does it aspire to educate or inform, is the intent to sell something, was it created simply as a forum to 'rant' about a particular subject?" (Wright & Grabowsky, 2011, p. 81). You can find this information in the "About Us," or "Mission Statement" link on the website. To evaluate the purpose you might also critique the site's relevance to your needs, the articulation of its target population, appropriateness of graphic images, and the timeliness of updates (Gorski, 2000). You should be suspicious if this information is not readily available from the home page. Next is determining *what* the information the site seeks to collect from you and how it will be used (Wright & Grabowsky, 2011), or if it requires registration or plug-in software (Gorski, 2000). Some sites ask you to enter personal information that may be used for another purpose or sold to other interested parties. Another important aspect of the site's credibility is *when* it was last updated. If you cannot easily find a statement or date indicating updating, you should be wary. Or, if the website has not been updated in months or years and has broken links, chances are you are not getting current information.

The last criteria advocated by Wright and Grabowsky (2011) is *how* the site reviews and selects information. They emphasize that a website should reveal how and by whom its content is selected. Editorial or review boards should be listed with credentials and any claims made should be backed with evidence and reference information. Gorski (2000) suggests that credible websites clearly indicate the author(s) names, highlight credentials, explain how quality is controlled, and identify all other affiliations of the website (educational institutions, businesses, associations, and so forth). Bias should also be identified through author or sponsoring organization statements, authority of authorship, and forthrightness in identification of commercial sites. You should also look for places for website users to discuss content and offer divergent views such as through discussion forums. Wright and Grabowsky caution us to be suspicious of sites promising cures, promoting just one product or idea, or offering vague endorsements such as "several research studies show" or "scientific research proves" (2011, p. 82).

Finding Reputable Information. The amount of information available via the Internet is irresistible, overwhelming, and even intimidating. September 2012 estimates of the size of the World Wide Web are at 9.26 billion websites (http://www.worldwidewebsize.com/). Returning to the depression example, a simple Google search of the term yields 62,400,000 hits, and a search on "depression AND treatment" yields 17,400,000 hits. How do we help learners find reputable sources among a sea of information? Wright and Grabowsky (2011) suggest seeking out professional organizations related to the topic as one strategy. The learner interested in depression would find the Anxiety and Depression Association of America as one source of trustworthy, unbiased information. If you are suspicious of the accuracy of the information on a particular website, follow the advice of Wilkas (2002) and seek out reputable fraud detection sites. Wright and Grabowsky (2011) also recommend using national libraries such as The National Library of Medicine for trustworthy information. Other such libraries might be National Library of Congress or local and state libraries. National libraries can provide access to major databases and reference material. Other types of websites include personal sites, message boards, and social networking. The same guidelines as listed in the evaluation section above apply to assessing these more independent sites. Mobile applications or "apps" are also very popular as mobile devices become more widespread, although they also need to be critically evaluated. Apps can be downloaded for free or purchased on every topic imaginable. The depression sufferer can find free apps such as WebMD, which provides reputable medical information, or 3DBrain, which shows images of the brain and how it is affected by mental illness. Dozens of apps are also available that help patients monitor moods, assess sadness levels, practice relaxation and breathing techniques, or identify positive affirmations and practices to ease depression.

How Technology Is Changing and Challenging Our Roles as Educators

Technology is affecting what we learn, how we learn, and how we teach. What can we expect on the one-to-five year horizon as educators? Based on a review of current articles, interviews, papers, and research, *The 2012 Horizon Report* by The New Media Consortium and EDUCAUSE (Johnson, Adams, & Cummins, 2012) annually identifies and ranks technology trends that affect teaching, learning, and creative inquiry. The longitudinal report began in 2002 and represents a cumulative assessment of technology's potential impact on education. The report identifies trends related to technology and education and ranks the "technologies to watch" in the next five years. According to the report, the access to online resources and relationships is challenging our conceptions of education and educators, and requires us to revisit how we facilitate sense-making, coaching, and credentialing. Today, people work, learn, and study whenever and wherever they choose. The workplace is increasingly made up of collaboration-centric mobile workers, necessitating that student learning activities be structured to prepare students for online collaboration in a global context. See the link to "The Future of Work" listed in the Resources section of this chapter for a perspective on how work is changing in the Digital Age.

Although great strides are being made in the growth of mobile workers and online collaboration, the trends are not without their challenges. *The 2012 Horizon Report* (Johnson, Adams, & Cummins, 2012) notes that with this shift, the importance of digital media literacy is increasing in every discipline. Yet, that access to technology and training is not available to everyone creates what is called The Digital Divide (Bennett & Bell, 2010), as discussed earlier in this chapter. Another issue is that appropriate evaluation metrics are lagging as new forms of authoring, publishing, and researching are being continuously created. Traditional higher education is under unprecedented pressure to meet learner demand for new educational models and delivery formats in a cost-effective manner. The more innovative institutions are prevailing especially as technology is considered a "disruptive innovation" (Selingo, 2012) for more traditional institutions of higher education. The report predicts continued emergence of new models in light of the challenges. Finally, both learners and educators are constantly challenged to keep pace with the deluge of new information, software tools, and devices.

The 2012 Horizon Report (Johnson, Adams, & Cummins, 2012) featured six technologies to watch along with what it termed "three adoption horizons," referring to the technology's likely acceptance by the mainstream within a one-year, two-to-three year, and four-to-five year time frame. The one-year horizon includes mobile applications (apps) and tablets. Mobile devices (also called handheld computers, mobile phones, smartphones, and tablets) are increasingly becoming our means of accessing the Internet. Mobile apps are the fastest growing technology in education. Smartphones such as the Android and iPhone or tablets such as the iPad have apps on every topic imaginable available for free or as little as 99 cents. More and more of you will find classroom and teaching apps for these devices for tasks such as attendance taking, vocabulary building, note taking, and clicking (conducting anonymous, electronic votes in a classroom). Apps exist for a range of adult learning topics from literacy to ESL, to math. Tablet computing is the other near-term horizon technology that will enhance learning. iPads, Galaxy, and Tablet S are being widely adopted in schools and universities as less disruptive tools than mobile phones because they do not have incoming calls. These devices are continually connected to the Internet with access to apps. Tablets support gesture-based computing (navigation of the computer using hand gestures directly on the screen, for example) and their size makes viewing videos, images and presentations easy for the user.

Along the two-to-three-year horizon are game-based learning and learning analytics. Game-based learning has grown out of the popularity of gaming and is very effective for learning. Aldrich (2009) notes we have been playing games since the beginning of time and that they have been proven to enhance learning and retention as compared to traditional lecture-based teaching. Educational games range from single-player or small-group card and board games to large-scale multiplayer online games and alternate reality games. Smaller-scale games are fairly easy to integrate with coursework. The report views games that promote collaboration, problem-solving, and procedural thinking as holding the most promise for learning. Learning analytics is the ability to mine data related to student engagement, performance, and progress in practice in a way that allows for the revision of curricula, teaching, and assessment in real time. The Khan Academy offers a good example of learning analytics that allows educators to see how learners are progressing with the use of a dashboard (a visual, at-a-glance summary of progress). The learning analytics data then allows for immediate adjustments to the learning plan.

Longer term, along the four-to-five-year horizon, are the more speculative and little known gesture-based computing and the Internet of things. Gesture-based computing moves the control of computers from a mouse and keyboard to the motions of the body via new input devices, similar to the iPad screen or Wii, but much more sophisticated, intuitive, and embodied. The latest iPhones have the Siri system that blends gesture computing with voice recognition and functions as the phone owner's virtual assistant with everything from finding directions to making reservations. Gesture-based computing holds promise in that it does not rely on specific language, but rather natural human movements. The report points out that such features are very compelling in countries like India where there are over 30 native languages each spoken by more than a million speakers. Gesture-based computing is also helpful for blind, dyslexic, or other types of disabled learners who have difficulty using a keyboard. "The Internet of Things has become a sort of shorthand for network-aware smart objects that connect the physical world with the world of information. A smart object has four key attributes: it is small, and thus easy to attach to almost anything; it has a unique identifier; it has a small store of data or information; and it has a way to communicate that information to an external device on demand" (Johnson, Adams, & Cummins, 2012, p. 30). For example, Northern Arizona University uses student cards that have tags that allow easy recording of their attendance in large classes. Such devices are also being used to track animal behavior and the location of lab equipment or computers.

Electronic learning (eLearning) opportunities are widespread and multiplying, whether learners are seeking continuing education, recreation, or degrees. Availability does not necessarily translate into accessibility or adaptability when it comes to eLearning, even though most adults are attracted to it due to its convenience and flexibility. Gorard, Selwyn, and Madden (2003) caution that access to computers and information technology is not a universal panacea for engaging all people in learning. Gorard and Selwyn (2005) analyzed U.K. participation in adult education and concluded that information and communications technology is best at "increasing levels of participation within the social groups that were learning anyway" (p. 85)—participation predicted by socio-economic status, gender, age, and level of schooling. Providing access to eLearning is not simply about attracting learners. It is also a matter of providing access to those who may be less able to participate due to the cost or other life-constraints.

A notable shift that has been facilitated by CMC is what is known as the flipped classroom. The flipped classroom is one where the traditional lectures and content-driven delivery are offered online and application exercises are completed during face-to-face sessions, essentially reversing the traditional order of lecturing during class and assigning application homework. This approach fits adult education's values of active learner engagement and self-direction. EDUCAUSE (2012) outlines several advantages of the flipped classroom including that it promotes learner inquiry and collaborative learning, provides opportunities for learners to test their skill and interact in hands-on activities, helps instructors detect errors in learners' understanding and application, and gives learners the opportunity to be more self-directed in their learning. It also offers the teacher more opportunity for one-on-one interaction and guiding of the learners (Webley, 2012). Some downsides include that it requires advance preparation by teachers and learning of new technologies such as podcasting, and some students lament the absence of in-class lectures.

Parker (2013) makes recommendations for empowering learners in the context of technology. She notes that learners need to develop the ability to discern what is important and focus on it. We need to help learners move away from seeking "right" answers because "now answers are everywhere." Rather, the new educational goal should be to "learn the process, evaluate the source, question" (p. 61). We must also help learners realize that information cannot be taken at face value and instead must be questioned. Finally, Parker cautions that technology may promote breadth of understanding over depth. A key competency to address all four of Parker's recommendations is critical reflection, which will be discussed in Chapter 11.

Capozzi (2000) notes that eLearning is at its best when "learning programs are technology-assisted, not technology-based" (p. 37). A daunting challenge for educators is to ensure that technology does not drive the learning, but rather that learner needs and goals do. In spite of the new challenges and changes technology brings, adult educators are still tasked to create safe virtual environments for learning where materials are relevant and appeal to a range of learning styles, just as they would in face-to-face settings.

Chapter Summary

This chapter considered how the Digital Age affects adult learning and education. It began by examining the impact of technology in our lives. We explored adult learners in the digital context to understand their characteristics and engagement with technology, and how they negotiate the challenges of a wired world. We closed by assessing the teaching context and how educators can help learners become critical consumers of information, and how technology is challenging and changing our role as educators. The importance of context to learning has been a theme threading throughout this book. Just as technology is a pervasive, virtual context that both drives and distracts our learning, so too are the social and global contexts in which we live. Chapter 11 examines the role of critical reflection and perspectives and how they help us make meaning out of social context, and Chapter 12 examines how culture and context shape learning from a global perspective.

Linking Theory and Practice: Activities and Resources

1. Join a social network such as Facebook (https://www.facebook.com/) or Twitter (https://twitter.com/) and begin using it.
2. Select a unit of instruction from your area of expertise and incorporate a technology-based component such as an online discussion, podcasts, presentation with audio using the feature inside PowerPoint, or a product such as Adobe Captivate (http://www.adobe.com/products/captivate.edu.html), video or links to YouTube videos (http://www.youtube.com/), or add social networking as discussed below.
3. Create social networking opportunities for learners:
    a. Create a class Twitter account and share relevant information in Tweets and invite students to Tweet questions, particularly in large lecture formats.
    b. Create a class Facebook page, invite students to "Like" it and post relevant information and links there.
    c. Create a class wiki using Wikispaces: http://www.wikispaces.com/
4. Resources and Web Links:
    a. Aleph Molinari: "Let's Bridge the Digital Divide" TED Talk: http://www.ted.com/talks/aleph_molinari_let_s_bridge_the_digital_divide.html
    b. Videos on eLearning and Technology:
        i. TED Talk by Daphne Koller on "What We're Learning from Online Education": http://www.ted.com/talks/lang/en/daphne_koller_what_we_re_learning_from_online_education.html
        ii. Salman Kahn TED Talk, "Let's Use video to Reinvent Education": http://www.ted.com/talks/salman_khan_let_s_use_video_to_reinvent_education.html
        iii. Educational video about "The Future of Work" in a collaborative virtually connected world: http://www.youtube.com/watch?v=G8Yt4wxSblc
    c. Use Khan Academy techniques (software is chomp http://chomp.com/) where you can also find access to 3,250 digital lectures.

   d. View these reports on eLearning and Technology:
      i. GROE Roadmap for Education Technology Final Report Global Resources for Online Education (GROE) is a project sponsored by the National Science Foundation (NSF) and the Computing Community Consortium (CCC). The primary mission of the GROE project was to envision the future of educational technology and to recommend research agendas for federal funding of that vision. http://www.cra.org/ccc/docs/groe/GROE%20Roadmap%20for%20Education%20Technology%20Final%20Report.pdf
      ii. National Education Technology Plan 2010, U.S. Department of Education, Office of Educational Technology, Transforming American Education: Learning Powered by Technology, Washington, D.C., 2010: http://www.ed.gov/technology/netp-2010
      iii. U.S. Department of Education, Office of Planning, Evaluation, and Policy Development. (2010). *Evaluation of Evidence-Based Practices in Online Learning: A Meta-Analysis and Review of Online Learning Studies.* Washington, D.C.: www.ed.gov/about/offices/list/opepd/ppss/reports.html

   e. Try these mobile/tablet applications
      i. Here is a good short video with some iPad tips: http://video.foxnews.com/v/974775312001/ipad-2-basics
      ii. Top 50 iPad Apps for Educators: http://oedb.org/library/features/top_50_iphones_for_educators
      iii. 10 Apps That Make Magic on Your iPad"—*New York Times* article: http://www.nytimes.com/2010/12/09/technology/personaltech/09smart.html

   f. Check out how you can use videos and podcasting in developing content (educators) and presenting your class assignments (learners):
      i. "How to Record Weekly Videos"—Dale Suffridge, Kennesaw State University http://www.youtube.com/watch?v=uTFPUCOS5cQ
      ii. Support for creating your own podcasts: http://www.profcast.com/support/publishing_podcast.php

   g. Try some of the free courses available on the Internet:
      i. Coursera: Entrepreneurial firm that partners with universities to bring over a hundred courses to the Internet for free. https://www.coursera.org/
      ii. Kahn Academy (where you can choose from 3250 digital lectures. The site also provides a great example of the use of learning analytics) http://www.khanacademy.org/

h. Check out the monthly "7 Things You Should Know About . . ." blogs by EDUCAUSE on technology tips that answers the following seven questions about a range of topics: (1) What is it? (2) How does it work? (3) Who's doing it? (4) Why is it significant? (5) What are the downsides? (6) Where is it going? (7) What are the implications for higher education? Check out the dozens of topics here: http://www.educause.edu/research-and-publications/7-things-you-should-know-about

i. Learn about web literacy. Penn Libraries has tutorials for evaluating web resources that examines the source's authority, accuracy, bias, currency and coverage: http://gethelp.library.upenn.edu/guides/tutorials/webliteracy/

j. Unplug. Check out the "Healthy Mind Platter" (mimicking the "Choose My Plate" campaign that replaces the Food Pyramid) for tips on keeping your brain healthy and to recover from information overload: http://www.mindplatter.com/. See one of the creators, Siegel, discuss it on YouTube: http://www.youtube.com/watch?v=3EQ2tzHl3Ks

Chapter Highlights

- Although some assume online learning occurs largely in a formal, higher education class, the majority of eLearning is informal.
- The context of technology is changing how we communicate, think, and learn. It has also created an overwhelming sense of information overload for adult learners.
- The Digital Divide is global with the United States being more privileged in terms of Internet access. Within the United States, age, income, and education are key variables determining technical literacy and access.
- Key skills that learners need to develop for savvy web consumption include developing effective search strategies, critically evaluating information, and finding reputable sources.
- Technology is changing and challenging the role of adult educators.

CHAPTER ELEVEN

CRITICAL THINKING AND CRITICAL PERSPECTIVES

We have all had moments in our lives that forced us to stop and reevaluate our beliefs. Many of us can relate to questioning the political party, religious views, gender-role expectations, or cultural attitudes we grew up accepting without a second thought. What is it that makes us stop and question, and perhaps change, our beliefs? This thought process is known as critical thinking, a central goal of adult education. Critical thinking is something everyone has the capacity to do. Yet, we may not consciously evaluate our assumptions or think about how they are influenced by the wider social environment. This chapter considers what it means to be "critical." Being critical in our learning, thinking, and acting shifts our focus from the individual learner to the social structures that shape our interactions and experiences in various settings. We will locate critical thinking in its broader context, considering its philosophical underpinnings and contemporary counterparts. The chapter begins with a discussion of what it means to be critical and introduces critical theory, critical thinking, and critical action as a framework for learning and teaching.

Critical education has been important in social movements and liberation such as Freire's work with sugar cane workers in Brazil (1970/2000), Horton's work with the Highlander School on civil rights issues in the United States (1989), and the more recent "Occupy" movements in the United States. "The potential for liberation always exists when students are encouraged to step outside of their individual world, to develop empathy, to think historically, and to think critically" (Zamudio, Rios, & Jamie, 2008, p. 216). Promoting critical thinking holds great promise for adult education, yet, do we know what it is or how to do it? "Research indicates that an overwhelming majority (89%) of university faculty claim that the promotion of critical thinking is a primary objective of their instruction (Paul, Elder, & Bartell, 1997). Yet, only 19% could define critical thinking and 77% had little or no conception of how to reconcile content coverage with the fostering of critical thinking" (Mandernach, 2006, p, 41). Brookfield (2012b) defines critical thinking in education:

> Critical thinking describes the process by which students become aware of two sets of assumptions. First, students investigate the assumptions held by scholars in a field of study regarding the way legitimate knowledge is created and advanced in that field. Second, students investigate their own assumptions and the way these frame their own thinking and actions. Thinking critically requires us to check the assumptions that we hold, by assessing the accuracy and validity of the evidence for these assumptions and by looking at ideas and actions from multiple perspectives. A person who thinks critically is much better placed to take informed actions; actions that are well grounded in evidence and that are more likely to achieve the results intended. (p. 157)

Although researchers and educators agree on the importance of teaching critical thinking (Roth, 2010), there is less agreement on the best ways for promoting it through teaching (Tsui, 2002).

Being Critical

When we talk about critical thinking, what do we really mean? Brookfield (2012b), in his book *Teaching for Critical Thinking*, starts with what it is *not*. Critical thinking does not require a college education or advanced understanding of philosophy, nor is it problem solving or creativity. It does not mean you criticize persons or things, nor is it associated with age or IQ. Being critical in adult education has at least three aspects. The first, *critical theory*, is the philosophy underlying critical perspectives and approaches. Critical theory gives us a basis for critical thinking. The second, *critical thinking*, is a reflective thought process of assessing what we believe or do. The third, *critical action*, is the ability to make timely and mindful interventions once you have critically assessed your thoughts, behaviors, and options. This framework is outlined in Table 11.1 and discussed in the following sections.

Critical Theory

Critical theorists talk about "hegemony" or the process of the dominant group creating "truths" that become accepted as the natural and right way to think about something. A hegemonic assumption is something we believe because we think it is in our best interest, but over time the belief can actually hurt us. For example, many of us growing up in the United States have been told that "The American Dream"—the idea that anyone can be economically successful here with hard work and determination—is accessible to all. The reality is that certain groups have more access to this opportunity if they are privileged in terms of race, social class, education level, or gender. The more the less privileged believe in the American Dream, the less critical they become of unjust social conditions, and the more difficult it becomes for them to attain "The American Dream" than if they had rejected the ideology.

Critical theory, as implied by its name, critiques social conditions based on a Marxist goal of unremitting critique. Brookfield (2012b)

TABLE 11.1 ASPECTS OF BEING CRITICAL

Critical Theory—A Philosophy	Critical Thinking—A Thought Process	Critical Action—A Mindful and Timely Intervention

• Critiquing social conditions and how they create unequal power relations based on attributes like race, gender, class, age, sexual orientation, physical ability, and so on
• Challenging "truth" that is advanced by dominant groups
• Seeking emancipation and elimination of oppression in society
	• Reflecting on assumptions and beliefs
	• Critiquing self-thought and action
	  • Hunting assumptions
	  • Checking assumptions
	  • Seeing things from different viewpoints
	• Connecting individual experience to broader social conditions
		• Taking informed action
		• Monitoring self and group process
		  • Clarifying or changing thought
		• Altering behavior
		• Making timely interventions
		• Justifying our actions

explains it as "describ[ing] the process by which people learn to recognize how unjust dominant ideologies are embedded in everyday situations and practices. These ideologies shape behavior and keep an unequal system intact by making it appear normal" (p. 48). Dominant ideologies are broadly accepted beliefs and practices that usually work to perpetuate an economically unequal, racist, homophobic, and sexist society with negligible resistance (Brookfield). To be a critical person from a critical theory perspective, you would "take action to create more democratic, collectivist, economic, and social forms" (Brookfield, p. 49). Critical theory has been embraced by adult education as an important lens to analyze learning dynamics and environments. Critical theory helps us do three important things: (1) it gives us a framework for critiquing social conditions, (2) it challenges universal truths or dominant ideologies, and (3) it seeks social emancipation and the elimination of oppression.

Critical theorists are interested in power and how the powerful shape what we accept as knowledge and truth in society by creating ideologies we all believe in, even when they are not necessarily good for us, like capitalism. Critical theory acknowledges that the social world creates structures that confer privilege to some and marginalizes others based on attributes such as race, ethnicity, gender, age, sexual orientation, religion, class, physical ability, and so on. Critical theorists ask questions about social conditions such as "Who benefits from these arrangements?" "Who says X is true?"

Consider a practical example of social conditions that went without critique for too long, resulting in an economic crisis here in the United States. In the spirit of Brookfield's (2001) words: *"Because capitalism will do its utmost to convince us that we should live in ways that support its workings, we cannot be fully adult unless we attempt to unearth and challenge the ideology that justifies this system"* (p. 16, italics in original). What Brookfield is suggesting is that we need to critique the more visible social conditions that accompany our underlying ideology of capitalism, an ideology which we leave unquestioned. A critical theorist would argue that the worldwide financial crisis at the beginning of the 21st century was caused by failure to critique the social conditions of our economy. Many of us participated in running up credit far above our means and by taking out mortgages that we really couldn't afford. We were convinced by "truths" of "More and Bigger Is Better" and "Charge It." The banking system allowed and encouraged participation in these "truths" that were bad for everyone, except some banks that profited handsomely by people taking out loans they could not afford. It is not difficult to find a person who has been adversely affected by this fiscal crisis through loss of income, a mortgage under water, decline of investments, unemployment, reorganization at work, explosive debt, or foreclosure. Yet, in spite of a national and international financial crisis, perceptions about wealth and money are still largely myths as poignantly shown by the video on "Wealth Inequality in America" (retrieved from http://www.youtube.com/watch?v=QPKKQnijnsM). Survey participants vastly misperceived wealth distribution. This misperception is caused by hegemonic assumptions, that is, we believe in certain "myths" about the distribution of wealth in America.

Yet, the disaster could have been averted with some strenuous critique of the social conditions that created the situation. Instead, it was much more comforting to believe in unstoppable growth, escalating real estate prices, and unlimited credit—until the bubble burst. The banks claim they were neutral and in no way talked people into loans they could not afford, but from a critical perspective, they were not innocent—although likely they had bought into their ideology just as vigorously as the rest of us. Ideology is something that we are often steeped in, yet unable to see. Ideology becomes reified as truth through mass media, religious teachings, schools, the government, and so forth, and we participate in "investing in our unhappiness" as Brookfield describes in the next section.

When critical theorists critique social conditions, what they are really seeking to expose are "truths" or underlying ideologies we have accepted without question that actually function to hurt us. In the preceding example, when we accepted the economic conditions as "true" it allowed the moneyed stakeholders in our economy to retain power while those less fortunate faced financial trauma. Brookfield (2001) suggests that a critical theory of adult learning must explore how adults learn to resist ideological manipulation or, in other words, question truths that seem immutable.

What are some of the ideologies or hegemonic assumptions that govern your thought and action? Some typical U.S. hegemonic assumptions might be: "A Woman's Place Is in the Home," "Everyone Is Equal Under the Law," "Pull Yourself Up from Your Bootstraps," or "What's Good for General Motors Is Good for America." We can take the truism, "What's Good for General Motors Is Good for America" to describe hegemony. During the 20th century, American corporations became more and more powerful, ignoring changing market conditions, and enjoying more rights than individual citizens. General Motors has a long history of mismanagement, such as not anticipating the demand for fuel-efficient cars, overincentivizing purchases, stopping electric car innovation, and not anticipating the demand for trucks that culminated in the corporation going bankrupt, needing an $85 billon government bailout early into the first Obama administration. Yet this "truth" about corporate profits being good for America results in individuals losing power and income as corporations and CEOs become richer and more powerful at the taxpayers' expense. Corporate power is not in the interest of most Americans, yet few question this particular ideology. When we begin to doubt and ultimately reject unquestioning support of corporate growth and excess (or any dominant ideology), we shift away from blind acceptance of the status quo to become more emancipated in how we think about and participate in capitalism or other "isms" we previously did not question.

Critical Perspectives

Before we move on to *Critical Thinking* and *Critical Action*, the two other dimensions of our *Being Critical Framework*, it is important to note that there are critical perspectives in addition to critical theory. Coming from many disciplines, these other perspectives seek to change inequitable social, organizational, and educational systems by recognizing and challenging ideological domination and manipulation. They may be termed postmodernism, critical theory, feminist pedagogy, critical race theory, queer studies, multiculturalism, critical management studies, or critical human resource development. Critical approaches "urge us to find ways of naming, knowing, and being in the world that move outside sites of revolutions and into spaces of transformation" (Fox, 2002, p. 198). Following is a brief list of definitions of these critical perspectives that you may come across in your studies.

Postmodernism

Postmodernism, like critical theory, emerged in the 20th century. Postmodernism critiques what are considered "absolute truths" or "metanarratives" (Lyotard, 1984). A metanarrative is a grand story or shared historical account of events that is not questioned. Postmodernism questions the validity of these metanarratives. An example of a metanarrative in the United States is that everyone has an equal chance to succeed, or that over-the-top consumerism and consumption are indicators of success. Brookfield (2000) notes metanarratives affecting our field with the following postmodernist critique: "Adult education grand narratives of self-direction, andragogy or perspective transformation are seen as illusory, representative chiefly of our desire to impose a fictional, conceptual order on the chaotic fragmentation of learning and practice" (p. 34). His postmodern analysis rejects the belief that educational meaning is transparent or shared.

Postmodernists believe that knowledge can emerge from a particular context or event, and it can shift as the context, learner, or events change. Postmodernists acknowledge that your experience of a particular context or event will be different from the next person's. Correspondingly, postmodernists do not believe that there is a single rule for judging the validity of knowledge and will question anything that is presented as knowledge. Postmodernists deconstruct "knowledge" to discover discourses or assertions about what is right, good, or normal. For example, postmodernists question our use of binaries such as good/bad, right/wrong, boy/girl, teacher/student in which the *order* of the terms (noting which terms are first) conveys which term is more powerful and preferred. Postmodern critique looks for distortion of meaning as a means to gain or retain power, with the understanding that power is present in relationships, rather than held by one individual.

Feminist Pedagogy

Feminism focuses on women and other marginalized social groups, bringing attention to inequality in politics, economics, and society. Feminist pedagogy seeks to create learning environments where learners can critique social conditions and understand how their gender, race, sexuality, or class affects their personal, work, and social lives. In other words, it is not simply concerned with the individual experience of women, but rather how social forces create conditions that marginalize all women into situations such as being segregated into gendered jobs or receiving less pay than men for comparable skill and work. Feminist pedagogy principles parallel good adult education. When educators teach from this perspective, you can expect them to: share authority and decision making with learners, candidly discuss how power dynamics affect the topic, honor the experience of the learners, analyze effects of background and status on social life, empower learners through creating respectful environments where they have multiple opportunities to be heard, help learners develop voice, address power relations and authority as they arise in the classroom, challenge learners to think critically, raise issues related to sexism and heterosexism, and consider how society can be transformed. See Maher and Tetreault (1994, 2001) for a classic discussion of feminist pedagogy.

Critical Race Theory (CRT)

Critical race theory emerged from a legal movement that evolved in the 1970s as a form of critique over delayed progress of civil rights litigation and racial reform. CRT challenges us to confront the role of law in upholding white supremacy. Today CRT has become a movement in other disciplines such as education, sociology, and women's studies that seeks to promote understanding of the social and experiential context of racism. It is considered *oppositional scholarship*, that is, it challenges the experience of whites as the normative standard. Zamudio, Russell, Rios, and Bridgeman (2010) explain, "As a society, we like to believe that racism is no longer a salient social problem since it has been illegal for over 50 years. Most of us have never lived in a society where slavery was accepted, land was stolen, and segregation was legally enforced. Critical race theorists believe that not only does racial inequality continue to be embedded in the legal system . . . but that racial inequality permeates every aspect of social life" (p. 3).

White privilege is a "truth" that goes unchallenged by whites who often are unaware of the advantages conferred by their skin color: "Whites don't see their viewpoints as a matter of perspective. They see it as truth" (Taylor, 1998, p. 122). CRT challenges us to recognize the pervasiveness and normalness of racism as a daily fact of life and how entrenched white supremacy is in our political and legal systems. It argues that whites are only interested in advocating for racial equality when their interests are accommodated in the process. Peggy McIntosh's groundbreaking article on "White Privilege: Unpacking the Invisible Knapsack" (1988) is a powerful statement on how white privilege is invisible to whites, and provides an excellent perspective for class dialogue. See the resources section for a link to the article.

Queer Studies

Different from Queer Theory (an analysis within queer studies that challenges how we socially construct categories of sexuality), queer studies emerged approximately 20 years ago. It is a multidisciplinary field grounded in critical theory that explores power relations related to sexuality and gender identity with a focus on LGBTI (lesbian, gay, bisexual, transgender, and intersex) individuals. Development of this critical perspective has been influenced by Michael Foucault, Gayle Rubin, Leo Bersani, Eve Kosofsky Sedwick, and Judith Butler, among many others

(Warner, 2012). Similar to critical theory's critique of social conditions and challenging of truths, queer studies confronts how ideologies of sexuality have developed to privilege heterosexuality as the norm. Queer studies examines queer influences in society and is also concerned with their relationship to the social and political oppression of marginalized people based on gender, race, and class.

Multiculturalism

Multiculturalism is a perspective that values diverse and multiple cultures within a society. Rather than seeking the "melting pot" status where many cultures meld together into one, multiculturalism respects the unique identities and contributions of individuals and their cultures. Multicultural education is concerned with providing strategies for educators to create democratic, inclusive learning environments that honor the cultural diversity of learners. Multicultural education recognizes that curricular decisions are political and that what and how material is chosen is influenced by the instructor's philosophical outlook and own culture. Educators who take a multicultural perspective reflect on the consequences of their philosophical outlook and chosen pedagogy and develop awareness of how their social status affects how they address multicultural issues. Multiculturally sensitive educators will strive to provide a range of readings by diverse authors rather than those who represent dominant groups. They will also honor diverse perspectives and create opportunities for learners to share their voices. An important outcome of multicultural education is the creation of inclusive learning environments for adult learners (see Tisdell, 1995, for a discussion of inclusion; and Sheared, Johnson-Bailey, Colin, Peterson, & Brookfield [2010] for an extensive discussion of multiculturalism in adult education).

Critical Management Studies (CMS)

Critical management studies emerged in 1992 with a book of the same title by Alvesson and Willmott. CMS critically evaluates management theory and practice and questions the "truths" that tend to preserve power among managers and executives, typically white males. Its goals include fostering insight, providing critique, and creating a "transformative redefinition" of organization practices, cultures and structures (Alvesson & Deetz, 1996). Critical theory informs CMS's effort to "challenge the legitimacy and counter the development of oppressive institutions and practices"

(Alvesson & Willmott, 1992, p. 13) and its vision is to emancipate workers and create more accountability for managers whose acts impact the lives of employees and other stakeholders (Alvesson & Willmott, 1992). Within this perspective, management and business are privileged above all other interests, sometimes referred to as *managerialism*. CMS concerns itself with any groups who are marginalized in organizations and management relationships.

Critical Human Resource Development (CHRD)

Critical HRD emerged in the early 2000s and shares goals similar to CMS with a focus on human resource activities and how they can create oppression in organizations. CHRD challenges the concept of HRD practice that privileges managers or the bottom line and advocates for HRD that is socially conscious and responsible to multiple stakeholders. Some key problems CHRD addresses are treating workers more like commodities than humans; privileging management and shareholder interests above all others such as employees, communities, families, customers, and the environment; unquestioning acceptance of managerial power and dominance; and adopting traditional organization structures and reward systems (Bierema, 2010).

So far, we have discussed what it means to be critical, defined critical theory, and identified some key critical perspectives that have been influenced by critical theory. Next we return to our *Being Critical Framework* to understand how critical thinking and critical action relate to adult learning.

Critical Thinking

The notion of critical thinking is traceable to ancient Greece, "where intellectuals generally believed that immutable 'truths' existed, and that it was the task of great minds to discover them. For Plato (427–347 BC) and his followers, truths were universal, eternal, remote from ordinary life, and accessible only to philosophers. Falsehoods, on the other hand, were commonplace and could, when unmanaged, cause untold mischief, especially when generally believed by citizens in that worst of all political systems, democracy" (Doughty, 2006, p. 1). Another Greek philosopher, Socrates (470–399 BC), "spent his time bantering with a local audience . . . He could be expected to undo the errors of his colleagues by the use of brisk "Socratic" cross examination. By these lights, critical thinking meant the exposure of foolishness by someone wise enough to engage winningly in discussion" (Doughty, 2006, p. 2). A more modern take on critical thinking is that it is not the sole province of the elite, nor are there universal "truths" as Plato believed. Further, there are more educational methods to stimulate critical thinking than just the Socratic method of questioning learners through vigorous discussion.

Defining Critical Thinking

Critical thinking—the ability to assess your assumptions, beliefs, and actions—is imperative to survival; failure to engage in it makes you a target of those who may wish to harm or manipulate you (Brookfield, 2012b). "Intellectually engaged, skillful and responsible thinking that facilitates good judgment, critical thinking requires the application of assumptions, knowledge, competence and the ability to challenge one's own thinking. Critical thinking skills require self-correction, monitoring to judge the reasonableness of thinking, and reflexivity" (Behar-Horenstein & Niu, 2011, p. 26). If you are not able to think critically, you will not be able to defend yourself or ultimately get the outcomes you desire. Effective critical thinking is important to making good decisions throughout life such as relationship choices (friendships, dating), career selection, political orientation, dietary options, financial strategies, living situation, and child rearing (Brookfield, 2012b). Several examples of the absence of critical thinking were on display during the national debate in the United States about the Obama health care plan. One notable example was retirement-age protesters who often disrupted town hall meetings to angrily shout, "Keep Your Government Hands off My Medicare!" (Cesca, 2009). What these protestors did not understand (and vehemently disputed) is that they were already beneficiaries of a highly successful government health care program. These adults had become convinced that any government involvement was bad, yet they were essentially advocating taking away something they were already benefiting from (Medicare) in their protests. This example shows a lack of critical thinking that could harm individuals economically or medically and illustrates just how powerful an ideology can be in convincing us to "invest in our own unhappiness."

Critical thinking "is a way of living that helps you stay intact when any number of organizations (corporate, political, educational, and cultural) are trying to get you to think and act in ways that serve their purposes" (Brookfield, 2012b, p. 2). We have already raised several examples of this phenomenon including women's status, inequities in continuing education, the Holocaust, and the recent world financial crisis. Issues that require critical thinking may be as personal as deciding what brand of coffee is most environmentally sustainable, to joining a local political campaign to elect a candidate who supports community issues, to demonstrating in national protests such as the "Occupy" movements in the United States, to supporting international protests over oppression, as many have over conflicts in Egypt, Syria, Somalia, and the Sudan.

Ennis (1989) posited that critical thinkers possess certain abilities that set them apart from those who do not exhibit critical thinking. These include:

> Assume a position or change it based on the evidence
>
> Remain relevant to the point
>
> Seek information and precision in the information sought
>
> Exhibit open-mindedness
>
> Consider the big picture
>
> Focus on the original problem
>
> Search for reason
>
> Orderly consider complex components of problems
>
> Seek a clear statement of the problem
>
> Seek options
>
> Show sensitivity to others' feelings and knowledge
>
> Use credible sources

What does critical thinking look like? The next sections follow the characteristics introduced in Table 11.1 and will discuss how critical thinking is grounded in reflection, involves critique of thought and action, and connects our individual experiences to broader social conditions.

Reflecting on Assumptions and Beliefs

Thinking critically begins with an examination of your assumptions. An assumption is a deeply held belief that guides your thought and action. Brookfield (2012b) classifies assumptions into three categories: prescriptive, paradigmatic, and causal. *Prescriptive assumptions* are our beliefs about how we should behave. As educators, we may have certain prescriptive beliefs about teaching ("I *should* be able to facilitate group conflict," "I *need* to treat everyone equally," and so on). What are some prescriptive assumptions you hold?

Paradigmatic assumptions are deeply held beliefs or mental models that shape how we view the world, like the ideologies discussed earlier in this chapter. These assumptions are so deeply embedded, it may be difficult to articulate them, or surprising once we discover what they are. A mental model or paradigmatic assumption that has permeated adult education is humanism—the belief in the inherent good and potential in all people. This paradigm underlies much of modern day adult education practice such as andragogy, self-directed learning, experiential learning, and transformational learning. Patriarchy is another example of a dominant paradigmatic assumption. All of us participate in this system that protects white male power. As educators, we may be shocked to discover that we call on men more often in the classroom, yet this is one unconscious way in which teachers, whether female or male, preserve male power. Laura and Sharan are still surprised by how often women students defer power to the males in the classroom (even when they are a distinct minority). For example, the person who reports on a group activity is more often than not a male student even though he may be the *only* male in the group. Students are often shocked and embarrassed when we point out that they just engaged in a patriarchy-preserving act with their deference to the male learners!

Causal assumptions allow us to both explain and predict circumstances. For instance, if I do "X," then "Y" will occur. Most of us have been told, "Do Unto Others as You Wish to Have Done Unto You." Yet, we have probably learned, through trial and error, that doing good deeds does not always mean they return to you. What are some causal assumptions that you hold?

Critiquing Thought and Action

The next important aspect of critical thinking is to shift critique to thought and action. Brookfield (2012b) offers an excellent framework for accomplishing this that includes hunting assumptions, checking assumptions, seeing things from different viewpoints, and taking informed action. *Hunting assumptions* involves trying to identify what underlies our thought and action. Hunting assumptions is an effort to unearth what you believe and determine its accuracy. We spend our days acting on assumptions that are grounded in our experience. These actions are often embedded in deeply socialized gender roles. Imagine a woman's dog barking and pacing near his dish. She assumes the dog is hungry and feeds him. You may not think that making assumptions about pet care are as deeply embedded as those linked to dominant ideology, like patriarchy. Yet, perhaps the woman has internalized feeding the dog as part of her role in the home. Like many other women, there are probably dozens of actions this woman takes daily that are deeply embedded in patriarchy that she does not stop to question such as caregiving, unpaid labor in the home, playing a nurturing role in your relationships, deferring to her male spouse when it comes to career decisions. Brookfield refers to this behavior as "instrumental reasoning," (p. 8) or figuring out how to fix something without questioning whose interests are served by the fixing.

Next, is *checking assumptions.* Once we become aware of assumptions, then we need to assess how accurate they are. We may seek out evidence from experience, authorities, or even disciplined research. We can consider another gendered home care example: mowing the lawn. This home maintenance activity is overwhelmingly considered "men's work." If we are in the critical thinking mode of checking assumptions, we might ask how other men (and women) expect men to unquestioningly accept and adopt the home-maintenance roles in their families. The third step is *seeing things from different viewpoints.* hooks (2010) suggests that an open mind is essential for critical thinking and asks her students to embrace "radical openness" (p. 10) because we become overly attached to our own ideas and discount other ideas without even assessing them. Taking a different viewpoint in the lawn mowing example might involve seeking out other men who do not play this role in their families or women who mow their lawns and understanding their perspectives and behaviors. Finally, *taking informed action* is the final step and key goal of critical thinking. The man who mows the lawn may decide it is time to renegotiate tasks in his home or discuss assumptions about his role with his family, as does the woman who is shouldered with the responsibility of feeding the dog and providing significant amounts of dependent care. Taking informed action will be more extensively discussed later in this chapter.

Connecting Individual Experience to Broader Social Conditions

Critical thinking might make you think of someone deep in thought as they contemplate ideas or events. Although this is often the case, individual critical thinking can be shared and sometimes merged into collective reflection on assumptions and beliefs. That is not to say that at the end of the collective dialogue everyone will agree, but that conditions were created for joint assessment of assumptions. Critical thinking becomes powerful when we understand how our individual experience is not unique to us, but that others may be caught in the same dominant ideology that is hurting them. Brookfield (2012b) emphasizes "critical thinking is a social learning process" (p. 229). hooks (2010) advocates, "Critical thinking is an interactive process, one that demands participation on the part of the teacher and students alike" (p. 9). She also argues that it requires full engagement of everyone.

These collective critical thinking conditions are often sought in our classrooms where we raise challenging issues for learners to consider. Critical thinking becomes most powerful when we are able to connect our individual ideas and experiences to broader social issues. For instance, Laura once worked in corporate America and at that point in her life was not a feminist and did not put much stock in the cause. Then she started constantly bumping up against patriarchy through being invisible, harassed, questioned, and singled out as representative of all women. For a long time, she felt isolated and alone and thought that something must be wrong with her. When she finally discovered feminist critique and learned that there were philosophies that questioned social conditions and truths like critical theory, it was cathartic. Suddenly she was able to connect her individual experience with social conditions and see how her participation in this culture was actually harmful. She has never been quite the same, embarking on a new academic career aimed at exposing inequities in the workplace—thinking critically and taking action for social change.

Critical Action—Mindful and Timely Intervention

The crux of critical thinking is not simply engaging in it. It is using our insights to inform our actions. Without acting on our new knowledge, all we have is a collection of thoughts. Critical action emerges in three ways: (1) taking informed action, (2) monitoring and correcting ourselves, and (3) justifying our actions.

Brookfield (2012b) views informed action as basing our action on some evidence that supports taking it. Of course the quality of evidence you rely on will be important in how accurate your assumption was in the first place. Take medical doctors, for example. Most of us would assume that since they are highly intelligent and highly trained, that they would be excellent critical thinkers. This is not necessarily so. The best predictor of how your physician will treat your blood pressure is not based on the latest medical evidence; it is the year she graduated from medical school (M. H. Ebell, M.D., personal communication, August 30, 2012). Physicians are much more likely to base their actions on experience ("I saw angina in a similar patient yesterday—that must be what this one has too") or antidote ("This is what Dr. So-and-So does, so it must be the best approach"). In this case, assumptions might have been hunted and checked, but the process stopped there when the physician settled on poor evidence to make decisions and take action. A more informed approach would be to seek out the best research available in making treatment decisions.

What are other ways that we can take action on our critical thinking? One way is to be in a continual state of critiquing our intentions, ideologies, and actions. Effective critical thinkers and actors monitor and correct themselves as well as their group when appropriate. Opportunities for such correction are plentiful in a classroom setting. Simple things like thinking out loud or articulating our assumptions go a long way in opening up reflection and dialogue on our ideas. Brookfield (2012b) stresses that it is essential for instructors to model these behaviors to foster critical thinking in learners. Once we are mindful of our assumptions, then we can move into Brookfield's process of hunting and checking assumptions and entertaining different viewpoints. When we do this, it creates conditions for individual and collective clarification of ideas and sometimes changes to ideology and behavior. Another key aspect of critical action is making interventions that are timely. Once we have completed the critical thinking process it is time to put our new perspectives into action in a way that does the most good.

Critical thinking is not a neutral process because it asks you to question values and who benefits from your actions. Brookfield (2012b) emphasizes that "part of critical thinking is making sure that the actions that flow from our assumptions are justifiable according to some notion of goodness or desirability" (p. 15). The act of critical thinking becomes more complicated when we begin to understand the power relations tied to it. He goes on to observe, "if critical thinking is understood only as a process of analyzing information so we can take actions that produce desired results, then some of the most vicious acts of human behavior could be defined as critical thinking" (p. 16). We cannot separate critical thinking from our morals and values. This is where it becomes important that the action be both mindful and timely: mindful in the sense that it has a moral or ethical basis, and timely in that we do not wait to overthink acting when intervention is needed.

Creating a Critical Classroom

How can we most effectively facilitate critical thinking for adults? Returning to our framework introduced in Table 11.1, Table 11.2 identifies a pedagogy for introducing learners to critical theory, critical thinking, and critical action. Each will be profiled in the following sections.

Brookfield, in his 2012 book *Teaching for Critical Thinking,* offers a wealth of explanation and exercises on fostering critical thinking with adult learners. Through his own practice, he has collected data from student testimonies about the best methods for fostering critical thinking, and categorized them in five areas including: "(1) critical thinking is best experienced as a social learning process, (2) that it is important for teachers to model the process for students, (3) that critical thinking is best understood when grounded in very specific events or experiences, (4) that some of the most effective triggers to critical thinking are having to deal with an unexpected event (or disorienting dilemma as it is sometimes called), and (5) that learning critical thinking needs to be incrementally sequenced" (p. xii). Fostering critical thinking does not necessarily take more time, although it requires us to plan and facilitate learning activities with the goal of developing learners' ability to think critically.

Introducing Critical Theory

Critical theory often intimidates learners who find it too esoteric and critique oriented to have practical value. Our task as educators is to help learners relate to it individually and then connect their own experience to that of others and the broader society. We suggest three foci to facilitate learners' understanding of critical theory including: understanding power relations, recognizing ideological manipulation and hegemony, and practicing democracy. It is important to keep in mind that critical theory

TABLE 11.2 ACTIVITIES FOR CREATING A CRITICAL CLASSROOM

Introducing Critical Theory	Facilitating Critical Thinking	Taking Critical Action
• Understanding power relations • Recognizing ideological manipulation and hegemony • Practicing democracy	• Fostering critical reflection • Building a learning community • Practicing dialogical conversation	• Classroom experiential learning • Lived experience learning

is a philosophy, so what we are helping learners do is to develop a critical stance toward the world that questions social conditions and "truths" that shifts their unit of analysis away from the self to the system.

The first focus, understanding power relations, involves defining power and helping learners understand how it is conferred, used, abused, and shifted in social relations. As discussed earlier in this chapter, power is conferred to individuals on the basis of race, gender, class, position, and other variables. Critical theory is interested in how social systems of oppression protect dominant groups. One exercise might be for learners to draw a mind map of the power relations in their lives and share it with a small group. For example, a learner may write his name in the middle of a paper and then draw lines to other systems or people that he interacts with in his personal, professional, and community life. From these relationships might be linkages drawn to show how the branches of intellectual power, positional power, political power and so forth intersect and connect across systems and people. The map could have multiple levels such as family, work, community, nation, and world. The important aspect here is to help a learner who is experiencing racism (or any other form of oppression) connect it to the larger social issues that embed racism through policy, culture, and economy. Concepts of power are more fully discussed in Chapter 12.

The next focus, recognizing ideological manipulation and hegemony, involves identifying dominant ideologies that may be operating individually or collectively. "Education as a tool of colonization that serves to teach students allegiance to the status quo has been so much the accepted norm that no blame can be attributed to the huge body of educators who simply taught as they were taught" writes hooks (2010, p. 29) as she discusses that educational integrity depends on questioning our biases as both educators and learners. Otherwise, we all risk reinforcing the dominant culture through preserving ideologies of sexism, racism, classism and so forth. It might be easier for learners to begin with commonly held social ideologies and critique them, such as economic, political, racial, or gender ideologies (for example, all economic growth is good, all politicians are the same, people of color or women in important roles got there through tokenism rather than through merit). You might ask small groups to come up with a list of ideologies together and then ask learners to identify some of their individually held ones. Next small groups should take one or two examples to understand the hegemony at work within the ideology—that is, how people have come to accept a particular belief as "true," and "the way it should be."

The third focus, practicing democracy, is at the core of critical theory the ultimate goal of which is to emancipate the oppressed and transform society. Creating a democratic classroom is a first step where learners have authority and participate in decision making. We also want to promote democratic behavior during small group discussions and projects. Some examples of democratic classrooms include creating an inclusive environment where all learners have the opportunity to speak and be heard, negotiation of issues that affect the group, and confrontation of behavior that is damaging to the democracy.

Facilitating Critical Thinking

Once learners have a grasp of critical theory, we can turn our focus to individual and collective thought processes through critical thinking. In some ways, it is a continuation of the competencies that were the focus of learning critical theory. Yet, facilitating critical thinking is more focused on creating conditions that promote individual and collective learning on challenging topics. These include fostering critical reflection, building a learning community, practicing dialogical conversation, and connecting individual experience to the collective.

Fostering Critical Reflection. Critical thinking depends on our ability to examine our assumptions. This reflection can take several forms. We reflect on previous action, we reflect in action as we are doing something, and we reflect on learning itself. All of these approaches to reflection are important for critical thinking. It is important both as learners and educators that we are continually flexing our reflexive muscles. Valentin (2007) writes, "Reflection on personal experience forms a starting point in critical pedagogy" (p. 178). How can we effectively foster reflection for ourselves as both learners and educators?

As we promote the use of critical thinking to explore ideologies and hunt assumptions, it is important to ensure that we are not simply replacing a dominant ideology with a feminist or critical one (Fox, 2002). We are not really teaching critical thinking if we are convincing learners to adopt our own assumptions and ideologies. bell hooks (2010) also writes that her goal is not for her students to "become little bell hooks" but rather to become "self-actualized and self-determining" through critical thinking (p. 183).

Reflection can be fostered in a number of ways. Individual journaling is a powerful exercise. hooks (2010) gives her students short spontaneous writing assignments where they have to write a paragraph on "my most courageous moment happened when . . ." (p. 20) and share their writing with each other. You could use a number of phrases for completion related to the course content for this type of activity such as "An assumption I disagree with is . . ." or "A question I want to raise is . . ." and use them as a springboard to promote dialogue in small groups or with the full class. Current events provide powerful opportunities to reflect on ambiguous issues that do not have easy answers. Case studies also provide excellent opportunities to reflect on situations and promote dialogue about assumptions and ideas. Questioning is also a potent reflective tool. You can have students generate questions about readings or issues. Or you could explore an assumption by merely asking questions about it.

Brookfield (2012b) suggests using a Critical Incident Questionnaire (pp. 54–55) at the end of each class to help learners think critically about the learning they just experienced. He asks learners to anonymously document: (1) the most engaged moment, (2) the most distanced moment, (3) the most helpful action, (4) the most puzzling action, and (5) what surprised them most. Brookfield reviews responses before class, notes key themes, and begins the next class with a synopsis of the forms. He uses the responses as a means of both evaluating learners' development with these concepts, as well as a launch pad for discussing other issues in the class.

Building a Learning Community. How do we create an atmosphere that is conducive to critical thinking? hooks (2010) writes about the idea of "engaged pedagogy" that welcomes students to be wholly present, honest, and radically open. She observes, "Engaged pedagogy begins with the assumption that we learn best when there is an interactive relationship between the student and teacher" (p. 19). We would add that the interactivity must also occur between students. hooks begins all of her teaching by laying the foundation for community and explains multiple strategies in her book *Teaching Critical Thinking*. She emphasizes, "When everyone in the classroom, teacher and students, recognizes that they are responsible for creating a learning community together, learning is at its most meaningful and useful. In such a community of learning there is no failure. Everyone is participating and sharing whatever resource is needed at a given moment in time to ensure that we leave the classroom knowing that critical thinking empowers us" (p. 11). An important aspect of building a learning community is for the instructor to model critical thinking. This can be done by talking out loud through our own critical thought process as instructors (Brookfield, 2012b). Another community-building strategy is to learn about, discuss, and explore how issues related to our social positions, power, and privilege affect our experiences as learners and educators. These issues are brought up in class with regularity, along with readings and articles that discuss the topic.

Practicing Dialogical Conversation. It has been our experience that learners do not often know how to have a conversation with someone with whom they disagree, so helping learners build competence in this area while working with challenging concepts is fundamental to the critical thinking process. Instead of engaging in mutual dialogue, learners are often anxious to advocate their own ideas and ideologies. To mitigate this lack of conversational skill, we advocate teaching learners the concepts of effective listening and dialogue (Brookfield & Preskill, 2005; Ellinor & Gerard, 1998). hooks (2010) observes "by choosing and fostering dialogue, we engage mutually in a learning partnership" (p. 43). Brookfield (2012b) uses an exercise called "Circle of Voices" to promote dialogue. The process begins with a minute of silence. Next learners speak their thoughts in a round-robin format for up to one minute each with no interruptions from others allowed. Next the group moves into open conversation that ties back to something someone said in the opening round. hooks notes that although engaged pedagogy assumes that each learner has something valuable to contribute, it does not assume "that all voices should be heard all the time or that all voices should occupy the same amount of time" (p. 21). Brookfield echoes this stance and suggests that valuing all experience and viewpoints as equally valid simply reinforces dominant ideologies in some instances. Again, this is where awareness of power relations helps build the community—when we can point out how a dynamic in the class might have reinforced a dominant ideology or marginalized a person or group.

Taking Critical Action

"Thinking is an action" (hooks, 2010, p. 7) and moving our thinking into mindful and timely intervention is key to critical thinking that matters. How do we create experiences that help learners connect critical theory and critical reflection to critical action? We recommend creating experiential learning experiences both inside and outside the classroom.

To help learners take critical action, we can create micro opportunities during formal instruction to enact learners' newfound ability to apply critical theory and thinking. These types of activities include dialogical conversation, following democratic principles in the classroom, modeling critical approaches as the instructor, or addressing classroom dynamics that illustrate oppression or dominant ideology. See Brookfield's *Teaching Critical Thinking* for an extensive listing of exercises for classroom settings.

We can also create learning experiences for students outside the classroom by assigning learning projects that give them real-life opportunities to grapple with critical issues. We have had success with individual change projects that involve learners embracing a change that is important to them and documenting the experience throughout the semester. Another approach is to create service learning projects where learners go into the community to volunteer or conduct research.

Critical thinking causes learners to begin questioning their assumptions, which in turn allows them to see injustice in the world. How can we help them learn from that experience? Thalhammer et al. (2007) published a report indicating that what prevents people from acting on social injustice is a sense of helplessness and lack of compassion and empathy toward others. Their work focuses on how to build what they term "courageous resistance" that would foster empathy and give learners a sense that they could take action on social injustice. There are six steps to courageous resistance:

1. Engage in activities that allow bonding between people
2. Practice empathy
3. Practice care
4. Diversify from our own experience (groups who are different from us)
5. Network with other groups for access to resources, services, and support
6. Practice new skills

Callahan (2012), for example, using a critical management education framework, designed a courageous resistance project assignment aimed at helping HRD students question assumptions, focus on socially embedded power relations that are unequal, take a social perspective, and hold emancipation and a more just society as guiding principles. Callahan has her students select a community project that serves those in need and engage with that project for the equivalent of at least four days during the course of the semester; such projects include volunteering at a homeless or women's shelter, an underprivileged school district, or other agency that is not part of the students' regular interactions. Learners maintain a reflective journal of their volunteer experiences that becomes the basis for a reflection paper that describes what they learned during their volunteer experience and how that experience will serve to influence their practice as HRD professionals.

In a similar vein, Fox (2002) developed a critical thinking assignment that helps learners see a current issue from multiple perspectives. She has learners identify a current local issue that is controversial. Learners research the history of the issue and various viewpoints and solutions on it. Learners are tasked with identifying a particular proposed solution to the problem and learning about its consequences from various stakeholders in the community. After learners research the solution, they are asked to formulate their own stances toward it. Learners are expected to find a way to enter the conflict, such as writing letters to the editor or elected officials, creating educational information such as a web page or brochure, and so forth. At the end of the semester, learners discuss the consequences of the options they selected to enter the conflict during class and talk about each other's design choices.

Experiential learning that involves learners in engaging with others as in the examples offered by Thalhammer (2007), Callahan (2012), and Fox (2002) spur learners into action and help build empathy. These highly experiential learning experiences are potentially transformational for the student and stimulate action within their communities.

Chapter Summary

This chapter examined the process of being "critical" in our learning and teaching. It considered critical thinking in its broader context of critical theory, critical perspectives, and taking critical action. It defined and described critical thinking and presented strategies for promoting critical thinking with adult learners. It concluded with applications for teaching and learning.

Linking Theory and Practice: Activities and Resources

1. "White Privilege: Unpacking the Invisible Knapsack" by Peggy McIntosh
   a. Have students read this classic anti-racist article at http://www .nymbp.org/reference/WhitePrivilege.pdf or view Peggy McIntosh describing the transformation that led her to write this piece http:// www.youtube.com/watch?v=DRnoddGTMTY

    b. Facilitate a dialogue about their reactions, unrealized privilege, or experience of marginalization.

2. Engage in a dialogue about positionality, privilege, context and power. "Quotes to Affirm and Challenge" (Adapted from Brookfield, 2012b, *Teaching for Critical Thinking*, pp. 114–118)

    a. The purpose of this assignment is to give learners an opportunity to critically reflect on the readings and experience a "critical thinking" activity intended to help them unearth assumptions.

    b. Learners review the assigned readings and:

        i. Choose one quote they wish to affirm

        ii. Choose one quote they wish to challenge

    c. During class you have students share their quotes in small groups (with appropriate credits to the source), along with a brief rationale for their selections.

    d. Learners discuss the quotes.

    e. Next learners engage in a reflective audit by discussing the following questions:

        i. What were the two quotes you selected and why did you originally pick them? If you had to do this exercise again on the same text, would you still choose these quotes? If "yes," what was it in other students' comments that convinced you your choice was a good one? If "no," what was it in other students' comments that convinced you to alter your original choice?

        ii. What was the pair of quotes posed by another person that you chose to discuss and why did you select them? As you dialogued with other students, what new information or perspectives did you learn about the topic? If nothing new emerged to you, what parts of your thinking were confirmed?

        iii. What does your participation in this exercise tell you about your own patterns of thinking on this topic? What arguments or what kinds of evidence, are you drawn to, and what constitutes good research or scholarship in this topic, and what constitutes poor research or scholarship?

3. Resources and Web Links:

    a. Brookfield, S. (2012b). *Teaching for critical thinking: Tools and techniques to help students question their assumptions.* San Francisco: Jossey-Bass. This is a comprehensive text on facilitating critical thinking with adult learners that has activities for beginning, intermediate and advanced critical thinking.

    b. Dr. Stephen Brookfield.

This website offers a portal to Dr. Brookfield's work, books, articles and interviews, critical incident questionnaire, visuals, papers and workshop materials.: http://www.stephenbrookfield.com/Dr._Stephen_D._Brookfield/Home.html

    c. Critical Thinking.NET

This site provides a rigorous collection of critical thinking resources and information and was developed by Robert H. Ennis and Sean F. Ennis. http://www.criticalthinking.net/

    d. The Critical Thinking Community

The homepage for the Foundation and Center for Critical Thinking where you can find resources, books, professional development opportunities, research, conferences, assessment and testing, and online learning related to critical thinking. http://www.criticalthinking.org/

    e. bell hooks.

This Infed (Informal Education) site features a biography of bell hooks and assesses her contributions to education. http://www.infed.org/thinkers/hooks.htm

    f. Dialogue and Conversation

Freire described dialogue as "the encounter between [people], mediated by the world, in order to name the world." This Infed entry describes his notions of dialogue and learning. http://www.infed.org/biblio/b-dialog.htm

    g. Critical Thinking Assessment

The Foundation and Center for Critical Thinking's link to assessment. http://www.criticalthinking.org/pages/critical-thinking-testing-and-assessment/594

Chapter Highlights

- Critical theory is a philosophical stance that critiques social conditions and challenges ideologies we have come to accept as "truth" as a means of ending oppression and promoting emancipation.
- Critical thinking is a thought process of evaluating and critiquing our assumptions.
- Critical theory and critical thinking help us connect individual experience to broader social conditions.

- Critical theory has influenced the development of critical perspectives across disciplines including: postmodernism, feminist pedagogy, critical race theory, queer studies, multiculturalism, critical management studies, critical human resource development, and others.
- We create critical classrooms by introducing critical theory, facilitating critical thinking, and helping learners take critical action.

CHAPTER TWELVE

CULTURE AND CONTEXT, THEORY AND PRACTICE IN ADULT LEARNING

The statement "Don't tell me how educated you are, tell me how much you have traveled" has been attributed to The Prophet Mohammed (http://www.beyondthevacation.com/#/travel-quotes/4536627397). Book knowledge will only get us so far in a complex world of diverse learners and multiple cultures. We began this book examining the necessity of learning in a globalizing world where the knowledge age has replaced the industrial age, technology advances faster than we can keep up, and demographic shifts are demanding that we acknowledge, celebrate, and embrace difference. "Book knowledge" has been balanced with practical examples, applications, and resources as a means of connecting theory and practice for your journey as adult learners and educators. Every field laments the disconnect between theory and practice, and adult education is no exception. This final chapter considers how culture and context affect learning, explores the role of theory and practice in adult education, and offers a framework that integrates culture, theory, and practice. Adult learning is a journey. This book offers a means of bridging various aspects of this dynamic, diverse process.

Culture and Context

The word *culture* may conjure different images: traveling to exotic places, learning a new language, eating ethnic food, feeling uneasy and out-of-place in unfamiliar surroundings, understanding a corporate culture, or making a cultural faux pas. Culture is "a pattern of shared basic assumptions that was learned by a group as it solved its problems of external adaptation and internal integration, that has worked well enough to be considered valued and, therefore, to be taught to new members as the correct way to perceive, think, and feel in relation to those problems" (Schein, 2004, p. 17). Culture deeply influences nations, ethnic groups, geographical regions, organizations, social groups, neighborhoods, and classrooms.

Consider some examples of how culture influences social phenomena in the cases of the gender gap worldwide, and continuing professional education in the United States. Each year the World Economic Forum releases a "Global Gender Gap" report that assesses the gap between men and women in 135 countries on four criteria: economic participation and opportunity, political empowerment, educational attainment, and health and survival (http://www3.weforum.org/docs/WEF_GenderGap_Report _2011.pdf). Consistently, the status of women is highest in Nordic countries—Iceland (1), Norway (2), Finland (3), and Sweden (4), while other developed countries lag behind such as the United States (17), France (48), Brazil (82), and South Korea (107). What is the nature of the culture in these nations that causes such a disparity in women's status? Might it be related to policy? Socialization? Gendered expectations? Economic variables? How might the national culture affect women's access to and participation in education?

Another social phenomenon is around continuing education in the United States. Why is it that continuing professional education for medical doctors takes place on luxury cruises or at tropical resorts, but for teachers it usually occurs in the school cafeteria? This scenario points to the uneven distribution of privilege based on profession, and likely gender, as the majority of teachers are women. A cultural analysis of this situation means that we do not simply attribute the status of teachers or doctors to individuals, but take a broader view to understand how social and cultural forces shape access to power and privilege. It also means we might examine non-Western views of teachers and their status and find a similar situation would not exist in a culture that reveres teachers, such as Confucian culture. What other examples can you think of where the stakes seemed unfair? What cultural rules might have been at play? How has your own culture affected your participation in education and learning?

Culture can be examined from several perspectives in adult education including positionality, privilege, context, and power. *Positionality* is a visible or invisible attribute such as ableness, age, class, culture, gender, race, religion, sexual orientation, language, and so forth. Positionality is unique for each person and is derived from and influences life experiences and relationships with others. Each of us has intersecting "positions" that combine in unique ways to shape how we both experience the world, and how the world experiences us. For example, Laura is a white Midwesterner of Western European descent who was born into a working class family that moved up to the middle class during her youth. She was privileged to receive an excellent education as a result of her family's social and economic position. Laura's positionality is a mixture of the racial, geographical, ethnic cultures she belongs to and her positions within the culture based on gender, race, sexuality, socioeconomic status, and so forth. If we refer back to the gender gap study described above, women's positionality confers different levels of privilege depending on the country in which they reside. Their position as women intersects with other variables to enhance or erode their economic, educational, and social equality with men.

Privilege is unearned power based on race, gender, class, or another positionality. Referred to by McIntosh (1988) as an invisible knapsack, privilege is something carried by certain people, often without awareness. For example, those who carry around the knapsack of white privilege "Can go shopping alone most of the time, pretty well assured that [they] will not be followed or harassed . . . [They] can choose blemish cover or bandages in "flesh" color and have them more or less match [their] skin . . . [They] can swear, or dress in second hand clothes, or not answer letters, without having people attribute these choices to the bad morals, the poverty, or the illiteracy of [their] race" (McIntosh, n.p.). Oppression, on the other hand, is the marginalization of a nondominant person or group by the privileged group. Within every culture you will find the dynamics of privilege and oppression between social groups. In the continuing professional education example, doctors are more privileged than teachers. Although such privilege may be invisible to doctors, it is likely that teachers are aware that other professions enjoy perks not available to them. Take a few moments and reflect on these ideas. What is your culture? What is your positionality? What gives you privilege in the world? What makes you marginalized in the world? These questions may be difficult to answer if you have been especially privileged, for instance, if you are white, male, able-bodied, heterosexual, or possess wealth. Because they offer insights into our thoughts and actions, becoming versed and aware of positionality and privilege, and comfortable talking about it, are key skills as an educator and learner. See the "Positionality Pie" exercise at the end of this chapter to examine your positionality more closely.

Culture is a set of shared, yet often unarticulated assumptions that permeate thought and action. Culture deeply affects social context. Education happens in contexts that are populated by humans who have multiple, conflicting agendas, and varying degrees of power and privilege. *Context* refers to the social system that shapes the thought and action of people within a particular setting such as a classroom, school, organization, community, or nation. "Context" in adult education has been equated with the history and culture of the learner (Malcolm & Zukas, 2001), the setting where adult education takes place (Hanson, 1996; McIntyre, 2000), and learning environments (Alheit, 1999; Field & Schuller, 1999). Consider the context of an English as a Second Language (ESL) classroom. The learners come from multiple cultures with multiple agendas such as to learn to speak a new language, get a job, understand what their children are learning, and so forth. The teacher also has an agenda such as to teach, make an income, or gain a promotion, and is often of a different cultural background from the learners. When two or more people engage within a social context, dynamics between their cultures, positionalities, and privileges result in power relations.

Power is the ability to influence others or to bring about change. The exercise of power happens through relationships, such as those among students or between the students and teacher. Within the ESL classroom, the male Hispanic student who speaks the best English may become the class leader based on his gendered privilege and speaking ability. This student may be more inclined to speak up and communicate with the teacher or school administrators on behalf of the other learners. The teacher may be a feminist, partial to the struggles that her women learners experience and willing to be more flexible when they ask for exceptions. Or, she may be insensitive to the cultural traditions and expectations of her learners. All individuals have some degree of power, although it may be equal or unequal, stable, shifting, or changing, depending on the context and their privilege.

Within a classroom, the instructor has formal power, but that is not to say the students are powerless. They can influence each other, the instructor, and the administration around classroom and institution issues. When we are able to exercise power in relationships, we are generally privileged. For example, the ESL male student leader may be looked up to by other students in his class for his language skills and finesse with the educational institution. He may also find kinship and understanding with other

Hispanics who are struggling in a new culture and country where there is a strong anti-immigrant sentiment. Yet this same man may see his power eroded in other settings. He may encounter discrimination at work based on ethnicity and language skills when he is overlooked for opportunities and promotions. He may be viewed with suspicion when he enters a department store to shop. His positionality creates different dynamics depending on the individuals within the particular context.

These dynamics of culture and context play out in adult education. For example, classrooms are increasingly multicultural. Teaching methods such as andragogy may be comfortable for learners who grew up in Western cultures and feel free to share personal experiences, but highly uncomfortable and foreign for learners from non-Western cultures. In another example, access to education is influenced by availability of funding and technology that are dependent on power and privilege. The ability to connect to the Internet is becoming increasingly important not only for learning, but also for making basic everyday transactions, as discussed in Chapter 10. Countries lacking the resources and technological infrastructure to connect to the Internet will fall further and further behind countries with better access. Educational practices and equal access to resources do not always effectively cross cultural borders, making teaching and learning increasingly challenging in a global context.

Culture and Learning

"Cultural background, assumptions, and view of the world influence our understanding of adult learning" (Johansen & McLean, 2006, p. 321) and the traditional Western philosophies of education such as liberalism, progressivism, humanism, behaviorism, and radicalism (Elias & Merriam, 2005) are foreign to many worldwide who view education and learning in other ways. For instance, "Andragogy has become *the* philosophical and practical dogma for many adult educators, particularly in the United States" (Johansen & McLean, p. 325) but does not cross many cultural borders. Epistemological systems—our ways of knowing—all have different ideas about the nature of knowledge and learning depending on your country and culture.

Chapman (2011) asks, "Does theory travel?" (p. 396), raising the issue that it is created in a particular time and context noting "Social theory . . . is a collection of overlapping, contending, and colliding discourses, or ways of speaking, thinking, and acting that tries to reflect explicitly on how social life is constituted and to make social practices intelligible" (p. 396). What counts for learning and knowledge in an African context is different from that in Latin American contexts, or religious contexts such as Hinduism, Buddhism, and Islam. Merriam and Kim (2011) describe Western knowledge as emerging out of Greek thought and being relatively young as compared to other global ways of knowing. They note that the terms *Western* and *non-Western,* though commonly used for lack of a better way to differentiate these perspectives, are problematic because they set up unnatural dichotomies between types of knowing. For example, learning from experience is common in all cultures, but it is less valued in the West where formal book knowledge predominates. In reviewing a number of non-Western perspectives on learning and knowing, they suggest that learning and knowing in non-Western cultures can be characterized as (1) communal, (2) lifelong and informal, and (3) holistic.

The perspective that learning is communal locates learning in the community and is a means of collective development based on the interrelationships and interdependency of community members. Knowledge in this sense is not sought for individual development, but rather to benefit the whole community. For example, this view toward learning is found in African Ubuntu—basic respect and compassion for others in society through spirituality, consensus building, and dialogue (Nafuko, 2006); in Confucianism—learning to serve society in harmony between beings and nature (Yang, Zheng, & Li, 2006); in Buddhism—a systems view where the community operates synergistically (Johansen & Gopalakrishna, 2006); and in Hinduism—a holistic view of how individuals, organizations, society, the universe, and the cosmos are interrelated and integrated (Ashok & Thimmappa, 2006).

The next theme, that learning is lifelong and informal (Merriam & Kim, 2011), extends far beyond the Western bias toward vocationalism where learning helps adults to do their jobs better and faster. Non-Western views of lifelong learning are situated in the communal ethic discussed above where community-based, informal learning is grounded in the Buddhist principles of mindfulness (intentionally attending to daily life) and African expectations that active citizens are continually sharing their knowledge with each other to benefit the community. The Islamic worldview also values lifelong learning as "The Prophet Muhammad . . . emphasized the importance of knowledge and encouraged all people, including men and women of all races and backgrounds to learn and teach knowledge through His sayings (*hadiths*). 'Seek knowledge from cradle to grave' (Al-Bukhari 2006), for example, encourages a continuous lifelong learning philosophy" (Akdere, Russ-Eft, & Eft, 2006, p. 357). Western views of learning also tend to be biased toward formalized, teacher-centered settings in contrast to the emphasis on informal learning that is situated in daily life in non-Western settings.

Finally, the perspective that learning is holistic (Merriam & Kim, 2011), shifts away from the Western emphasis on cognitive knowing to acknowledge other ways of knowing such as somatic, spiritual, emotional, moral, experiential, and social learning as discussed in earlier chapters of this book. Non-Western views do not separate these ways of knowing. Holism is sought in Buddhism, Confucianism, Hinduism, and African and Native American cultures. Holistic learning practices include yoga in Hindu tradition, balancing the mind and body in the Buddhist pursuit of enlightenment, or using the Native American medicine wheel to represent the balance of the spiritual, emotional, physical, and mental to achieve whole personhood (Merriam & Kim).

An ongoing lament as globalization takes hold and classrooms are increasingly multicultural, diverse, and multilingual is that learning cultures often clash, particularly between East and West. Much of educational psychology is grounded in Western culture where the learner is individualistic and independent (Hu & Smith, 2011), whereas non-Western approaches view the self as more interdependent (Watkins, 2000). Eastern approaches are steeped in Confucianism, which places a high value on education where teachers not only impart a subject, but also develop learners into people of virtue, and there is a strong ethic that all individuals have a right to an education (Hu & Smith). Some key differences between the East and West respectively include: long-term versus short-term thinking, harmony and community versus individualism, artistic versus scientific inquiry, and interdependence versus independence (Trinh & Kolb, 2011–2012).

Watkins examined the literature on Western and Eastern teaching and learning to identify cross-cultural differences. Highlights of Watkins's study include that Western learners tend to view understanding as "a process of sudden insight" whereas Eastern learners view it as a lengthy process requiring significant mental energy. Eastern learners view academic success as tied primarily to effort rather than ability, in contrast to Western views. Motivation in Western societies tends to be highly individualistic and ego-driven, as compared to the concept of success being a collective venture involving peers and family in Eastern cultures and a matter of "family face" (Ho, 1993, in Watkins, 2000, p. 167).

Eastern teachers also assume different roles than they do in the West, taking on more of a parental role—one of authority and wisdom (Watkins, 2000). Western learners show their cultural bias toward cognitive learning by identifying good teaching with the ability to motivate interest, clearly explain concepts, and blend effective and varied instructional strategies. Eastern learners instead prefer teachers with deep subject knowledge, ability to answer questions, and good role modeling who are concerned with the moral development of their students. Group work is also viewed differently across these two hemispheres. Western learners are accustomed to simultaneous small-group work whereas Easterners are more inclined to use sequential small groups where two students would stand in front of the others and share a dialogue or comment on the subject while the other learners listen intently. Finally, learner questioning is also different among these teaching and learning traditions. Eastern students ask questions after they have learned independently, thus drawing on their base of new knowledge, whereas Western students are encouraged to ask questions from a place of not knowing or ignorance that is viewed as rude by Easterners. Yet in Western culture, Eastern students appear unengaged when they do not readily participate in small groups or questioning. These differences create misunderstandings and culture clashes in multicultural, global learning contexts.

Culturally Relevant Teaching

Although we often draw contrasts between Eastern and Western approaches to teaching and learning, Confucius placed a high value on applied learning, similar to the pragmatism valued in the West. "He believed that learning, thinking, and acting should go hand in hand for a complete education. He asked, 'Isn't it a pleasure to study and then to repeatedly apply what you have learned into practice?' (Analects, 1.1)" (Hu & Smith, 2011, p. 20). Trinh and Kolb (2011–2012) also point out that Eastern principles are embedded in the experiential learning theory of Kolb (1984) (see Chapter 6). They note that to accomplish more holistic learning raises the stakes for educators to build accessible and motivating learning environments for a range of learners. Citing Confucius, "'By three methods we may learn wisdom: First, by reflection, which is noblest, second by imitation, which is easiest, and third, by experience, which is the bitterest'" (Trinh & Kolb, p. 30), they show how the Kolb Learning Cycle parallels these ideas with its stages of experience, reflection, thinking, and acting. It seems there is more benefit in merging the cultural practices to achieve highly effective, varied learning for diverse learners than in maintaining they are dichotomous approaches.

How can we be more culturally sensitive for increasingly diverse adult learners? Merriam and Kim (2011) recommend that we approach learning holistically and recognize ways of knowing beyond cognitive to include somatic, emotion, and spirituality. Next it is important to recognize how learning is embedded in everyday life. We can do this by honoring the experiences and informal learning people encounter in daily life and by providing opportunities to reflect on this learning. They also recommend being responsive to learners from other cultures than our own. This means that we need to understand teaching and learning within these cultures. Pratt and Associates (2005) discuss five perspectives on teaching that reflect different culturally based beliefs about the instructor's role and responsibilities. The five perspectives are: (1) transmission, emphasizing effective delivery of content; (2) apprenticeship, involving modeling ways of being and learning through experience; (3) developmental, cultivating ways of thinking about content, discipline, or practice; (4) nurturing, facilitating self-efficacy, encouraging the learner to build confidence; and (5) social reform, seeking a better society.

McLean (2006), in summing up a special issue of *Advances in Developing Human Resources,* focused on "Worldviews of Adult Learning in the Workplace" concludes that given the diversity and distinctions among worldviews, it is unlikely that a unitary theory of adult learning will emerge. Instead, he calls for a major rethinking of our understandings of adult learning theory. He urges us to recognize the complexity of approaches to adult learning, and to acknowledge that many worldviews are incompatible with the Western notions of andragogy. He also notes that Western philosophies of humanism, behaviorism, liberalism, and radicalism are present in many learning worldviews and that we should embrace this mix in our understandings of adult learning. He also recommends, like Merriam and Kim (2011) and Pratt (2005), that we acknowledge the diversity of worldviews in our practices, and expect each learner to have a unique worldview that is an amalgam of cultures such as national, family, religious, ethnic, local, gender, and so forth. McLean notes that we cannot do this important, challenging work if we ourselves are not lifelong learners who are open to and continually exploring new views. The dynamics and conflicts that ensue when East Meets West in teaching and learning is but an example of the role of culture and context. Fortunately, there is a growing body of literature bringing in very different cultural perspectives on learning and knowing. Some of these resources are listed at the end of this chapter.

The Relationship Between Theory and Practice

Just as nations, social groups, and learners have culture, so too do fields of practice, such as adult education. Referring back to Schein's definition (2004) of culture as "A pattern of shared basic assumptions that was learned by a group . . ." (p. 17), the theories and practices we use in adult education are part of our culture as learners and educators. What are some key things you believe or do when you are teaching or learning? Perhaps you regard small-group exercises as superior to large classroom discussions. Or, you follow a particular program planning routine. Although you may not have thought much about these actions, decisions, and beliefs that you enact daily, they are your theories. "Theorizing is one of the most practical things adult educators do" (Brookfield, 2010, p. 71). By this he means that we all make assumptions, use our instincts, and rely on our theories to make decisions about what to learn or how to teach.

Lewin is credited with the saying, "Nothing is so practical as good theory," yet many of our eyes glaze over when people start discussing it. He was right though, as Brookfield (2010) points out that "all adult educators are theorists" (p. 71). We are constantly creating and acting on theories. A theory is a "coherent description, explanation, and representation of observed or experienced phenomena" (Gioa & Pitre, 1990, p. 587). Theories are created every day and embedded in our culture. For example, you might have a theory that the teacher must develop presence in an online learning environment to keep the learners motivated and engaged. We have many false assumptions of theory, such as that it is disconnected from practice, it gets created in isolation from the "real world," and theory creators do not actually practice (Lynham, 2002). Yet in reality, we are continually creating, trying, and refuting theories in our daily practice, whether we call it "theory" or not. What makes a theory "good"? "Good theory is of value precisely because if fulfills one primary purpose: That purpose is to explain the meaning, nature, and challenges of a phenomenon, often experienced, but unexplained in the world in which we live, so that we may use that knowledge and understand it to act in more informed and effective ways" (Lynham, 2002, p. 222). The idea of "good theory" is also relative, depending on your cultural background and views toward learning and teaching.

U.S. baseball player and manager Yogi Berra's famous line, "In theory there is no difference between theory and practice. In practice there is," suggests the value of practical knowledge in making tactical decisions under pressure. This practical knowledge constitutes our "theories-in use" which can often be distinguished from our "espoused theories" which are what we say or think guides our actions (see Chapter 6). Working from what we actually do in practice, Brookfield (2010) offers three conditions that can turn our practical decisions into practical "theories": (1) Theories generalize beyond individual experience and allow us to compare experiences or options; (2) theories have predictive value (if we do x, then y will occur); and (3) theories allow us to classify events. For example, take transformative learning. This theory allows us to (1) compare transformative experiences with each other. You might share pivotal learning experiences with a friend and find commonalities. (2) The theory predicts that if you have a disorienting dilemma, it is possible that your perspective may transform. Finally, (3) transformative learning allows us to classify events that might result in transformation such as unanticipated life change, life-threatening illness, shocking revelation, and so forth. Think about some area of your practice such as program or curriculum development or instructional design. How can you apply Brookfield's three conditions to develop a "practical theory"?

Cervero (1991) notes that although adult education theory and practice should be closely linked, a great disparity exists between the two, much to the frustration of both practitioners and theoreticians. Cervero points out that the relationship between theory and practice is a human invention that is influenced by history, social relations, and culture. He offers four different viewpoints about this theory-practice relationship in adult education that trace the field's historical evolution and show how this relationship is fluid and changing. The first, *Adult Education Without Theory*, emerged during the early 20th century, when there was no organized theory of adult education or professional body. Adult education was practiced by many educators of adults with no awareness of the field. Cervero notes that the notion of "practice" would assume membership in an occupational group with shared traditions and knowledge—things that did not exist at the time. In the absence of a defined theory or practice, "educators base[d] their work on a set of ideals and practical knowledge that they . . . developed through direct experience" (p. 21). This would be similar to how a practitioner who trained adults would work, but was unaware a field of adult education existed. Even in this situation, theories emerge from practice and they are culturally bound.

The first doctorate in adult education was awarded in 1935 by Columbia University, and it was 20 years later that professors of adult education met to consider what the body of knowledge of the field might be. The field has always been challenged by its diversity and the reality that many educators of adults do not view themselves as adult educators. Imel, Brockett, and James (2000) observed "many who practice adult education do not identify with adult education as a field because they do not see its relevance to their work and the learners they serve" (p. 632). The problem of adult education being widely practiced by those who neither identify with the field nor ascribe to our theories and practices is widespread.

Theory as the Foundation of Practice is the second of the four theory-practice viewpoints outlined by Cervero (1991). In this view, practical knowledge is not viewed as a sufficient basis for practice. Instead, theory is developed scientifically and applied to improve practice. "Like engineers, who do not decide whether to construct a building, but rather how to build it most effectively, the body of knowledge would be a set of value-free principles about how to conduct adult education most effectively" (Cervero, 1991, p. 24). This viewpoint gained prominence in the 1950s, corresponding with the formation of the Commission of Professors of Adult Education in the United States, and remains a dominant view today. The discourse you often hear about "gaps" between theory and practice can be traced back to this viewpoint and the drive by some to create theories comes out of this perspective. This viewpoint values theory development and assumes that a solid theory should stand, regardless of the context. Contrary to that context-free view, Kasworm, Rose, and Ross-Gordon (2010) observe that thinking about theory and practice has shifted from a belief that a general theory could be universally applied, to a more context-sensitive approach to understanding adult education.

The third viewpoint, *Theory in Practice*, involves identifying and critiquing the informal theories or tacit knowledge practitioners apply to their work as a means of improving practice. This view assumes that practitioners base their work on theory, and theory can be derived from practice. Argyris and Schön (1974) developed this idea with professionals in organizations using action inquiry and identifying learning loops to examine espoused theory versus theory-in-use. Action inquiry is a process of reflecting both *in* action and *on* action. Reflection-in-action occurs when you are in the midst of problem solving where individuals or group members might ask: "What is happening right now?" or "What assumptions are we making?" Reflection-on-action happens after-the-fact, where an individual or group members might ask, "What happened?" or "What assumptions were dominating our thinking?" or "Why did our actions contradict our words?" Action inquiry may also evaluate the level of learning by examining learning loops according to three levels. The first, *single-loop learning* involves following the rules. Argyris and Schön use the example of a thermostat set to 68 degrees and problem solving around it. When the temperature varies, our first reaction is to make sure that the deviation from the norm is corrected. We act to restore equilibrium by resetting the temperature. There is no critical reflection in this example; we simply act to restore order. In an educational sense, if the learners are not learning the content, we may push the content harder the next time. The next loop, *double-loop learning*, will cause us to question, if not change the rules. In this case we would reflect on the rules and their utility, not just deviations. We would ask, "Why is the thermostat set on 68?" Double-loop learning requires creativity and critical thinking. In the educational example, we would question why the learners are not learning and question the relevance of the content and effectiveness of the pedagogy. Finally, Triple-Loop feedback is learning about the learning itself. In this case we would reflect on how well we learned and would ask, "How well did we learn about the thermostat?" or "What assumptions impaired our ability to learn/teach effectively?"

The fourth viewpoint, *Theory and Practice for Emancipation*, unites theory and practice, recognizing that knowledge is ideological,—that is, it always reflects certain beliefs and is never a neutral phenomenon, and the goal of practice is emancipation through education. Theory and practice are conjoined in this view since they make up a single, connected reality. Rather than arguing about theory and practice, proponents of this view would question whose interests are being served by the knowledge whether the ideas came from theory or practice. This viewpoint also assumes that knowledge is the product of social and cultural relations and is aligned with critical theory. Freire is the best-known proponent of this view. This view challenges us to trace the historical and cultural underpinnings of the assumptions behind our practice.

Cervero (1991) emphasizes that this "problem" some perceive between theory and practice is not one to be solved. Instead, we need to view the theory-practice relationship as a highly conflicted matter where contradictory ideologies will collide and views of knowledge will clash. Indeed, there are cultural differences and power struggles when it comes to defining the relationship between theory and practice. Skirmishes over the meanings of theory and practice are not neutral exchanges, rather they are social and political processes of negotiation that are dealt with by real people working with real problems.

Theories are always in progress. We apply the best theories and practices until new information verifies, refines, or refutes them. Dominant groups often have power to determine theoretical frameworks. That may be one explanation for the pervasiveness of Western educational practices in education today. Chapman (2011) urges:

> If we want to exist, we need to not just take theory, but produce it. Wouldn't it be better to encourage our students and our colleagues to be good at theory and practice, to try new things, to think differently and, against the ways we've always thought, to see where it takes us[?] . . . We should still not stay home, surrounded by our old, well-worn theories. We need to get out more, invite more novel theories home for dinner, bring them into our classes, and yes, challenge ourselves and our students out of their comfort of the known and easily understood. If we want there to be an adult education field that is seen and understood and accepted in the academy, one that works to make things intelligible and better, we need some theory to do it . . . [We want] students who travel into new work and new classrooms and are welcomed there because they can think, they can theorize, they can critique, because they can make themselves understood, and they can make it different. (pp. 398–399)

A Framework for Adult Learning

As we come to a close of our exploration of the theory and practice of adult learning, let us step back and consider these ideas from multiple perspectives. Merriam, Caffarella, and Baumgartner (2007) offered a framework for adult learning that distinguishes it from child learning according to characteristics of the learner, process, and context. Here we expand that framework to consider the additional variables of the educator and the design and facilitation of the learning itself.

Oftentimes the *educator* is overlooked in discussions of teaching and learning in adult education. We believe this is a mistake as the work of helping adults learn begins with the well-being and mindset of the educator, and where he or she is involved in the learning. Throughout this book we have addressed both the educator and learner since the roles are intertwined. We also think it is important to acknowledge that all educators are learners first. Being an educator is an honor and responsibility, and striving to continually improve as educators is a lifelong learning endeavor.

Outstanding educators embody Schön's notion (1983) of the reflective practitioner stance in which they are engaged in an ongoing examination and adjustment of practice. This reflective practice gives the educator a keen sense of self and how her or his values translate into educational thought and action. As noted above, educators are in a continual state of creating and testing theories as they strive to meet learner needs. Both non-Western and Western teaching approaches have much to offer learners and we can more effectively reach diverse learners across cultures through multiple methods and by embracing multiple perspectives and worldviews.

The *learner* tends to get most of our attention, and for good reason. This book has addressed many aspects of the learner from who participates in adult education to what motivates learners. Early theoretical work in adult education focused on describing the learner. These contributions dominated from the 1960s through the 1980s and include Houle's work (1961) on understanding learner goals, Knowles' popularization (1970) of the andragogy concept, the advancement of self-directed learning as a key feature of adult learning (Knowles, 1975), and the development of lesser-known theories such as McClusky's Theory of Margin (1950). Adults participate for multiple reasons, although work-related learning remains a significant focus. Adults are also engaged in English as a second language (ESL), adult basic education (ABE), general education development (GED), credential programs, apprenticeship programs, continuing professional education, and personal development courses. Adults have high expectations for timely and relevant learning. Although adult learning has common characteristics, the diversity of learning styles and varied cultures of learners must be acknowledged and valued in the learning process. Adulthood is full of multiple demands so learning will most likely be sought when it is relevant to a life issue or problem. The learning must also be about something adults care about and find useful. Adult motivation to learn is likely to be intrinsic, that is, adults learn to meet unmet needs, resolve unwanted conditions, or reach desired goals.

Educators and learners are key stakeholders in the learning process. Just how does the learning happen? The *process* of learning is concerned with what goes on in the learner's head, heart, body, and soul that leads to change in behavior or perspective. We have seen, particularly in this chapter, that the process of learning is culturally bound and ways of learning and knowing are different and sometimes contradictory between and among cultures. Change is a major catalyst for learning in all cultures. Adulthood is characterized by constant change that may prompt an identity crisis, challenge relationships, and affect a person's sense of legacy—what will be left for the next generation. Learning helps us cope with change whether it is expected or unanticipated. For example, we might expect to leave home for the first time, become a college student, commit to a relationship, join a cause, start a family, take a new job, or assume an important community role. All of these anticipated life events are learning opportunities. We are less prepared for life's unexpected changes such as the breakup of a relationship, sudden death of a loved one, loss of a job, change in financial circumstances, or new insights gained from events, travel, or relationships. Some of these changes could evoke transformative learning, that is, shifting our way of thinking and being in the world. Change often requires us to reframe our understanding of circumstances and ideas. Adults learn through making meaning of life situations and reorganizing their understandings of ideas, and at times changing their behaviors and beliefs as a result of learning. The chapters in this book have dealt with various aspects of this learning process including motivation, the role of experience, self-directed learning, transformative learning, the brain and cognitive functioning, embodied and spiritual learning, and critical thinking.

Context has already been described in this chapter and it affects every learning exchange. Context is the social system that permeates the thinking and actions of all human beings within a particular situation such as a classroom, school, organization, community, or nation. Context may incorporate physical conditions, political conditions, economic conditions, power dynamics, and other influences that impact the people occupying that space. The physical or psychological context may also require its inhabitants to modify their thinking and action when they are occupying the space. For example, the physical context such as a classroom setup affects the exchange. A traditional lecture format with all learners facing the front will create very different interpersonal dynamics than a room where learners can sit around a table and face each other or a room that just has chairs without tables. Of course, learners from cultures that are more teacher-centered may be uncomfortable with a room set-up that turns their gaze away from the teacher and toward their peers. By the same token, the psychological environment, such as one marked by interpersonal conflict creates very different dynamics than one where there is collaboration and respect.

Effective learning for adults is cognizant of the intersecting roles the educator, learner, process, and context play in the *design and facilitation* of learning. The design and facilitation of learning is the bridge between theory and practice in adult education. It is the moment we must take our theories and concepts of adult learning and put them into practice to create relevant, timely, and engaging learning experiences for diverse learners. There is no single formula for creating powerful programs that will optimize learning for all learners. Yet, as discussed throughout this book, there are several things that educators can do to ensure that each participant has an opportunity to learn from the experience.

The impact of culture continues to be important for educators and learners as we strive to appreciate diverse ways of knowing. Although the traditional theories of adult learning are here to stay such as andragogy, self-directed learning, and transformative learning, the field is turning its focus to more contemporary emerging understandings of learning such as holistic learning, embodied learning, spirituality, non-Western ways of knowing, and technology. We would like to think this is a result of our increasingly globalized and technologically connected world. Smith (2010) suggests that holism is the most effective means of facilitating learning as it promotes a "natural state of the human being . . . [an] interconnectedness within the human being (mind, body, spirit), between humans, and between humans and the universe" (p. 150). Smith explains that the technical rational Western approach to learning fails to honor the intellectual, emotional, physical, social, aesthetic, and spiritual aspects that are important in many non-Western cultures. She notes that Western approaches privilege the intellect over other ways of knowing and value autonomy and independence over collective ways of learning. Holism, on the other hand is experiential, interdependent, community-oriented and culturally responsive. It values using the learner's culture within her learning context while inviting the learning community to engage in the learning.

Chapter Summary

Adult learning is a key survival skill in an increasingly complex world that is becoming more global, technological, and diverse on a daily basis. Learning is crucial to preparing for employment, providing a secure home for loved ones, and participating fully in society. Our individual and collective cultures affect our attitudes and opportunities for learning, as well as our expectations for the roles of learners and educators. Although Western educational theories and practices have dominated, our increasingly global, multicultural world is creating opportunities to design and facilitate more holistic teaching and learning. This book has provided a path through the vast theory and practice of adult learning. When we are designing and facilitating learning it is important to consider the educator, learner, process and context, as well as the broader culture and diversity of learners. As Mahatma Gandhi observed, "No culture can live, if it attempts to be exclusive" (in Chakrabarti, 1992). Education and learning cannot be exclusive either—our future depends on more holistic, inclusive theories and practices of adult learning for all learners.

Linking Theory and Practice: Activities and Resources

1. Interview someone from another culture and compare and contrast it with your own.
   a. What are the key social differences?
   b. How is learning and education viewed?
   c. What is the role of teachers?
2. Positionality Pie Chart Exercise
   a. Part 1: Create a pie chart to identify your group affiliations (positionalities) that have some importance to your self-concept (Examples: "Educational Degree," "woman," "Muslim," "Christian," "Asian," "Secretary," "Sorority Member," "Mother," "Caucasian," "American."

FIGURE 12.1 EXAMPLE PIE CHART

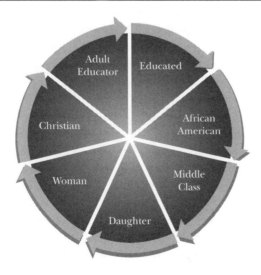

   b. Pie-Chart Exercise, Part 2: Ask learners to "fill in the blanks" of the
      following questions:
      i. Because I am _____ (a major
         group identity according to your pie chart), I have a tendency
         to _____ in relationships with other people
         who are_____.
      ii. Because I am _____ other people who are
          _____ have a tendency to _____ in their inter-
          actions with me.
   c. Part 3: Ask learners to pair off and share their respective pie charts
      and answers to these questions.
3. Visit with learners who represent a different worldview or culture from
   your own and ask them about what helps them learn.
4. Read about other learning and teaching worldviews (see Resources
   below).
5. Participate in workshops or courses taught by instructors who have a
   different worldview from your own. Reflect on the differences from
   your own views and behaviors in a classroom.
6. Read a chapter in one of the books listed in the resources on different
   religious views on teaching and learning from your own.
7. Reflect on the questions below either individually or in small groups.
   a. What are some of the theories you hold about the world around
      you?
   b. How did you derive these theories?
   c. What makes a theory "good"?
   d. Lewin was known for saying: *There is nothing quite as practical as good
      theory.* Do you agree? Why or why not?
8. Identify Theories-in-Use. Interview a practitioner about how she or he
   plans a program or instruction and try to get at their theory-in-use of
   adult education. See if it matches their espoused theory, that is, what
   they say they believe.
9. Reflect on your own program planning or instruction and see if you
   can identify your own theories and tie them to formal theories.
10. Consider some learning you have either facilitated or participated in
    as a learner. Describe the educator, learner, process, context, and
    facilitation and delivery. How can you analyze these different facets of
    learning?
11. Read one of Parker Palmer's books, such as *The Courage to Teach*
    (1998), and reflect on the role of the educator and how you see your-
    self as an educator in terms of his ideas.

12. A simple instructional design formula Laura has used for years is what she calls the "POP." This mnemonic is an easy to remember design trick that reminds us to decide the learning purpose, outcome(s), and process. The POP can be applied by both educators designing instruction and learners planning self-directed learning. To complete a POP you need to answer three questions: (1) what is the overarching *purpose* of the educational program? The *purpose* is the overarching goal and should be established with the learners and context in mind. Next, (2) what are the key learning *outcomes* desired? The *outcomes* should attend to needs of the learner, educator and context and incorporate the various learning domains (such as Affective, Behavioral, Cognitive) and accommodate diverse learning styles (sensory or experiential). Finally, (3) what is the best *process* for attaining the purpose and outcomes? The *process* should maximize different learning procedures and be sensitive to adult learners and context. Write a POP for your next teaching event or critique an existing one and see if you want to make changes.

13. Resources for Further Study:
    a. McLean, G. N. & Johansen, B.C.P. (Eds.). (2006). Worldviews of adult learning in the workplace. *Advances in Developing Human Resources: Worldviews of adult learning in the workplace, 8*(3).
    b. Merriam, S. B. (Ed.). (2007). *Non-Western perspectives on knowing and learning.* Malabar, FL: Krieger.
    c. Reagan, T. G. (2005). *Non-Western educational traditions: Indigenous approaches to educational thought and practice* (3rd ed.). Mahwah, NJ: Lawrence Erlbaum.
    d. *The Handbook of Transformative Learning,* and the six chapters in Part Three on "Culture, Positionality, and International Perspectives," Taylor, E. W. & Cranton, P. (Eds.). (2012). San Francisco: Jossey-Bass.
    e. The Center for Courage and Renewal—Based on Parker Palmer's principles. http://www.couragerenewal.org/
    f. The University of Georgia College of Education Diversity Resources http://www.coe.uga.edu/diversity/resource/

Chapter Highlights

- Culture is a set of assumptions that govern how a group perceives, thinks, and feels. It is passed on to new members of the group.

- Elements of culture include positionality, privilege, context, and power. These dynamics intersect to create power relations within a social context, including educational settings.
- Western educational theories and methods may be culturally at odds for increasingly diverse learners who come from non-Western cultures.
- Although Western and non-Western teaching and learning approaches differ, both have valuable contributions that can heighten the learning experience when blended in a more holistic manner.
- There are several ways to understand the relationship between theory and practice, each a product of the historical and cultural development of the field of adult education.
- The design and facilitation of adult learning is the moment we bridge theory and practice to engage the educator, learner, process, and context in meaningful ways for diverse learners.

REFERENCES

ADEA Commission on Change and Innovation in Dental Education, et al. (2006). Educational strategies associated with development of problem solving, critical thinking and self-directed learning. *Journal of Dental Education, 70*(9), 925–936.

Ahl, H. (2006). Motivation in adult education: A problem solver or euphemism for direction and control? *International Journal of Lifelong Education, 25*(4), 385–405.

Akdere, M., Russ-Eft, D., & Eft, N. (2006). The Islamic worldview of adult learning in the workplace: Surrendering to God. *Advances in Developing Human Resources: Worldviews of Adult Learning in the Workplace, 8*(3), 416–423.

Ala-Mutka, K. (2010). *Learning in informal online networks and communities* (EUR 24149 EN). Luxembourg: Office for Official Publications of the European Communities.

Aldrich, C. (2009). *Learning online with games, simulations and virtual worlds: Strategies for online instruction.* San Francisco: Jossey-Bass.

Alfred, M. V. (2004). Immigration as a context for learning: What do we know about immigrant students in adult education? In E. E. Clover (Ed.), *Proceedings of the Joint International Conference of the 45th Annual Adult Education Research Conference and the Canadian Association for the Study of Adult Education* (pp. 13–18), Victoria, Canada: University of Victoria.

Alheit, P. (1999). On a contradictory way to the Learning Society: A critical approach. *Studies in the Education of Adults, 31*(1), 66–82.

Allen, I. E., & Seaman, J. (2011). *Going the distance: Online education in the United States, 2011.* Babson Park, MA: Babson Survey Research Group. http://babson.qualtrics. com/SE/?SID=SV_6Xpu84FGPyTh6CM&SaveButton=1&SSID=SS_3eIMbPwGYb AxRyt

Allen, S. J. (2007). Adult learning theory & leadership development. *Leadership Review, 7*, 26–37.

Alvesson M., & Deetz, S. (1996). Critical theory and postmodernism approaches to organizational studies. In S. Clegg, C. Hardy, and W. Nord (Eds.), *Handbook of organizational studies* (pp. 191–217). Thousand Oaks, CA: Sage.

Alvesson, M., & Willmott, H. (Eds.). (1992). *Critical management studies.* London: Sage.

Alvesson, M., & Willmott, H. (Eds.). (2003). *Studying management critically.* London: Sage.

Amann, T. (2003). Creating space for somatic ways of knowing within transformative learning theory. In C. A. Wiessner, S. R. Meyer, N. L. Pfhal, & P. G. Neaman (Eds.). *Proceedings of the Fifth International Conference on Transformative Learning* (pp. 26–32). New York: Teacher's College, Columbia University.

Anderson, L. W., & Krathwohl, D. R. (Eds.). (2001). *A taxonomy for learning, teaching, and assessing: A revision of Bloom's taxonomy of education objectives.* New York: Longman.

Argyris, C. (1991, May-June). Teaching smart people how to learn. *Harvard Business Review,* 99–109.

Argyris, C., & Schön, D. A. (1974). *Theory in practice: Increasing professional effectiveness.* San Francisco: Jossey-Bass.

Arlin, P. K. (1975). Cognitive development in adulthood: A fifth stage? *Developmental Psychology, 11,* 602–606.

Arlin, P. K. (1984). Adolescent and adult thought: A structural interpretation. In M. L. Commons, F. A. Richards, & C. Armon (Eds.), *Beyond formal operations: Late adolescent and adult cognitive development* (pp. 258–271). New York: Praeger.

Arnett, J. J. (2000). Emerging adulthood: A theory of development from the late teens through the twenties. *American Psychologist, 55*(5), 469–480.

Arnett, J. J., & Tanner, J. L. (Eds.). (2006). *Emerging adulthood in America: Coming of age in the 21st century.* Washington, D.C.: American Psychological Association.

Artis, A. B., & Harris, E. G., (2007). Self-directed learning and sales force performance: An integrated framework. *Journal of Personal Selling & Sales Management, XXVII*(1), 9–24.

Ashmos, D. P., & Duchon, D. (2000). Spirituality at work: a conceptualization and measure. *Journal of Management Inquiry, 9*(2), 134–45.

Ashok, H. S., & Thimmappa, M. S. (2006). A Hindu worldview of adult learning in the workplace. *Advances in developing human resources: Worldviews of adult learning in the workplace, 8*(3), 329–336.

Aspin, D. N., Evans, K., Chapman, J., & Bagnall, R. (2012). Introduction and overview. In D. N. Aspin, J. Chapman, K. Evans, & R. Bagnall (Eds.), *Second international handbook of lifelong learning,* Part 1 (pp. xlv–lxxxiv). New York: Springer.

Astin, A. W. (2004). Why spirituality deserves a central place in liberal education. *Liberal Education, 90*(2), 34–41.

Aued, B. (February 18, 2012). Caterpillar plant will bring 4200 jobs, 2.4 billion to region. *Athens Banner Herald.* Http://onlineathens.com/local-news/2012-02-17/caterpillar-plant-will-bring-4200-jobs-24-billion-region#.UAV24bioGjA.email.

Ausubel, D. P. (1967). A cognitive structure theory of school learning. In L. Siegel (Ed.), *Instruction: Some contemporary viewpoints* (pp. 207–260). San Francisco: Chandler.

Avoseh, M.B.M. (2001). Learning to be active citizens: Lessons of traditional Africa for lifelong learning. *International Journal of Lifelong Education, 20*(6), 479–486.

Baltes, P. B., & Smith, J. (1990). Toward a psychology of wisdom and its ontogenesis. In R. J. Sternberg (Ed.), *Wisdom: Its nature, origins, and development* (pp. 87–120). Cambridge: Cambridge University Press.

Baltes, P. B., & Staudinger, U. M. (1993). The search for a psychology of wisdom. *Current Directions in Psychology Science, 2,* 75–80.

Bandura, A. (1976). Modeling theory. In W. S. Sahakian (Ed.). *Learning: Systems, models, and theories* (2nd ed., pp. 391–409). Skokie, IL: Rand McNally.

Bandura, A. (1986). *Social foundations of thought and action: A social cognitive theory.* Englewood Cliffs, NJ: Prentice Hall.

Barbour, K. (2011). *Dancing across the page: Narrative and embodied ways of knowing.* Bristol: Intellect Bristol, Great Britain.

Basseches, M. (1984). *Dialectical thinking and adult development.* Norwood, NJ: Ablex.

Bassett, C. L. (2006). Laughing at gilded butterflies: Integrating wisdom, development, and learning. In Hoare, C. (Ed.), *Handbook of adult development and learning* (pp. 281–306). New York: Oxford University Press.

Baum, J. (1978). An exploration of widowhood: Implications for adult educators. In *Proceedings of the Annual Adult Education Research Conference.* San Antonio, TX.

Baumgartner, L. M. (2012). Mezirow's theory of transformative learning from 1975 to present. In E. W. Taylor & P. Cranton (Eds.), *The handbook of transformative learning* (pp. 99–115). San Francisco: Jossey-Bass.

Behar-Horenstein, L. S., & Niu, L. (2011). Teaching critical thinking skills in higher education: A review of the literature. *Journal of College Teaching & Learning, 8*(2), 25–41.

Belenky, M. F., Clinchy, B. M., Goldberger, N. R., & Tarule, J. M. (1986). *Women's ways of knowing: The development of self, voice, and mind.* New York: Basic Books.

Bennett, E. E. (2012). A four-part model of informal learning: Extending Schugurensky's conceptual model. In J. Buban & D. Ramdeholl (Eds.), *Proceedings of the 53rd Annual Adult Education Research Conference May 31–June 3, 2012* (pp. 24–31) Saratoga Springs, N. Y.: SUNY Empire State College.

Bennett, E. E., & Bell, A. A. (2010). Paradox and promise in the knowledge society. In C. K. Kasworm, A. D. Rose, & J. M. Ross-Gordon (Eds.), *Handbook of adult and continuing education* (pp. 411–420). Thousand Oaks, CA: Sage.

Bergsteiner, H., Avery, G. C., & Neumann, R. (2010). Kolb's experiential learning model: critique from a modeling perspective. *Studies in Continuing Education, 32*(1), 29–46.

Bierema, L. L. (2010). *Implementing a critical approach to organization development.* Malabar, FL: Krieger.

Bierema, L. L. (2008). Adult learning in the workplace: Emotion work or emotion learning? In Dirkx, J. M. (Ed.). *Adult learning and the emotional self* (pp. 55–65), New Directions for Adult and Continuing Education, no. 120. San Francisco: Jossey-Bass.

Bierema, L. L., & Rand, S. (2008, May). Women's leadership development: Understanding the value of on-line social networks in corporate America. *Proceedings of the 9th International Conference on Human Resource Development Research and Practice across Europe.* Lille, France.

Billett, S. (2002). Critiquing workplace learning discourses: Participation and continuity at work. *Studies in the Education of Adults, 34*(1), 56–68.

Birzer, M. L. (2004). Andragogy: Student centered classrooms in criminal justice programs. *Journal of Criminal Justice Education, 15*(2), 393–410.

Bjorklund, B. R. (2011). *The journey of adulthood.* (7th ed.), Boston: Prentice Hall.

Bloom, B. S. (Ed.). (1956). *Taxonomy of educational objectives: Handbook I: Cognitive domain.* New York: David McKay.

Boshier, R. (1991). Psychometric properties of the alternative form of the education participation scale. *Adult Education Quarterly, 41*(3), 113–130.

Boshier, R., & Collins, J. B. (1985). The Houle Typology after twenty-two years: A large-scale empirical test. *Adult Education Quarterly, 35*(3), 113–130.

Bowman, W. (2010). Living philosophy, knowing bodies, embodied knowledge. *Action, Criticism & Theory for Music Education, 9*(1), 2–8.

Boyd, R. D., & Myers, J. B. (1988). Transformative education. *International Journal of Lifelong Education, 7,* 261–284.

Brain Metrix http://www.brainmetrix.com/

Brandon, A. F., & All, A. C. (2010). Constructivism: Theory analysis and application to curricula. *Nursing Education Perspectives, 31*(2), 89–92.

Brockett, R. G. (1994). Resistance to self-direction in adult learning: Myths and mis-understandings. In R. Hiemstra & R. G. Brockett (Eds.), *Overcoming resistance to self-direction in adult learning* (New Directions for Adult and Continuing Education, no. 64, pp. 5–12.

Brockett, R. G. (2009). Moving forward: An agenda for future research on self-directed learning. In M. G. Derrick & M. K. Ponton (Eds.), *Emerging directions in self-directed learning* (pp. 37–50). Chicago, IL: Discovery Association Publishing House.

Brockett, R. G., et al. (2000). Two decades of literature on self-directed learning: A content analysis. Paper presented at the International Self-Directed Learning Symposium, Boynton Beach, Florida.

Brockett, R. G., & Hiemstra, R. (1991). *Self-direction in adult learning: Perspectives on theory, research, and practice.* New York: Routledge, Chapman, and Hall.

Brockett, R. G., & Hiemstra, R. (2012). Reframing the meaning of self-directed learning. *Proceedings of the Adult Education Research Conference,* USA, pp. 155–162.

Brookfield, S. D. (1984). Self-directed learning: A critical paradigm. *Adult Education Quarterly, 35,* 59–71.

Brookfield, S. D. (1991). Using critical incidents to explore learners' assumptions. In J. Mezirow and Associates. *Fostering critical reflection in adulthood* (pp. 177–193). San Francisco: Jossey-Bass.

Brookfield, S. (2000). The concept of critically reflective practice. In A. L. Wilson, & E. R. Hayes (Eds.), *Handbook of adult and continuing education* (pp. 33–49). San Francisco: Jossey-Bass.

Brookfield, S. D. (2001). Repositioning ideology critique in a critical theory of adult learning. *Adult Education Quarterly, 51*(1), 7–22.

Brookfield, S. D. (2009). Engaging critical reflection in corporate America. In J. Mezirow, E. W. Taylor, & Associates. *Transformative learning in practice* (pp. 125–135). San Francisco: Jossey-Bass.

Brookfield, S. D. (2010). Theoretical frameworks for understanding the field. In C. E. Kasworm, A. D. Rose, & J. M. Ross-Gordon (Eds.), *Handbook of adult and continuing education: 2010 edition* (pp. 71–81). Thousand Oaks, CA: Sage.

Brookfield, S. D. (2012a). Critical theory and transformative learning. In E. W. Taylor & P. Cranton (Eds.), *The handbook of transformative learning* (pp. 131–146). San Francisco: Jossey-Bass.

Brookfield, S. D. (2012b). *Teaching for critical thinking: Tools and techniques to help students question their assumptions.* San Francisco: Jossey-Bass.

Brookfield, S. D., & Preskill, S. (2005). *Discussion as a way of teaching: Tools and techniques for democratic classrooms.* San Francisco: Jossey Bass.

Brooks, J. G., & Brooks, M. G. (1999). *The case for constructivist classrooms.* Alexandria, VA: Association for Supervision and Curriculum Development.

Brown, J. S., Collins, A., & Duguid, P. (1989). Situated cognition and the culture of learning. *Educational Researcher, 18*(1), 32–42.

Bryan, V. C. (2013). The power, peril, and promise of information technology to community education. In V. C. Bryan & V.C.X. Wang, (Eds.), *Technology use and research applications for community education and professional development,* pp. 1–23. Hershey: PA: IGI Global. doi:10.4018/978-1-4666-2955-4.ch001

Bryan, V. C., & Wang, V.C.X. (Eds.). (2013). *Technology use and research applications for community education and professional development.* Hershey: PA: IGI Global.

Butin, D. W. (2010). *Service learning in theory and practice: The future of community engagement in higher education.* New York: Palgrave Macmillan.

Butterwick, S., & Lawrence, R. L. (2009). Creating alternative realities: Arts-based approaches to transformative learning. In J. Mezirow, E. W. Taylor, & Associates. *Transformative learning in practice* (pp. 35–45). San Francisco: Jossey-Bass.

Bye, D., Pushkar, D., & Conway, M. (2007). Motivation, interest, and positive affect in traditional and nontraditional undergraduate students. *Adult Education Quarterly, 57*(2), 141–158.

Caffarella, R. S. (1993). Self-directed learning. In S. B. Merriam (Ed.), *An update on adult learning theory* (pp. 25–36). New Directions for Adult and Continuing Education, No. 57. San Francisco: Jossey-Bass.

Caffarella, R. S. (2000). Goals of self-directed learning. In G. A. Straka (Ed.), *Conceptions of self-directed learning: Theoretical and conceptual considerations* (pp. 37–48). Berlin, Germany: Waxmann.

Callahan, J. L. (2012). Learning to become critical: The courageous resistance project. Proceedings of the University Forum on Human Resource Development 2012 Conference. Famalicão, Portugal.

Candy, P. C. (1991). *Self-direction for lifelong learning: A comprehensive guide to theory and practice.* San Francisco: Jossey-Bass.

Capozzi, M. (2000). eLearning that starts with the learner, not the "e." *TechTrends, 44*(5), 37–39.

Carr, N. (2008). Is Google making us stupid? *Yearbook of the National Society for the Study of Education, 107*(2), 89–94. Doi: 10.1111/j.1744–7984.2008.00172.x

Cattell, R. B. (1963). Theory of fluid and crystallized intelligence: A critical experiment. *Journal of Educational Psychology, 54,* 1–22.

Cervero, R. (1991). Changing relationships between theory and practice. In J. M. Peters & P. Jarvis (Eds.). *Adult education: Evolution and achievements in a developing field of study.* San Francisco: Jossey-Bass.

Cesca, B. (August 9, 2009). Keep your Goddamed government hands off my Medicare! *Huffington Post.* http://www.huffingtonpost.com/bob-cesca/get-your-goddamn -governme_b_252326.html

Chang, B. (2010). Local administrative districts serving as lifelong learning communities: A case study on the Zhabei Learning Community. *Adult Learning, 21*(3–4), 27–33.

Chapman, V. L. (2011). Attending to the theoretical landscape in adult education. In S. B. Merriam & A. P. Grace (Eds.), *The Jossey-Bass reader on contemporary issues in adult education,* pp. 395–400. San Francisco: Jossey-Bass.

Chakrabarti, M. (1992). *Ghandian humanism*. New Delhi, India: Concept Publishing Company.

Charaniya, N. K. (2012). Cultural-spiritual perspective of transformative learning. In E. W. Taylor & P. Cranton (Eds.), *The handbook of transformative learning* (pp. 231–244). San Francisco: Jossey-Bass.

Cheville, J. (2005). Confronting the problem of embodiment. *International Journal of Qualitative Studies in Education, 18*(1), 85–107.

Chickering, A. W., Dalton, J. C., & Stamm, L. (2006). *Encouraging authenticity and spirituality in higher education*. San Francisco: Jossey-Bass.

Chisholm, C. U., Harris, M.S.G., Northwood, D. O., & Johrendt, J. L. (2009). The characterisation of work-based learning by consideration of the theories of experiential learning. *European Journal of Education, 44*(3), 319–337.

Chu, R. J-C., & Tsai, C-C. (2009). Self-directed learning readiness, Internet self-efficacy, and preferences towards constructivist Internet-based learning environments among higher-aged adults. *Journal of Computer Assisted Learning, 25*, 489–501.

Clardy, A. (2000). Learning on their own: Vocationally oriented self-directed learning projects. *Human Resource Development Quarterly, 11*(2), 105–125.

Clark, M. C. (1993). Transformational learning. In S. B. Merriam (Ed.), *An update on adult learning theory* (pp. 47–56). New Directions for Adult and Continuing Education, No. 57. San Francisco: Jossey-Bass.

Clark, M. C. (2001). Off the beaten path: Some creative approaches to adult learning. In S. B. Merriam (Ed.), *The new update on adult learning theory* (pp. 83–92). New Directions for Adult and Continuing Education, No. 89. San Francisco: Jossey-Bass.

Clark, M. C. (2012). Transformation as embodied narrative. In E. W. Taylor & P. Cranton (Eds.), *The handbook of transformative learning* (pp. 425–438), San Francisco: Jossey-Bass.

Clinchy, B. M. (2002). Revisiting women's ways of knowing. In B. K. Hofer & P. R. Pintrich (Eds.), *Personal epistemology: The psychology of beliefs about knowledge and knowing* (pp. 63–88). Hillsdale, NJ: Erlbaum.

Clinton, G., & Rieber, L. P. (2010). The Studio experience at the University of Georgia: an example of constructionist learning for adults. *Education Tech Research Development, 58*, 755–780.

Collins, A. S., Brown, J. S., & Holum, A. (1991). Cognitive apprenticeship: Making thinking visible. *American Educator, 15*(3), 6–11, 38–46.

Conner, T. R., Carter, S. L., Dieffenderfer, V., & Brockett, R. G. (2009). A citation analysis of self-directed learning literature: 1980–2008. *International Journal of Self-Directed Learning, 6*(2), 53–75.

Conti, G. J. (2004). Identifying your teaching style. In M. W. Galbraith (Ed.), *Adult learning methods: A guide for effective instruction* (3rd ed., pp. 75–91). Malabar, FL: Krieger.

Coombs, P. H. (1985). *The world crisis in education: A view from the eighties*. New York: Oxford University Press.

Coombs, P. H., with Prosser, R. C., & Ahmed, M. (1973). *New paths to learning for children and youth*. New York: International Council for Educational Development.

Cornelius, S., & Macdonald, J. (2008). Online informal professional development for distance tutors: Experiences from The Open University in Scotland. *Open Learning, 23*(1), 43–55.

Costa, A. L., & Kallick, B. (2004). *Assessment strategies for self-directed learning.* Thousand Oaks, CA: Corwin Press/Sage.

Cowen, T. (2003). Does globalization kill ethos and diversity? *Phi Kappa Phi Forum, 83*(4), 17–20.

Cozolino, L. (2002). *The neuroscience of psychotherapy: Building and rebuilding the human brain.* New York: Norton.

Cranton, P. (2006). *Understanding and promoting transformative learning: A guide for educators of adults* (2nd ed.). San Francisco: Jossey-Bass.

Cranton, P. (in press). Transformative learning. In P. Mayo (Ed.), *Learning with adults: A reader.* Rotterdam: Sense Publishers.

Cranton, P., & Hoggan, C. (2012). Evaluating transformative learning. In E. W. Taylor & P. Cranton (Eds.), *The handbook of transformative learning* (pp. 520–535). San Francisco: Jossey-Bass.

Cranton, P., & Kasl, E. (2012). A response to Michael Newman's "Calling transformative learning into question: Some mutinous thoughts," *Adult Education Quarterly, 62*(4), 393–398.

Cranton, P., & Taylor, E. W. (2012). Transformative learning theory: Seeking a more unified theory. In E. W. Taylor & P. Cranton (Eds.), *The handbook of transformative learning* (pp. 3–20). San Francisco: Jossey-Bass.

Crowdes, M. S. (2000). Embodying sociological imagination: Pedagogical support for linking bodies to minds. *Teaching Sociology, 28*(1), 24–40.

Crowther, J. (2012). 'Really useful knowledge' or 'merely useful' lifelong learning? In D. N. Aspin, J. Chapman, K. Evans, & R. Bagnall (Eds.), *Second International Handbook of LifelongLearning,* Part 2 (pp. 801–811). New York: Springer.

Csikszentmihalyi, M. (1990). *Flow: The psychology of optimal experience.* New York: Harper & Row.

Dall'Alba, G., & Barnacle, R. (2005). Embodied knowing in online environments. *Educational Philosophy and Theory, 37*(5), 719–744.

Daloz, L. A. (2012). *Mentor: Guiding the journey of adult learners* (2nd ed.). San Francisco: Jossey-Bass.

Daloz, L. A., Keen, C. H., Keen, J. P., & Parks, S. D. (1996). *Common fire: Leading lives of commitment in a complex world.* Boston: Beacon Press.

Darling-Hammond, L., Barron, B., Pearson, P. D., Schoenfeld, A. H., Stage, E. K., Zimmerman, T. D., Cervetti, G. N., & Tilson, J. L. (2008), *Powerful learning: What we know about teaching for understanding.* San Francisco: Jossey-Bass.

Das, K., Malick, S., & Khan, K. S. (2008). Tips for teaching evidence-based medicine in a clinical setting: Lessons from adult learning theory. Part one. *Journal of the Royal Society of Medicine, 101*, 493–500.

Deeley, S. J. (2010). Service-learning: Thinking outside the box. *Active Learning in Higher Education, 11*(1), 43–53.

Dewey, J. (1963). *Experience and education.* New York: Collier Books. First published 1938.

Dia, D., Smith, C. A., Cohen-Callow, A., & Bliss, D. L. (2005). The education participation scale–modified: evaluating a measure of continuing education. *Research on Social Work Practice, 15*(3), 213–222.

Dirkx, J. M. (1998). Transformative learning theory in the practice of adult education: An overview. *PAACE Journal of Lifelong Learning, 7*, 1–14.

Dirkx, J. M. (2001). The power of feelings: Emotion, imagination and the construction of meaning in adult learning. In S. B. Merriam (Ed.), *The new update on adult learning theory* (pp. 63–72). New Directions for Adult and Continuing Education, No. 89. San Francisco: Jossey-Bass.

Dirkx, J. M. (Ed.). (2008). *Adult learning and the emotional self.* New Directions for Adult and Continuing Education, No. 120. San Francisco: Jossey-Bass.

Dirkx, J. M. (2012a). Nurturing soul work: A Jungian approach to transformative learning. In E. W. Taylor & P. Cranton (Eds.), *The handbook of transformative learning* (pp. 116–130). San Francisco: Jossey-Bass.

Dirkx, J. (2012b). Self-formation and transformative learning: A response to Michael Newman's "Calling transformative learning into question: Some mutinous thoughts," *Adult Education Quarterly, 62*(4), 399–405.

Dirkx, J. M., & Smith, R. O. (2009). Facilitating transformative learning: Engaging emotions in an online context. In J. Mezirow, E. W. Taylor, & Associates. *Transformative learning in practice* (pp. 57–66). San Francisco: Jossey-Bass.

Doidge, N. (2007). *The brain that changes itself: Stories of personal triumph from the frontiers of brain science.* New York, NY: Penguin Group.

Doughty, H. A. (2006). Critical thinking vs. critical consciousness. *College Quarterly, 9*(2), 1–54.

Drago-Severson, E. (2009). *Leading adult learning: Supporting adult development in our schools.* Thousand Oaks, CA: Corwin.

Driscoll, M. P. (2005). *Psychology of learning for instruction* (3rd ed.). Boston: Allyn and Bacon.

Dumont, H., & Istance, D. (2010). Analysing and designing learning environments for the 21st century. In Dumont, H., Istance, D. & Benavides, F. (Eds.), *The nature of learning: Using research to inspire practice* (pp. 19–34). OECD Publishing: Organisation for Economic Co-operation and Development.

Dupré, B. (2007). *50 philosophy ideas you really need to know.* London: Quercus Publishing.

Dyke, M. (2006). The role of the "Other" in reflection, knowledge formation and action in late modernity. *International Journal of Lifelong Education, 25*(2), 105–123.

Dyke, M. (2009). An enabling framework for reflexive learning: Experiential learning and reflexivity in contemporary modernity. *International Journal of Lifelong Education,28*(3), 289–310.

EDUCAUSE (February, 2012). 7 things you should know about the flipped classroom. http://www.educause.edu/research-and-publications/7-things-you-should-know -about

Elias, J., & Merriam, S. B. (2005). *Philosophical foundations of adult education.* Malabar, FL: Krieger.

Ellinger. A. D. (2004). The concept of self-directed learning and its implications for human resource development. *Advances in Developing Human Resources, 5*(1), 158–177.

Ellinor, L., & Gerard, G. (1998). *Dialogue: Creating and sustaining collaborative partnerships at work.* New York: Wiley.

English, L. M. (2000). Spiritual dimensions of informal learning. In L. M. English & M. A. Gillen (Eds.), *Addressing the spiritual dimensions of adult learning: What educators can do* (pp. 29–38). New Directions for Adult and Continuing Education, No. 85.San Francisco: Jossey-Bass.

English, L. M. (Ed.). (2001). Contestations, invitations, and explorations: Spirituality in adult learning [Special issue]. *Adult Learning, 12*(3).

English, L. M. (2005). Historical and contemporary explorations of the social change and spiritual directions of adult education. *Teachers College Record, 107*(6), 1169–1192.

English, L. M., Fenwick, T. J., & Parsons, J. (2003). *Spirituality of adult education and training.* Malabar, FL: Krieger.

Ennis, R. H. (1989). Critical thinking and subject specificity: Clarification and needed research. *Educational Researcher, 18*(3), 4–10.

Erikson, E. (1963). *Childhood and society* (2nd ed., rev.). New York: Horton.

Ettling, D. (2012). Educator as change agent: Ethics of transformative learning. In E. W. Taylor & P. Cranton (Eds.), *The handbook of transformative learning* (pp. 536–551). San Francisco: Jossey-Bass.

European Commission. (2006). *Communication for the Commission: Adult learning: it is never too late to learn.* COM(2006)614 Final: Brussels. www.ComEuropean2006_0614en01.pdf.

Fenwick, T. (2003). *Learning through experience: Troubling orthodoxies and intersecting questions.* Malabar, FL: Krieger.

Fenwick, T. (2004). The practice-based learning of educators: A co-emergent perspective. *Scholar-Practitioner Quarterly, 2*(4), 43–59.

Fenwick, T. (2008). Workplace learning: Emerging trends and new perspectives. In S. B. Merriam (ed.), *Third update on adult learning theory* (pp.17–20), New Directions for Adult and Continuing Education, No. 119. San Francisco: Jossey-Bass.

Field, J., & Schuller, T. (1999). Investigating the learning society. *Studies in the Education of Adults, 31*(1), 1–9.

Fisher-Yoshida, B. (2009). Coaching to transform perspective. In J. Mezirow, E. W. Taylor, & Associates. *Transformative learning in practice* (pp. 148–159). San Francisco: Jossey-Bass.

Fleming, J. J., & Courtenay, B. C. (2006). The role of spirituality in the practice of adult education leaders. In M. Hagen & E. Goff (Eds.), *Proceedings of the 47th Annual Adult Education Research Council* (pp. 124–129). Minneapolis, MN: University of Minnesota.

Foer, J. (2011). *Moonwalking with Einstein: The art and science of remembering everything.* New York: Penguin Press.

Foley, G. (Ed.). (2004). *Dimensions of adult learning: Adult education and training in a global era.* Berkshire, England: Open University Press.

Foos, P. W., & Clark, M. C. (2008). *Human aging.* Boston: Pearson.

Forrest III, S. P., & Peterson, T. O. (2006). It's called andragogy. *Academy of Management Learning & Education, 5*(1), 113–122.

Fowler, J. W. (1981). *Stages of faith: The psychology of human development and the quest for meaning.* New York: HarperCollins.

Fox, C. (2002). The race to truth: Disarticulating critical thinking from whiteliness. *Pedagogy: Critical Approaches to Teaching Literature, Language, Composition, and Culture, 2*(2), 197–212.

Fox, S. (January 15, 2013). Health online 2013: Survey data as vital sign. http://e-patients.net/archives/2013/01/health-online-2013-survey-data-as-vital-sign.html

Freiler, T. J. (2008). Learning through the body. In S. B. Merriam (Ed.), *Third update on adult learning theory* (pp. 37–48). New Directions for Adult and Continuing Education, No. 119. San Francisco: Jossey-Bass.

Freire, P. (1970/2000). *Pedagogy of the oppressed.* New York: Continuum.

Friedman, T. L. (2005). *The world is flat: A brief history of the twenty-first century.* New York: Farrar, Straus & Giroux.

Friedman, T. L. (August 13, 2011). A theory of everything (sort of). *The New York Times Sunday Review.* http://www.nytimes.com/2011/08/14/opinion/sunday/Friedman -a-theory-of-everyting-sort-of.html

Friedman, T. L. (January 27, 2013). Revolution hits the universities. *The New York Times, Sunday Review,* pp. 1, 11.

Gagne, R. M. (1985). *The conditions of learning.* (4th ed.). New York: Holt, Rinehart, and Winston.

Gallagher, S. (2005). *How the body shapes the mind.* New York: Oxford University Press.

Gardner, H. (1993). *Multiple intelligences: The theory in practice.* New York: Basic Books.

Gardner, H. (2000). A case against spiritual intelligence. *International Journal for the Psychology of Religion, 10*(1), 27–34.

Gardner, H., & Moran, S. (2006). The science of multiple intelligences theory: A response to Lynn Waterhouse. *Educational Psychologist, 41*(4), 227–232.

Garrison, D. R. (1997). Self-directed learning: Toward a comprehensive model. *Adult Education Quarterly, 48,* 18–33.

Garrison, D. R., & Archer, W. (2000). *A transactional perspective on teaching and learning: A framework for adult and higher education.* Oxford: Elsevier Science.

Gharibpanah, M., & Zamani, A. (2011). Andragogy and pedagogy: differences and applications. *Life Science Journal, 8*(3), 78–82.

Gibson, S. K. (2004). Social learning (cognitive) theory and implications for human Resource development. In B. Yang (Ed.), *Advances in Developing Human Resources, 6*(2), 193–210.

Ginsberg, M. B., & Wlodkowski, R. J. (2010). Access and Participation. In C. E. Kasworm, A. D. Rose, and J. M. Ross-Gordon (Eds.), *Handbook of adult and continuing education: 2010 edition.* Thousand Oaks, CA: Sage.

Gioa, D. S., & Pitre, E. (1990). Multiparadigm perspective on theory building. *Academy of Management Review, 15*(4), 584–602.

Goldberger, N. R., Tarule, J. J., Clinchy, B. M., & Belenky, M. F. (Eds.). (1996). *Knowledge, difference and power: Essays inspired by women's ways of knowing.* New York: Basic Books.

Goldenberg, J. L., Pyszczynski, T., Greenberg, J., & Solomon, S. (2000). Fleeing the body: A terror management perspective on the problem of human corporeality. *Personality and Social Psychology Review, 4*(3), 200–218.

Goleman, D. (1995). *Emotional intelligence: Why it can matter more than IQ.* New York: Bantam Books.

Gorard, S., & Selwyn, N, (2005). Towards a le@rning society? The impact of technology on patterns of participation in lifelong learning. *British Journal of Sociology of Education, 26*(1), 71–89.

Gorard, S., Selwyn, N., & Madden, L. (2003). Logged onto learning? Assessing the impact of technology on participation in lifelong learning. *International Journal of Lifelong Education, 22*(3), 281–296.

Gorski, P. (2000). Toward a multicultural approach for evaluating educational web sites. *Multicultural Perspectives, 2*(3), 44–48.

Gravett, S. (2001). *Adult learning.* Pretoria, SA: Van Schaik Publishers.

Gravett, S., & Petersen, N. (2009). Promoting dialogic teaching among higher education faculty in South Africa. In J. Mezirow, E. W. Taylor, & Associates. *Transformative learning in practice* (pp. 100–110). San Francisco: Jossey-Bass.

Gredler, R. L. (1997). *Learning and instruction: Theory into practice* (3rd ed.). Englewood Cliffs, NJ: Prentice Hall.

Green, G., & Ballard, G. H. (2010–2011). No substitute for experience: Transforming teacher preparation with experiential and adult learning practices. *SRATE Journal, 20*(1), 12–19.

Griffin, V. (2001). Holistic learning. In T. Barer-Stein & M. Kompf (Eds.), *The craft of teaching adults* (3rd ed.) (pp. 107–36). Toronto: Irwin/Culture Concepts.

Grippin, P., & Peters, S. (1984). *Learning theory and learning outcomes.* Lanham, MD: University Press of America.

Gross, R. (1999). *Peak learning* (rev. ed.). New York: Putnam.

Grow, G. (1991). Teaching learners to be self-directed: A stage approach. *Adult Education Quarterly, 41*(3), 125–149.

Grow, G. (1994). In defense of the staged self-directed learning model. *Adult Education Quarterly, 44*(2), 109–114.

Guglielmino, L. M. (1977). *Development of the self-directed learning readiness scale.* Unpublished doctoral dissertation. University of Georgia.

Gunnlaugson, O. (2008). Metatheoretical prospects for the field of transformative learning. *Journal of Transformative Education, 6*(2), 124–135.

Hanson, A. (1996). The search for a separate theory of adult learning: Does anyone really need andragogy? In R. Edwards, A. Hanson, & P. Braggett (Eds.), *Boundaries of adult learning* (pp. 99–108). New York: Routledge.

Hasan, A. (2012). Lifelong learning in OECD and developing countries: An interpretation and assessment. In D. N. Aspin, J. Chapman, K. Evans, & R. Bagnall (Eds.), *Second international handbook of lifelong learning,* Part 2 (pp. 471–498). New York: Springer.

Havighurst, R. J. (1972). *Developmental tasks and education* (3rd ed.). New York: McKay. First published 1952.

Henschke, J. A. (2011). Considerations regarding the future of andragogy. Futures Column, *Adult Learning, 22*(1–2), 34–37.

Hergenhahn, B. R., & Olson, M. H. (2005). *An introduction to theories of learning* (7th ed.). Englewood Cliffs, NJ: Prentice Hall.

Hersey, P., & Blanchard, K. (1988). *Management of organizational behavior: Utilizing human resources* (5th ed.). Englewood Cliffs, NJ: Prentice Hall.

Hiemstra, R., & Sisco, B. (1990). *Individualizing instruction.* San Francisco: Jossey-Bass.

Hill, W. F. (2002). *Learning: A survey of psychological interpretations* (7th ed.), Needham Heights, MA: Allyn & Bacon.

Holton, E. F. III, Wilson, L. S., & Bates, R. A. (2009). Toward development of a generalized instrument to measure andragogy. *Human Resource Development Quarterly, 20*(2), 169–193.

hooks, b. (2010). *Teaching critical thinking: Practical wisdom.* New York: Routledge.

Horn, J. L., & Cattell, R. B. (1966). Refinement and test of the theory of fluid and crystallized intelligence. *Journal of Educational Psychology, 57,* 253–270.

Horton, M. (1989). *The Highlander Folk School: A history of its major programs.* New York: Carlson.

Houle, C. O. (1961). *The inquiring mind.* Madison, University of Wisconsin Press.

Howard, B. (2012). Age-proof your brain: 10 easy ways to stay sharp forever. *AARP The magazine, 55*(2B), 53–54, 56.

Hu, R., & Smith. J. J. (2011). Cultural perspectives on teaching and learning: A collaborative self-study of two professors' first year teaching experiences. *Studying Teacher Education, 7*(1), 19–33.

Humes, K. R., Jones, N. A., & Ramirez, R. R. (2011). Overview of race and Hispanic origin: 2010. 2010 Census Briefs. United States Census Bureau.

Huynh, D., et al. (2009). The impact of advanced pharmacy practice experiences on students' readiness for self-directed learning. *American Journal of Pharmaceutical Education, 74*(4), 1–8.

Hye-Jin (Ed.). (2000). *Unblossomed flower: A collection of paintings by former military comfort women.* Kwangjiu-kun, Republic of Korea: The Historical Museum of Sexual Slavery by the Japanese Military.

Illeris, K. (2004a). *Adult education and adult learning.* Malabar, FL: Krieger.

Illeris, K. (2004b). *The three dimensions of learning.* Malabar, FL: Krieger.

Imel, S., Brocket, R. G., & James, W. B. (2000). Defining the profession: A critical appraisal. In A. L. Wilson & E. R. Hayes (Eds.), *Handbook of adult and continuing education* (pp. 628–642). San Francisco: Jossey-Bass.

Infed. (n. d.). Howard McClusky and educational gerontology. *Infed: The encylopaedia of informal education.* http://www.infed.org/thinkers/mcclusky.htm

INTEL. (2012). *Women and the Web: Bridging the Internet gap and creating new global opportunities in low and middle-income countries.* INTEL Corporation, Dalberg Global Advisors, & Globescan. http://www.intel.com/content/dam/www/public/us/en/documents/pdf/women-and-the-web.pdf

Jablonski, M. A. (Ed.). (2001). *The implications of students' spirituality for student affairs practice: New directions for student services.* San Francisco: Jossey-Bass.

Jarvis, P. (1987). *Adult education in the social context.* London: Croom Helm.

Jarvis, P. (2006). *Towards a comprehensive theory of human learning.* London: Routledge.

Jarvis, P. (2008). The consumer society: Is there a place for traditional adult education? *Convergence, 51*(1), 11–27.

Jensen, A. R. (2002). Psychometric g: Definition and substantiation. In R. J. Sternberg & E. L. Grigorenko (Eds.), *The general factor of intelligence: How general is it?* (pp. 39–53). Hillsdale, NJ: Erlbaum.

Johansen, B.C.P., & Gopalakrishna, D. (2006). A Buddhist view of adult learning in the workplace. *Advances in Developing Human Resources: Worldviews of Adult Learning in the Workplace, 8*(3), 337–345.

Johansen, B. P., & McLean, G. N. (2006). Worldviews of adult learning in the workplace: A core concept in human resource development. *Advances in Developing Human Resources, 8*(3), 321–328.

Johnson, L., Adams, S., & Cummings, M. (2012). *The NMC Horizon Report: 2012 Higher Education Edition.* Austin, Texas: The New Media Consortium. http://net.educause.edu/ir/library/pdf/HR2012.pdf

Johnstone, J.W.C., & Rivera, R. J. (1965). *Volunteers for learning: A study of the educational pursuits of adults.* Hawthorne, NY: Aldine de Gruyter.

Joosten, T. (2012). *Social media for educators: Strategies and best practices.* San Francisco: Jossey-Bass.

Kahneman, D. (2011). *Thinking, fast and slow.* New York: Farrar, Straus, and Giroux.

Kallenbach, S., & Viens, J. (2004). Open to interpretation: Multiple intelligences theory in adult literacy education. *Teachers College Record, 106*(1), 58–66.

Karakas, F. (2010). Spirituality and performance in organizations: A literature review. *Journal of Business Ethics, 94,* 89–106.

Kasworm, C. E., & Bowles, T. A. (2012). Fostering transformative learning in higher education settings. In E. W. Taylor & P. Cranton (Eds.), *The handbook of transformative learning* (pp. 388–407). San Francisco: Jossey-Bass.

Kasworm, C. E., Rose, A. D., & Ross-Gordon, J. M. (Eds.). (2010). *Handbook of adult and continuing education: 2010 edition.* Thousand Oaks, CA: Sage.

Kasworm, C. E., Rose, A. D., & Ross-Gordon, J. M. (2010). Looking back, looking forward. In C. E. Kasworm, A. D. Rose, & J. M. Ross-Gordon (Eds.), *Handbook of adult and continuing education: 2010 edition* (pp. 441–451). Thousand Oaks, CA: Sage.

Kee, Y. (2007). Adult learning from a Confucian way of thinking. In S. B. Merriam (Ed.), *Non-western perspectives on learning and knowing* (pp. 153–172). Malabar, FL: Krieger.

Kegan, R. (1982). *The evolving self: Problem and processes in human development.* Cambridge, MA: Harvard University Press.

Kegan, R. (1994). *In over our heads: The mental demands of modern life.* Cambridge, MA: Harvard University Press.

Kegan, R. (2000). What "form" transforms? A constructive-developmental perspective on Transformational learning. In J. Mezirow & Associates (Eds.), *Learning as transformation: Critical perspectives on a theory in progress* (pp. 35–70). San Francisco: Jossey-Bass.

Keller, J. M. (1983). Motivational design of instruction. In C. M. Reigeluth (Ed.), *Instructional-design theories and models: An overview of their current* status (pp. 383–434). Mahwah, NJ: Lawrence Erlbaum Associates.

Kemmer, D. (2011/12). Blended learning and the development of student responsibility for learning: A case study of a "widening access" university. *Widening Participation in Lifelong Learning, 133,* 60–73.

Kendall, J., Kendall, C., Catts, Z. A., Radford, C., & Dasch, K. (2007). Using adult learning theory concepts to address barriers to cancer genetic risk assessment in the African American community. *Journal of Genetic Counseling, 16*(3), 279–288.

Kenney, J. L., Banerjee, P., & Newcombe, E. (2010). Developing and sustaining positive change in faculty technology skills: Lessons learned from an innovative faculty development initiative. *International Journal of Technology in Teaching and Learning, 6*(2), 89–102.

Kezar, A. (2001). Theory of multiple intelligences: Implications for higher education. *Innovative Higher Education, 26*(2), 141–154.

Kidd, J. R. (1973). *How adults learn* (rev. ed.). New York: Association Press.

Kim, K., Hagedorn, M., Williamson, J., & Chapman, C. (2004). National Household Education Surveys of 2001: Participation in adult education and lifelong learning: 2000–01. U.S. Department of Education Institute of Education Sciences NCES 2004–050. http://nces.ed.gov/pubs2004/2004050.pdf

Kim, Y. S., & Merriam, S. B. (2010). Situated learning and identity development in a Korean Older Adults' Computer Classroom. *Adult Education Quarterly, 60*(5), 438–455.

King, K. P. (2010). Informal learning in a virtual era. In C. K. Kasworm, A. D. Rose & J. M. Ross-Gordon (Eds.), *Handbook of adult and continuing education* (pp. 421–429). Thousand Oaks, CA: Sage.

King, K. P. (2012). The mind-body-spirit learning model: Transformative learning connections to holistic perspectives. *International Journal of Adult Vocational Education and Technology, 3*(3), 37–51.

King, P. M., & Kitchener, K. S. (1994). *Developing reflective judgment.* San Francisco: Jossey-Bass.

King, P. M., & Kitchener, K. S. (2002). The reflective judgment model: Twenty years of research on epistemic cognition. In B. K. Hofer & P. R. Pintrich (Eds.). *Personal Epistemology: The psychology of beliefs about knowledge and knowing* (pp. 37–61). Hillsdale, NJ: Erlbaum.

King, P. M., & Kitchener, K. S. (2004). Reflective judgment: Theory and research on the Development of epistemic assumptions through adulthood. *Educational Psychologist, 39*(1), 5–18.

Kleiner, B., Carver, P., Hagedorn, M., & Chapman, C. (2005). *Participation in adult education for work-related reasons: 2002–03* (NCES 2006–040). U.S. Department of Education, National Center for Education Statistics. Washington, DC: U.S. Government Printing Office.

Knight, C. C., & Sutton, R. E. (2004). Neo-Piagetian theory and research: Enhancing pedagogical practice for educators of adults. *London Review of Education, 2*(1), 47–60.

Knowles, M. S. (1968). Andragogy, not pedagogy. *Adult Leadership, 16*(10), 350–352, 386.

Knowles, M. S. (1970). *The modern practice of adult education: Andragogy versus pedagogy.* New York: Cambridge Books.

Knowles, M. S. (1973). *The adult learner: A neglected species.* Houston: Gulf.

Knowles, M. S. (1975). *Self-directed learning: A guide for learners and teachers.* New York: Association Free Press.

Knowles, M. S. (1980). *The modern practice of adult education: From pedagogy to andragogy.* (2nd ed.). New York: Cambridge Books.

Knowles, M. S. (1984). *The adult learner: A neglected species* (3rd ed.). Houston: Gulf.

Knowles, M. S., & Associates (1984). *Andragogy in action: Applying modern principles of adult learning.* San Francisco: Jossey-Bass.

Knowles, M. S., Holton, E. F. III, & Swanson, R. A. (2011). *The adult learner* (7th ed.). Houston, TX: Gulf

Kohlberg, L. (1973). Continuities in childhood and adult moral development. In P. Baltes & K. Schaie (Eds.), *Life-Span developmental psychology: Personality and socialization* (pp. 180–204). Orlando: Academic Press.

Kohlberg, L. (1981). *The philosophy of moral development: Moral stages and the idea of justice.* San Francisco: Harper San Francisco.

Kokkos, A. (2012). Transformative learning in Europe: An overview of the theoretical perspectives. In E. W. Taylor & P. Cranton (Eds.), *The handbook of transformative learning* (pp. 289–303). San Francisco: Jossey-Bass.

Kolb, D. A. (1984). *Experiential learning: Experience as the source of learning and development.* Englewood Cliffs, NJ: Prentice Hall.

Kolb, D. A., Boyatzis, R. E., & Mainemelis, C. (1999), Learning Theory: Previous Research and New Directions. http://learningfromexperience.com/media/2010/08/experiential-learning-theory.pdf

Kolb, D. A., & Yeganeh, B. (2012). Deliberate experiential learning. In K. Elsbach, C. D. Kayes, & A. Kayes (Eds.), *Contemporary Organizational Behavior in Action* (pp. 1–10). Upper Saddle River, NJ: Pearson Education. http://learningfromexperience.com/research/

Komblatt, S., & Vega, F. (2009). *A better brain at any age: The holistic way to improve your memory, reduce stress, and sharpen your wits.* San Francisco, CA: Conari Press.

Kucukaydin, I., & Cranton, P. (2013). Critically questioning the discourse of transformative learning theory. *Adult Education Quarterly, 63*(1), 43–56.

Kuh, G. D. (2003). What we're learning about student engagement from NSSE. *Change, 35*(2), 24–32.

Küpers, W. (2005). Phenomenology of embodied implicit and narrative knowing. *Journal of Knowledge Management, 9*(6), 114–133.

Lanter-Johnson, Y. M. (2010). A conceptual approach to inclusive design of online learning communities: Voices of feminist professors. Unpublished doctoral dissertation, Northern Illinois University.

Lauzon, A. C. (2007). A reflection on an emergent spirituality and the practice of adult education. *Canadian Journal of University Continuing Education, 33*(2), 35–48.

Lave, J. (1988). *Cognition in practice: Mind, mathematics, and culture in everyday life.* Cambridge, UK: Cambridge University Press.

Lave, J., & Wenger, E. (1991). *Situated learning: Legitimate peripheral participation.* Cambridge, UK: Cambridge University Press.

Lawrence, R. L. (Ed.). (2012a). *Bodies of knowledge: Embodied learning in adult education.* New Directions for Adult and Continuing Education, No. 134. San Francisco: Jossey-Bass.

Lawrence, R. L. (2012b). Transformative learning through artistic expression: Getting out of our Heads. In E. W. Taylor & P. Cranton (Eds.), *The handbook of transformative learning* (pp. 471–485). San Francisco: Jossey-Bass.

Leach, L. (2005). Self-directed learning. In L. M. English (Ed.), *International encyclopedia of adult education* (pp. 565–569), New York: Palgrave Macmillan.

Lee, H. J. (2012). Rocky road: East Asian international students' experience of adaptation to critical thinking way of learning at U.S. universities. In J. Buban & D. Ramdeholl (Eds.), *Proceedings of the 53rd Annual Adult Education Research Conference*, (pp. 395–397). Saratoga Springs: NY: SUNY Empire State College.

Lee, M. (2003). Andragogy and foreign-born learners. In L. M. Baumgartner, M. Lee, S. Birden, & D. Flowers (Eds.), *Adult learning theory: A primer* (pp. 11–16). Information Series No. 392. Columbus, OH: Center on Education and Training for Employment. (ERIC Document Reproduction Service No. ED 482 337).

Lemkow, A. F. (2005). Reflections on our common lifelong learning journey. In J. P. Miller, S. Karsten, D. Denton, D. Orr, & I. C. Kates (Eds.), *Holistic learning and spirituality in education* (pp. 17–26). Albany: State University of New York Press.

Lewin, K. (1935). *A dynamic theory of personality.* New York: McGraw-Hill.

Lewin, K. (1951). *Field theory in social science.* New York: Harper & Row.

Light, T. P., Chen, H. L., & Ittelson, J. C. (2012). *Documenting learning with eportfolios: A guide for college instructors.* San Francisco: Jossey-Bass.

Lindeman, E. C. (1926/1961). *The meaning of adult education in the United States.* New York: Harvest House.

Livingstone, D. (2002). Mapping the iceberg. NALL Working Paper #54-2002. http://www.nall.ca/res/54DavidLivingstone.pdf.

Livingstone, D. W. (1999). Exploring the icebergs of adult learning: Findings of the first Canadian survey of informal learning practices. *Canadian Journal for the Study of Adult Education, 13*(2), 49–72.

Loevinger, J. (1976). *Ego development.* San Francisco: Jossey-Bass.

Long, H. B. (1998). Theoretical and practical implications of selected paradigms of self-directed learning. In H. B. Long & Associates (Eds.), *Developing paradigms for self-directed learning* (pp. 1–14). Norman, OK: Public Managers Center, College of Education, University of Oklahoma.

Long, H. B. (2009). Trends in self-directed learning research paradigms. In M. G. Derrick & M. K. Ponton (Eds.), *Emerging directions in self-directed learning* (pp. 19–36). Chicago, IL: Discovery Association Publishing House.

Lorge, I. (1944). Intellectual changes during maturity and old age. *Review of Educational Research, 14*(4), 438–443.

Loyens, S.M.M., Magda, J., & Rikers, R.M.J.P. (2008). Self-directed learning in problem-based learning and its relationship with self-regulated learning. *Educational Psychology Review, 20*, 411–427.

Lumosity http://www.lumosity.com/

Lynham, S. A. (2002). The general method of theory-building research in applied disciplines. In S. A. Lynham (Ed.) *Advances in Developing Human Resources, 4*(3), 221–241.

Lyotard, J. (1984). *The postmodern condition: A report on knowledge.* Minneapolis: University of Minnesota Press.

Mackeracher, D. (2004). *Making sense of adult learning* (2nd ed.), Toronto: University of Toronto Press.

Maher, F. A., & Tetreault, M.K.T. (1994). *The feminist classroom: A look at how professors and students are transforming higher education for a diverse society.* New York: Basic Books.

Maher, F. A., & Tetreault, M.K.T. (2001). *The feminist classroom: Dynamics of gender, race and privilege. Expanded edition.* Lanham, MD: Rowman & Littlefield Publishers.

Main, K. (1979). The power-load-margin formula of Howard Y. McClusky as the basis for a model of teaching. *Adult Education Quarterly 30*(1), 19–33.

Malcolm, I. (2012). "It's for us to change that": Emotional labor in researching adults' learning: Between Feminist Criticality and complicity in temporary, gendered employment. *Adult Education Quarterly, 62*(3), 252–271.

Malcolm, J., & Zukas, M. (2001). Bridging pedagogic gaps: Conceptual discontinuities in higher education. *Teaching in Higher Education, 6*(1), 33–42.

Mandell, A., & Herman, L. (2009). Mentoring: When learners make the learning. In J. Mezirow, E. W. Taylor, & Associates. *Transformative learning in practice* (pp. 78–89). San Francisco: Jossey-Bass.

Mandernach, B. J. (2006). Thinking critically about critical thinking: Integrating online tools to promote critical thinking. *InSight: A Journal of Scholarly Teaching, 1*, 41–50.

Marsick, V. J., & Maltbia, T. E. (2009). The transformative potential of action learning conversations: Developing critically reflective practice skills. In J. Mezirow, E. W. Taylor, & Associates. *Transformative learning in practice* (pp. 160–171). San Francisco: Jossey-Bass.

Marsick, V. J., & Watkins, K. E. (1990). *Informal and incidental learning.* London: Routledge.

Martinez, J., & Patel, M. (April 5, 2012). The blog of the John S., & James L. Knight Foundation: Five lessons in bridging the digital divide. http://www.knightfoundation.org/blogs/knightblog/2012/4/5/five-lessons-bridging-digital-divide/

Masden, S. R., John, C., Miller, D., & Warren, E. (2004). The relationship between an individual's margin in life and readiness for change. *Proceedings of the Academy of Human Resource Development, USA,* (pp. 759–766). Austin, TX City.

Maslow, A. H. (1954). *Motivation and personality.* New York: Harper and Row.

Maslow, A. H. (1970). *Motivation and personality* (2nd ed.). New York: HarperCollins.

Mayo, E. (1933). *The human problems of an industrial civilization.* New York: MacMillan.

McCarthy, M. (2010). Experiential learning theory: From theory to practice. *Journal of Business & Economics Research, 8*(5), 131–139.

McClusky, H. Y. (1963) The course of the adult life span. In W. C. Hallenbeck (Ed.), *Psychology of adults.* Chicago: Adult Education Association of the U.S.A.

McClusky, H. Y. (1970). A dynamic approach to participation in community development. *Journal of Community Development Society, 1,* 25–32.

McClusky, H. Y. (1971). The adult as learner. In R. J. McNeil & S. E. Seashore (Eds.), *Management of the urban crisis.* New York: The Free Press.

McEnrue, M. P., & Groves, K. (2006). Choosing among tests of emotional intelligence: What is the evidence? *Human Resource Development Quarterly, 17*(1), 9–42.

McIntosh, P. (1988). *White privilege: Unpacking the invisible knapsack.* http://www.nymbp.org/reference/WhitePrivilege.pdf

McIntyre, J. (2000). Research in adult education and training. In G. Foley (Ed.), *Understanding adult education and training.* Sydney: Allen and Unwin.

McLean, G. N. (2006). Rethinking adult learning in the workplace. *Advances in Developing Human Resources: Worldviews of Adult Learning in the Workplace, 8*(3), 416–423.

Mejiuni, O. (2012). International and community-based transformative learning. In E. W. Taylor & P. Cranton (Eds.), *The handbook of transformative learning* (pp.304–320). San Francisco: Jossey-Bass.

Merriam, S. B. (Ed.). (2007). *Non-Western perspectives on knowing and learning.* Malabar, FL: Krieger.

Merriam, S. B. (Ed.). (2008). Third update on adult learning theory. *New Directions for Adult and Continuing Education.* No. 199. San Francisco: Jossey-Bass.

Merriam, S. B., & Brockett, R. G. (2007). *The profession and practice of adult education.* San Francisco: Jossey-Bass.

Merriam, S. B., & Grace. A. P. (Eds.). (2011). *The Jossey-Bass reader on contemporary issues in adult education.* San Francisco: Jossey-Bass.

Merriam, S. B., & Kim, Y. S. (2011). Non-western perspectives on learning and knowing. In S. B. Merriam & A. P. Grace (Eds.), *The Jossey-Bass reader on contemporary issues in adult education,* pp. 378–389. San Francisco: Jossey-Bass.

Merriam, S. B., Caffarella, R. S., & Baumgartner, L. M. (2007). *Learning in adulthood* (3rd ed.). San Francisco: Jossey-Bass.

Merriam, S. B., Courtenay, B. C., & Cervero, R. M. (Eds.). (2006). *Global issues and adult education: Perspectives from Latin America, Southern Africa, and the United States.* San Francisco: Jossey-Bass.

Merriam, S. B., Mott, V. W., & Lee, M. (1996). Learning that comes from the negative interpretation of life experience. *Studies in Continuing Education, 18*(1), 1–23.

Metcalf, B. D. (2008). A feminist poststructuralist analysis of HRD: why bodies, power and reflexivity matter. *Human Resource Development International, 11*(5), 447–463.

Meyer, P. (2012). Embodied learning at work: Making the mind-set shift from workplace to playspace. In R. L. Lawrence (Ed.), Bodies of knowledge: Embodied learning in adult education (pp. 25–32). *New Directions for Adult and Continuing Education,* No. 134. San Francisco: Jossey-Bass.

Mezirow, J. (1978). *Education for perspective transformation: Women's re-entry programs in community colleges.* New York: Teachers College, Columbia University.

Mezirow, J. (1991). *Transformative dimensions of adult learning.* San Francisco: Jossey-Bass.

Mezirow, J. (1992). Transformation theory: Critique and confusion. *Adult Education Quarterly, 42*(2), 250–252.

Mezirow, J. (1996). Contemporary paradigms of learning. *Adult Education Quarterly, 46*(3), 158–172.

Mezirow, J. (2000). Learning to think like an adult: Core concepts of transformation theory. In J. Mezirow & Associates, *Learning as transformation: Critical perspectives on a theory in progress* (pp. 3–33), San Francisco: Jossey-Bass.

Mezirow, J., & Associates. (2000). *Learning as transformation: Critical perspectives on a theory in process.* San Francisco: Jossey-Bass.

Mezirow, J., Taylor, E. W., & Associates (2009). *Transformative learning in practice.* San Francisco: Jossey-Bass.

Michelson, E. (1998). Re-membering: The return of the body to experiential learning. *Studies in Continuing Education, 20*(2), 217–233.

Miettinen, R. (2000). The concept of experiential learning and John Dewey's theory of reflective thought and action. *International Journal of Lifelong Education, 19*(1), 54–72.

Miller, L. (Ed.). (2009). Present to possibility: The classroom as a spiritual space [Special issue]. *Teachers College Record, 111*(12).

Muirhead, R. J. (2007). E-learning: Is this teaching at students or teaching with students? *Nursing Forum, 42*(4), 178–184.

Mullen, C. (2005). *The mentorship primer.* New York: Peter Lang.

Mulvihill, M. K. (2003). The Catholic Church in crisis: Will transformative learning lead to social change through the uncovering of emotion? In C. A. Wiessner, S. R. Meyer, N. L. Pfhal, & P. G. Neaman (Eds.), *Proceedings of the Fifth International Conference on Transformative Learning* (pp. 320–325). New York: Teacher's College, Columbia University.

Musolino, G. M. (2006). Fostering reflective practice: Self-assessment abilities of physical therapy students and entry-level graduates. *Journal of Allied Health, 351*(1), 30–42.

Nafukho, F. (2006). Ubunto worldview: A traditional African view of adult learning in the workplace. *Advances in Developing Human Resources: Worldviews of Adult Learning in the Workplace, 8*(3), 408–415.

Nasser, H. E. (January 18–20, 2013). Changing Faces. *USA Weekend.* Pp. 6, 8–9.

Newman, M. (2012a). Calling transformative learning into question: Some mutinous thoughts. *Adult Education Quarterly, 62*(1), 36–55.

Newman, M. (2012b). Michael Newman's final comments in the forum on his article "Calling transformative learning into question: Some mutinous thoughts," *Adult Education Quarterly, 62*(4), 406–411.

Noel-Levitz, Inc. (2011). *The 2011 national online learners priorities report.* Coralville, IA: Noel-Levitz, Inc. https://www.noellevitz.com/upload/Papers_and_Research/2011/PSOL_report%202011.pdf

Ntseane, P. G. (2012). Transformative learning theory: A perspective from Africa. In E. W. Taylor & P. Cranton (Eds.), *The handbook of transformative learning* (pp. 274–288). San Francisco: Jossey-Bass.

O'Bannon, T., & McFadden, C. (2008). Model of experiential andragogy: Development of a non-traditional experiential learning program model. *Journal of Unconventional Parks, Tourism & Recreation Research, 1*(1), 23–28.

O'Sullivan, E. (2012). Deep transformation: Forging a planetary worldview. In E. W. Taylor & P. Cranton (Eds.), *The handbook of transformative learning* (pp. 162–177). San Francisco: Jossey-Bass.

Oddi, L. F., (1986). Development and validation of an instrument to identify self-directed continuing learners. *Adult Education Quarterly, 36*(2), 97–107.

Oddi, L. F., Ellis, A. J., & Roberson. J.E.A. (1990). Construct validity of the Oddi continuing learning inventory. *Adult Education Quarterly, 40*(3), 139–145.

Oh, J. R., & Park, C. H. (2012). Self-directed learning in the workplace. *Proceedings of the Adult Education Research Conference,* USA, pp. 265–271.

Ollis, T. (2010). The pedagogy of activism: Learning to change the world. *The International Journal of Learning, 17*(8), 239–249.

Orr, J. A. (2000). Learning from Native adult education. In L. English and M. A. Gillen (Eds.), Addressing the spiritual dimensions of adult learning: What educators can do (pp. 59–67). *New Directions For Adult & Continuing Education* No. 85. San Francisco: Jossey-Bass.

Ozuah, P. O. (2005). First, there was pedagogy and then came andragogy. *Einstein Journal of Biology and Medicine, 21,* 83–87.

Palloff, R. M., & Pratt, K. (2009) *Building learning communities in cyberspace: Effective strategies for the online classroom* (2nd ed.). San Francisco: Jossey-Bass.

Panhofer, H., Payne, H., Meekums, B., & Parke, T. (2011). Dancing, moving and writing in clinical supervision? Employing embodied practices in psychotherapy supervision. *The Arts in Psychotherapy, 38,* 9–16.

Parker, J. (2013). Examining adult learning assumptions and theories in technology-infused communities and professions. In V. Bryan, & V. Wang (Eds.), *Technology use and research approaches for community education and professional development* (pp. 53–65). Hershey, PA.: IGI Global. doi:10.4018/978-1-4666-2955-4.ch004

Parrish, M. M., & Taylor, E. W. (2007). Seeking authenticity: Women and learning in the Catholic worker movement. *Adult Education Quarterly, 57*(3), 221–247.

Paul, R., Elder, L., & Bartell, T. (1997). California teacher preparation for instruction in critical thinking: Research findings and policy recommendations. The Foundation for Critical Thinking: Dillon Beach, CA.

Pawar, B. S. (2009). Individual spirituality, workplace spirituality and work attitudes. *Leadership and Organization Development Journal, 30*(8), 759–777.

Perry, W. G. (1981). Cognitive and ethical growth: The making of meaning. In A. W. Chickering (Ed.), *The modern American college* (pp. 76–116). San Francisco: Jossey-Bass.

Perry, W. G. (1999). *Forms of intellectual and ethical development in the college years: A scheme.* San Francisco: Jossey-Bass.

Piaget, J. (1966). *The origins of intelligence in children.* New York: International Universities Press.

Piaget, J. (1972). Intellectual evolution from adolescent to adulthood. *Human Development, 16,* 346–370.

Pink, D. H. (2009). *Drive: The surprising truth about what motivates us.* New York: Riverhead Books.

Pintrich, P. R., Smith, D. A., Garcia, T., & McKeachie, W. J. (1991). *A manual for the use of the Motivated Strategies for Learning Questionnaire (MSLQ).* Ann Arbor: University of Michigan, National Center for Research to Improve Postsecondary Teaching and Learning.

PositScience http://www.positscience.com/

Pratt, D. D. (1993). Andragogy after twenty-five years. In S. B. Merriam (Ed.), *An update on adult learning theory* (pp. 15–24). New Directions for Adult and Continuing Education, No. 57, San Francisco: Jossey-Bass.

Pratt, D., & Associates, (2005). *Five perspectives on teaching in adult and higher education.* Malabar, FL: Krieger Publishing.

Pring, C. (2012). The social skinny: 100 social media, mobile and internet statistics for 2012 (March). http://thesocialskinny.com/100-social-media-mobile-and-internet-statistics-for-2012/

Quinney, K. L., Smith, S. D., & Galbraith, Q. (December, 2010). Bridging the gap: Self-directed staff technology training. *Information Technology and Libraries,* 205–213.

Rachal, J. (2002). Andragogy's detectives: A critique of the present and a proposal for the future. *Adult Education Quarterly, 52*(3), 210–227.

Rager, K. B. (2004). A thematic analysis of the self-directed learning experiences of thirteen breast cancer patients. *International Journal of Lifelong Education, 23*(1), 95–109.

Rager, K. B. (2006). Self-directed learning and prostate cancer: A thematic analysis of the experiences of twelve patients. *International Journal of Lifelong Education, 25*(5), 447–461.

Raidal, S. L, & Volet, S. E. (2009). Preclinical students' predispositions towards social forms of instruction and self-directed learning: A challenge for the development of autonomous and collaborative learners. *Higher Education, 57,* 577–596.

Reese, H. W., & Overton, W. F. (1970). Models of development and theories of development. In L. R. Goulet & P. B. Baltes (Eds.), *Life-span Developmental Psychology: Interventions* (pp. 115–145). Orlando: Academic Press.

Riggs, C. J. (2010). Taming the pedagogy dragon. *The Journal of Continuing Education in Nursing, 41*(9), 388–389.

Roberson, D. N., & Merriam. S. B. (2005). The self-directed learning of older, rural adults. *Adult Education Quarterly, 55*(4), 269–287.

Rock, D. (2009). *Your brain at work: Strategies for overcoming distraction, regaining focus, and working smarter all day long.* New York: Harper Collins.

Rock, D. (February 20, 2013). How to heal our smartphone-addled, overworked brains. *CNN Money.* http://management.fortune.cnn.com/2013/02/20/office-brain-health -smartphones/?goback=%2Egde_1782164_member_218115357

Rock, D., & Siegel, D. (2011). The healthy mind platter. http://www.mindplatter.com/

Roessger, K. M. (2012). Re-conceptualizing adult education's monolithic behaviourist interpretation: Toward a new understanding of radical behaviourism. *International Journal of Lifelong Education, 31*(5), 569–589.

Rogers, C. (1969). *Freedom to learn.* Columbus, OH: Charles E. Merrill.

Rogers, C. (1983). *Freedom to learn for the 80s.* Columbus, OH: Charles E. Merrill.

Rostami, K., & Khadjooi, K. (2010). The implications of behaviorism and humanism theories in medical education. *Gastroenterology and Hepatology, 3*(2), 65–70.

Roth, M. S. (January 3, 2010). Beyond critical thinking. *The Chronicle of Higher Education.* http://chronicle.com/article/Beyond-Critical-Thinking/63288/

Salovey, P., & Mayer, J. D. (1990). Emotional intelligence. *Imagination, Cognition and Personality, 9*(3), 185–211.

Sandlin, J. (2005). Andragogy and its discontents: An analysis of andragogy from three critical perspectives. *PAACE Journal of Lifelong Learning, 14,* 25–42.

Sandmann, L. R. (2010). Adults in four-year colleges and universities: Moving from the margin to mainstream? In C. K. Kasworm, A. D. Rose, & J. M. Ross-Gordon (Eds.), *Handbook of adult and continuing education* (pp. 221–230). Thousand Oaks, CA: Sage.

Savicevic, D. (1991). Modern conceptions of andragogy: A European framework. *Studies in The Education of Adults, 23*(2), 179–201.

Savicevic, D. (2008). Convergence or divergence of ideas on andragogy in different countries. *International Journal of Lifelong Education, 27*(4), 361–378.

Sawchuk, P. H. (2008). Theories and methods for research on informal learning and work: Towards cross-fertilization. *Studies in Continuing Education, 30*(1), 1–16.

Schapiro, S. A., Wasserman, I. L., & Gallegos, P. V. (2012). Group work and dialogue: Spaces and processes for transformative learning in relationships. In E. W. Taylor & P. Cranton (Eds.), *The handbook of transformative learning* (pp. 355–373). San Francisco: Jossey-Bass.

Schein, E. (2004). *Organizational culture and leadership* (3rd ed.). San Francisco: Jossey-Bass.

Scherer, A. G., Palazzo, G., & Matten, D. (2010), Introduction to the Special Issue: Globalization as a Challenge for Business Responsibilities. *Business Ethics Quarterly, 19*(3), pp. 327–347, 2009. Available at SSRN: http://ssrn.com/abstract=1430392

Schlesinger, R. (2005). Better myself: Motivation of African Americans to participate in correctional education. *The Journal of Correctional Education, 56*(3), 228–252.

Schön, D. A. (1983). *The reflective practitioner: How professionals think in action.* New York: Basic Books.

Schön, D. A. (1987). *Educating the reflective practitioner.* New York: Basic Books.

Schoonmaker, F. (2009). Only those who see take off their shoes: Seeing the classroom as a spiritual space. *Teachers College Record, 111*(12), 2713–2731.

Schunk, D. H. (1996). *Learning theories: An educational perspective.* Englewood Cliffs, NJ: Prentice Hall.

Schuyler, K. G. (2010). Increasing leadership integrity through mind training and embodied learning. *Counseling Psychology Journal: Practice and Research, 62*(1), 21–38.

Selingo, J. (January 26, 2012). A disrupted higher education system. *Chronicle of Higher Education.* http://chronicle.com/blogs/next/2012/01/26/a-disrupted-higher-ed -system/

Senge, P. M. (1990). *The fifth discipline: The art and practice of the learning organization.* New York: Currency/Doubleday.

Seuss, Dr. (1978). *I can read with my eyes shut.* New York: Random House.

Shapiro, S. L., Brown, K. W., & Astin, J. (2011). Toward the integration of meditation into higher education: A review of research evidence. *Teachers College Record, 113*(3), 493–528.

Sheared, V., Johnson-Bailey, J., Colin, S.A.J., Peterson, E., & Brookfield, S. D. (Eds.). (2010). *The handbook of race and adult education: A resource for dialogue on racism.* San Francisco: Jossey-Bass Higher Education.

Sherer, P. D., Shea, T. P., & Kristensen, E. (2003). Online communities of practice: A catalyst for faculty development. *Innovative Higher Education, 27*(3), 183–194.

Shieh, R. (2010). A case study of constructivist instructional strategies for adult online learning. *British Journal of Educational Technology, 41*(5), 706–720.

Siegel, D. (2012). *A pocket guide to neurobiology: An integrative handbook of the mind.* New York: Mind Your Brain, Inc., W. W. Norton.

Silen, C., & Uhlin, L. (2008). Self-directed learning—a learning issue for adults and faculty! *Teaching in Higher Education, 13*(4), 461–475.

Simmering, M. J., Posey, C., & Piccoli, G. (2009). Computer self-efficacy and motivation to learn in a self-directed online course. *Decision Sciences Journal of Innovative Education, 7*(1), 99–121.

Sinnott, J. D. (2010). *The development of logic in adulthood: Postformal thought and its applications.* New York: Plenum Press.

Skinner, B. F. (1971). *Beyond freedom and dignity.* New York: Knopf.

Slaughter, S., & Rhoades, G. (2004). *Academic capitalism and the new economy.* Baltimore, M.D.: The Johns Hopkins University Press.

Sleezer, C. M., Conti, G. J., & Nolan, R. E. (2003). Comparing CPE and HRD programs: Definitions, theoretical foundations, outcomes, and measures of quality. *Advances in Developing Human Resources, 6*(1), 20–34.

Smears, E. (2009). Breaking old habits: professional development through an embodied approach to reflective practice. *Journal of Dance and Somatic Practices, 1*(1), 99–110.

Smith, A. (2000). *The wealth of nations.* New York: Random House. Originally published 1776.

Smith, A., Rainie, L., & Zickuhr, K. (2011). *College students and technology.* Pew internet report. http://pewinternet.org/Reports/2011/College-students-and-technology.aspx

Smith, P. J., Sadler-Smith E., Robertson, I., & Wakefield, L. (2007). Leadership and learning: Facilitating self-directed learning in enterprises. *Journal of European Industrial Training, 31*(5), 324–335.

Smith, R. O. (2010). Facilitation and design of learning. In C. E. Kasworm, A. D. Rose, & J. M. Ross-Gordon (Eds.), *Handbook of adult and continuing education: 2010 edition* (pp. 147–155). Thousand Oaks, CA: Sage.

Smith, R. O. (2012). Fostering transformative learning online. In E. W. Taylor & P. Cranton (Eds.), *The handbook of transformative learning* (pp. 408–422). San Francisco: Jossey-Bass.

Snowber, C. (2012). Dance as a way of knowing. In R. L. Lawrence (Ed.), Bodies of knowledge: Embodied learning in adult education (pp. 53–60). *New Directions for Adult and Continuing Education*, No. 134. San Francisco: Jossey-Bass.

Soares, L. (January, 2013). Post-traditional learners and the transformation of postsecondary education: A manifesto for college leaders. American Council on Education. http://www.acenet.edu/news-room/Pages/Post-traditional-Learners-and-the-Transformation-of-Postsecondary-Ed.aspx. Accessed February 9, 2013.

Somerville, M. (2004). Tracing bodylines: The body in feminist poststructural research. *International Journal of Qualitative Studies in Education, 17*(1), 47–63.

Song, L., & Hill, J. R. (2007). A conceptual model for understanding self-directed learning in online environments. *Journal of Interactive Online Learning, 6*(1), 27–42.

Sonwalker, N. (2008). Adaptive individualization: The next generation of online education. *On the Horizon, 16*(1), 44–47.

Spear, G. E. (1988). Beyond the organizing circumstance: A search for methodology for the study of self-directed learning. In H. B. Long & others, *Self-directed learning: Application and theory*. Athens: Department of Adult Education: University of Georgia.

Spear, G. E., & Mocker, D. W. (1984). The organizing circumstance: Environmental determinants in self-directed learning. *Adult Education Quarterly, 35*, 1–10.

Spring, J. (2008). Research on globalization and education. *Review of Educational Research, 78*(2), 330–336.

Stavredes, T. (2011). *Effective online teaching: Foundations and strategies for student success*. San Francisco: Jossey-Bass.

Sternberg, R. J. (1988). *The triarchic mind: A new theory of human intelligence*. New York: Viking/Penguin.

Sternberg, R. J. (2003). *Wisdom, intelligence, and creativity synthesized*. Cambridge, UK: Cambridge University Press.

Sternberg, R. J. (2005). Older but not wiser? The relationship between age and wisdom. *Ageing International, 30*(1), 5–26.

Sternberg, R. J., Forsythe, G. B., Hedlund, J., Horvath, J. A., Wagner, R. K., Williams, W. M., et al. (2000). *Practical intelligence in everyday life*. New York: Cambridge University Press.

Stevens, K., Gerber, D., & Hendra, R. (2010). Transformational learning through prior learning assessment. *Adult Education Quarterly, 60*(4), 377–404.

Stevenson, J. S. (1982). Construction of a scale to measure load, power, and margin in life. *Nursing Research, 31*(4), 222–225.

Stewart, J., Rigg, C., & Trehan, K. (Eds.) (2006). *Critical human resource development: Beyond orthodoxy*. Harlow, England: Prentice Hall.

Stockdale, S. L., & Brockett, R. G. (2010). Development of the PRO-SDLS: A measure of self-direction in learning based on the Personal Responsibility Orientation Model. *Adult Education Quarterly, 20*(10), 1–20.

Swartz, A. L., & Tisdell, E. J. (2012). Wisdom, complexity, and adult education: Emerging theory and meanings for practice. In J. Buban & D. Ramdeholl (Eds.), *Proceedings of the 53rd Annual Adult Education Research Conference May 31–June 3, 2012* (pp. 321–327). Saratoga Springs, N.Y.: SUNY Empire State College.

Swindell, R. (2000). A U3A without walls: Using the internet to reach out to isolated people. *Education and Aging, 15*, 251–263.

Taylor, B., & Kroth, M. (2009). Andragogy's transition into the future: Meta-analysis of andragogy and its search for a measureable instrument. *Journal of Adult Education, 38*(1), 1–11.

Taylor, E. (1998). A primer on critical race theory. *The Journal of Blacks in Higher Education, 19*(Spring), pp. 122–124.

Taylor, E. W. (2005). Teaching beliefs of nonformal consumer educators: A perspective of teaching in home improvement retail stores in the United States. *International Journal of Consumer Studies, 29*(5), 448–457.

Taylor, E. W. (2008). Transformative learning theory. In S. B. Merriam (Ed.), Third update on adult learning theory (pp. 5–16). *New Directions for Adult and Continuing Education*, No. 119. San Francisco: Jossey-Bass.

Taylor, E. W. (2012). *Teaching adults in public places: Museums, parks, consumer education sites.* Malabar, FL: Krieger Publishing Company.

Taylor, E. W., & Cranton, P. (Eds.) (2012). *The handbook of transformative learning.* San Francisco: Jossey-Bass.

Taylor, E. W., & Snyder, M. J. (2012). A critical review of research on transformative learning theory, 2006–2010. In E. W. Taylor & P. Cranton (Eds.), *The handbook of transformative learning* (pp. 37–55). San Francisco: Jossey-Bass.

Taylor, F. W. (1911). *The principles of scientific management.* San Francisco: Jossey-Bass.

Taylor, J. B. (2009). *My stroke of insight.* New York: Plume/Penguin.

Taylor, K., & Lamoreaux, A. (2008). Teaching with the brain in mind. In S. B. Merriam (Ed.), Third update on adult learning theory (pp. 49–61). *New Directions for Adult and Continuing Education*, No. 119. San Francisco: Jossey-Bass.

Taylor, K., Marienau, C., & Fiddler, M. (2000). *Developing adult learners.* San Francisco: Jossey-Bass.

Tennant, M. (2012). *The learning self: Understanding the potential for transformation.* San Francisco: Jossey-Bass.

Tennant, M., & Pogson, P. (1995). *Learning and change in the adult years.* San Francisco: Jossey-Bass.

Thalhammer, K. E., O'Loughlin, P. L., Glazer, M. P., Glazer, P. M., McFarland, S., Shepela, S. T., & Stoltzfus, N. (Eds.) (2007). *Courageous resistance: The power of ordinary people.* New York: Palgrave MacMillan.

Thorndike, E. L., Bregman, E. O., Tilton, J. W., & Woodyard, E. (1928). *Adult learning.* New York: Macmillan.

Thory, K. (2013). Teaching managers to regulate their emotions better: Insights from emotional intelligence training and work-based application. *Human Resource Development International, 16*(1), 4–21.

Thurstone, L. L. (1938). *Primary mental abilities.* Chicago: University of Chicago Press.

Time. (August 27, 2012). The wireless issue.

Tisdell, E. J. (1995). *Creating inclusive adult learning environments: Insights from multicultural education and feminist pedagogy, Information series No. 361.* Columbus, OH: ERIC Clearing House on Adult, Career and Vocational Education.

Tisdell, E. J. (2001). *Spirituality in adult and higher education. ERIC Digest. [Identifier: ED 459370].* Columbus, OH: ERIC Clearinghouse on Adult, Career, and Vocational Education.

Tisdell, E. J. (2003). *Exploring spirituality and culture in adult and higher education.* San Francisco: Jossey-Bass.

Tisdell, E. J. (2007). In the new millennium: The role of spirituality and the cultural imagination in dealing with diversity and equity in the higher education classroom. *Teachers College Record, 109*(3), 531–560.

Tisdell, E. J. (2008). Spirituality and adult learning. In S. B. Merriam (Ed.), Third update on adult learning theory (pp. 27–36). *New Directions for Adult and Continuing Education,* No. 119. San Francisco: Jossey-Bass.

Tisdell, E. J. (2011). The wisdom of webs a-weaving: Adult education and the paradoxes of complexity in changing times. In E. J. Tisdell & A. L. Swartz (Eds.), Adult education and the pursuit of wisdom (pp. 5–14). *New Directions for Adult and Continuing Education,* No. 131. San Francisco: Jossey-Bass.

Tisdell, E. J., & Swartz, A. L. (Eds.). (2011). Adult education and the pursuit of wisdom. *New Directions for Adult and Continuing Education,* No. 131. San Francisco: Jossey-Bass.

Tough, A. (1967). *Learning without a teacher.* Toronto: Ontario Institute for Studies in Education.

Tough, A. (1971). *The adult's learning projects: A fresh approach to theory and practice in adult learning.* Toronto: Ontario Institute for Studies in Education.

Tough, A. (1978). Major learning efforts: Recent research and future directions. *Adult Education, 28*(4), 250–236.

Trinh, M. P., & Kolb, D. A. (Winter 2011–2012). Eastern experiential learning: Eastern principles for learning wholeness. *Career Planning and Adult Development Journal,* 29–43.

Tsui, L. (2002). Fostering critical thinking through effective pedagogy: Evidence from four case studies. *Journal of Higher Education, 73*(3), 740–763.

Tulving, E. (1985). How many memory systems are there? *American Psychologist, 40,* 385–98.

Turkle, S. (2011). *Alone together: Why we expect more from technology and less from each other.* New York: Perseus Book Group.

Tyler, J. A. (2009). Charting the course: How storytelling can foster communicative learning in the workplace. In J. Mezirow, E. W. Taylor, & Associates. *Transformative learning in practice* (pp. 136–147). San Francisco: Jossey-Bass.

U.S. Bureau of the Census (2012). Statistical Abstract, 2012 Press Notes. http://www.census.gov/newsroom/releases/pdf/cb11-tps30_pressnotes12.pdf

U.S. Department of Education, Office of Planning, Evaluation, and Policy Development. (2010). *Evaluation of evidence-based practices in online learning: A meta-analysis and review of online learning studies.* Washington, D.C.

U.S. Department of Education, National Center for Educational Statistics (2007). *The condition of education 2007 (NCES 2007–064).* Washington, DC: US Government Printing Office. http://nces.ed.gov/programs/coe/indicator_aed.asp

UNESCO Institute for Lifelong Learning. (2009). *Global report on adult learning and education.* http://uil.unesco.org/fileadmin/keydocuments/AdultEducation/en/GRALE_en.pdf

UNESCO. (2008). *EFA global monitoring report 2009: Overcoming inequality: why governance matters.* Oxford/Paris: Oxford University Press/UNESCO Publishing. http://unesdoc.unesco.org/images/0017/001776/177683e.pdf

Usher, R., Bryant, I., & Johnston, R. (1997). *Adult education and the post-modern challenge: Learning beyond the limits.* New York: Routledge.

Valentin, C. (2007). How can I teach critical management in this place? A critical pedagogy for HRD: Possibilities, contradictions and compromises. In C. Rigg, J. Steward, & K. Trehand (Eds.), *Critical human resource development: Beyond orthodoxy.* Harlow, UK: Pearson Education Limited.

Vella, J. (2000). A spirited epistemology: Honoring the adult learner as subject. In L. English& M. Gillen (Eds.), Addressing the spiritual dimensions of adult learning: What educators can do (pp. 7–16). *New Directions for Adult and Continuing Education,* No. 85. San Francisco: Jossey-Bass.

Vermunt, J. D., & Vermetten, Y. J. (2004). Patterns in student learning: Relationships between learning strategies, conceptions of learning, and learning orientations. *Educational Psychology Review, 16*(4), 459–384.

Viens, J., & Kallenbach, S. (2004). *Multiple intelligences and adult literacy: A sourcebook for practitioners.* New York: Teachers College, Columbia University.

Vroom, V. H. (1964/1995). *Work and motivation.* San Francisco: Jossey-Bass.

Vygotsky, L. S. (1978). *Mind in society: The development of higher psychological processes.* Cambridge, MA: Harvard University Press.

Walters, P. (2009). Philosophies of adult environmental education. *Adult Education Quarterly, 60*(1), 3–25.

Walters, S. (2005). Learning region. In L. M. English (Ed.), *International encyclopedia of adult education* (pp. 360–362). New York: Palgrave Macmillan.

Wang, V., & Farmer, L. (2008). Adult teaching methods in China and Bloom's Taxonomy. *International Journal for the Scholarship of Teaching and Learning, 2*(2), 1–15.

Wang, V.C.X., & Sarbo, L. (2004). Philosophy, role of adult educators, and learning. *Journal of Transformative Education, 2*(3), 204–214.

Warner, M. (January 1, 2012). Queer and then? *The Chronicle of Higher Education.* http://chronicle.com/article/QueerThen-/130161/

Watkins, D. (2000). Learning and teaching: A cross-cultural perspective. *School Leadership and Management, 20*(2), 161–173.

Watkins, K. E., Marsick, V. J., & Faller, P. G. (2012). Transformative learning in the workplace: Leading learning for self and organizational change. In E. W. Taylor & P. Cranton (Eds.), *The handbook of transformative learning* (pp. 373–387). San Francisco: Jossey-Bass.

Watson, C., & Temkin, S. (2000). Just-in-time teaching: Balancing the compelling demands of corporate America and academe in the delivery of management education. *Journal of Management Education, 24*(6), 763–778.

Webley, K. (July 9, 2012). Reboot the school. *Time* (pp.36–41).

Wenger, E. (1998). *Communities of practice: Learning, meaning, and identity.* Cambridge, UK: Cambridge University Press.

Wenger, E. (2000). Communities of practice and social learning systems. *Organization, 7*(2), 225–246.

Wenger, E., & Snyder, W. M. (2000). Communities of practice: The organizational frontier. *Harvard Business Review, 78*(1), 139–145.

Wiessner, C. A., & Sullivan, L. G. (2007). Constructing knowledge in leadership training programs. *Community College Review, 35*(2), 88–112.

Wilkas, L. R. (2002). Evaluating health web sites for research and practice. *Journal for Specialists in Pediatric Nursing, 7*(1), 38–41.

Wilner, A. S., & Dubouloz, G. J. (2011). Transformative radicalization: Applying learning theory to Islamist radicalization. *Studies in Conflict and Terrorism, 34*(5), 418–438.

Wilner, A. S., & Dubouloz, G. J. (2012). Violent transformations: Can adult learning theory help explain radicalization, political violence and terrorism? In J. Buban & D. Ramdeholl (Eds.). *Proceedings of the 53rd adult education research conference, May 31–June 3, 2012.* Saratoga Springs, NY: SUNY Empire State College.

Wilson, K. L., & Halford, W. K. (2008). Process of change in self-directed couple education. *Family Relations, 571*(5), 625–635.

Wink, P., & Dillon, M. (2002). Spiritual development across the adult life course: Findings from a longitudinal study. *Journal of Adult Development, 9*(1), 79–94.

Winter, A. J., McAuliffe, M. B., Hargreaves, D. J., & Chadwick, G. (2009). *The transition to academagogy.* Paper presented at the Philosophy of Education Society of Australasia (PESA) Conference Brisbane, Queensland. http://eprints.qut.edu.au/17367/1/17367.pdf

Withnall, A. (2012). Lifelong or longlife? Learning in the later years. In D. N. Aspin, J. Chapman, K. Evans, & R. Bagnall (Eds.), *Second international handbook of lifelong learning,* Part 2 (pp. 649–664). New York: Springer.

Wlodkowski, R. J. (2008). *Enhancing adult motivation to learn: A comprehensive guide for teaching all adults* (3rd ed.). San Francisco: Jossey-Bass.

World Economic Forum (2012). *Global population ageing: Peril or promise?* Global Agenda Council on Aging Society. World Economic Forum. www.WEF_GAC_GlobalPopulationAgeing_Report-2012.

World Health Organization (WHO). (1999). *Aging: Exploding the myths.* Aging and Health Program, World Health Organization. www.WHO_HSC_AHE_99.1

Wright, D., & Brajtman, S. (2011). Relational and embodied knowing: Nursing ethics within the interprofessional team. *Nursing Ethics, 18*(1), 20–30.

Wright, M., & Grabowsky, A. (2011). The role of the adult educator in helping learners access and select quality health information on the internet. *New Directions for Adult and Continuing Education,* No. *130,* 79–88.

Yeganeh, B., & Kolb, D. A. (2009). Mindfulness and experiential learning. *OD Practitioner, 41*(3), 8–14.

Yang, G., Zheng, W., & Li, M. (2006). Confucian view of learning and implications for developing human resources. *Advances in Developing Human Resources: Worldviews of Adult Learning in the Workplace, 8*(3), 346–354.

Zamudio, M., Rios, F., & Jamie, A. M. (2008). Thinking critically about difference: Analytical tools for the 21st Century. *Equity and Excellence in Education, 41*(2), 251–229.

Zamudio, M., Russell, C., Rios, F., & Bridgeman, J. L. (2010). *Critical race theory matters: Education and ideology.* New York: Routledge.

Zelinski, E. M., & Kennison, R. K. (2007). Not your parents' test scores: Cohort reduces psychometric aging effects. *Psychology and Aging, 22*(3), 546–557.

Zhang, L. F. (2004). The Perry scheme: Across cultures, across approaches to the study of human psychology. *Journal of Adult Development, 11*(2), 123–138.

Zickuhr, K., & Smith, A. (April 13, 2012). *Digital differences.* Washington, DC: Pew Research Center's Internet & American Life Project. http://pewinternet.org/~/media//Files/Reports/2012/PIP_Digital_differences_041312.pdf

Zinn, L. (1990). Identifying your philosophical orientation. In M. W. Galbraith (Ed.), *Adult learning methods: A guide for effective instruction* (pp. 39–77). Malabar, FL: Krieger.

Zull, J. E. (2006). Key aspects of how the brain learns. In S. Johnson & K. Taylor (Eds.), The neuroscience of adult learning (pp. 3–10). *New Directions for Adult and Continuing Education*, No. 110, San Francisco: Jossey-Bass.

NAME INDEX

A

Adams, S., 205, 207
Ahl, H., 147, 148–149, 150, 162
Ahmed, M., 16
Akdere, M., 244
Ala-Mutka, K., 195–196
Aldrich, C., 206
Alfred, M. V., 10
Alheit, P., 241
All, A. C., 37–38
Allen, I. E., 193, 199
Allen, S. J., 40
Alvesson, M., 220, 221
Amann, T., 133
Anderson, L. W., 34
Archer, W., 26
Argyris, C., 69, 116, 249
Aristotle, 44, 105
Arlin, P. K., 32, 183
Arnett, J. J., 12
Artis, A. B., 73
Ashmos, D. P., 140–141
Ashok, H. S., 243
Aspin, D., 20, 22
Astin, A. W., 138
Astin, J., 138

Aued, B., 3
Ausubel, D. P., 34, 49
Avery, G. C., 111
Avoseh, M.B.M., 1

B

Bagnall, R., 20, 22
Ballard, G. H., 110
Baltes, P. B., 185
Bandura, A., 35
Banerjee, P., 191
Barbour, K., 133
Barnacle, R., 127–128, 135
Barron, B., 5
Bartell, T., 213
Basseches, M., 95, 183
Bassett, C. L., 185–186
Bates, R. A., 58, 59
Baum, J., 153
Baumgartner, L. M., xiv, 19, 26, 52, 62, 69, 71, 85, 88–89, 181, 251
Behar-Horenstein, L. S., 222
Belenky, M. F., 32, 184
Bell, A. A., 6, 191, 205

Bennett, E. E., 6, 19, 191, 205
Bergsteiner, H., 111
Berra, Y., 248
Bersani, L., 219
Bierema, L. L., xviii, 94, 131–132, 197–198, 221
Billett, S., 18
Birzer, M. L., 59
Bjorklund, B. R., 33, 173, 176
Blanchard, K., 69
Bliss, D. L., 152
Bloom, B. S., 34
Bohm, D., 137
Boshier, R., 152
Bowles, T. A., 83, 91, 92
Bowman, W., 128
Boyatzis, R. E., 110
Boyd, R. D., 86
Brajtman, S., 133
Brandon, A. F., 37–38
Bregman, E. O., 27
Bridgeman, J. L., 219
Brockett, R. G., 11, 62, 63, 65, 66, 67, 68, 69, 71, 77, 78, 249

SUBJECT INDEX

e represents exhibit; *f* represents figure; *t* represents table.